Transnational Marketing Strategy

Transnational Marketing Strategy

Dr. Biswajit Das
Professor - Marketing Management
& Business Communication and Chairperson
Doctoral Programme of KIIT School of Management
KIIT University, Bhubaneswar, India

Dr. Ipseeta Satpathy
Associate Professor-OB and HRM
KIIT School of Management
KIIT University, Bhubaneswar, India

Dr. Sanjay Sharan
Professor, ICFAI Business School, Hyderabad
Full Bright Scholar
Wharton Business School, USA

NEW AGE
MANAGEMENT

An Imprint of

NEW AGE INTERNATIONAL (P) LIMITED, PUBLISHERS
New Delhi • Bangalore • Chennai • Cochin • Guwahati
Hyderabad • Kolkata • Lucknow • Mumbai
Visit us at **www.newagepublishers.com**

Published by New Age International (P) Ltd., Publishers
First Edition: 2014

BRANCHES

- **Bangalore** 37/10, 8th Cross (Near Hanuman Temple), Azad Nagar, Chamarajpet Bangalore-560 018, Tel.: (080) 26756823, Telefax: 26756820 **E-mail: bangalore@newagepublishers.com**
- **Chennai** 26, Damodaran Street, T. Nagar, Chennai-600 017, Tel.: (044) 24353401 Telefax: 24351463, **E-mail: chennai@newagepublishers.com**
- **Cochin** CC-39/1016, Carrier Station Road, Ernakulam South, Cochin-682 016 Tel.: (0484) 2377004, Telefax: 4051303 **E-mail: cochin@newagepublishers.com**
- **Guwahati** Hemsen Complex, Mohd. Shah Road, Paltan Bazar, Near Starline Hotel Guwahati-781 008, Tel.: (0361) 2513881, Telefax: 2543669 **E-mail: guwahati@newagepublishers.com**
- **Hyderabad** 105, 1st Floor, Madhiray Kaveri Tower, 3-2-19, Azam Jahi Road Nimboliadda, Hyderabad-500 027, Tel.: (040) 24652456 Telefax: 24652457, **E-mail: hyderabad@newagepublishers.com**
- **Kolkata** RDB Chambers (Formerly Lotus Cinema) 106A, 1st Floor S.N. Banerjee Road, Kolkata-700 014, Tel.: (033) 22273773 Telefax: 22275247, **E-mail: kolkata@newagepublishers.com**
- **Lucknow** 16-A, Jopling Road, Lucknow-226 001, Tel.: (0522) 2209578, 4045297 Telefax: 2204098, **E-mail: lucknow@newagepublishers.com**
- **Mumbai** 142C, Victor House, Ground Floor, N.M. Joshi Marg, Lower Parel Mumbai-400 013, Tel.: (022) 24927869, Telefax: 24915415 **E-mail: mumbai@newagepublishers.com**
- **New Delhi** 22, Golden House, Daryaganj, New Delhi-110 002 Tel.: (011) 23262368, 23262370, Telefax: 43551305 **E-mail: sales@newagepublishers.com**

ISBN: 978-81-224-3590-0

₹ 250.00

C-13-04-7040

Printed in India at Ajit Printers, Delhi.

Typeset at In-house, New Delhi.

PUBLISHING FOR ONE WORLD
NEW AGE INTERNATIONAL (P) LIMITED, PUBLISHERS
7/30 A, Daryaganj, New Delhi - 110002
Visit us at **www.newagepublishers.com**

Preface

This unique book named 'Transnational Marketing Strategy'(TMS) is born out of the indigenous thought process associated with the study of marketing management. All the perspectives are mooted to the basics and emerging to the transnational platforms of business. It shares and disseminates the essential know how's of the sciences of marketing.

TMS is a comprehensive book for most of the universities in India and abroad hosting business management as a subject. The recent spurt of cross-border shift and transfer in business has become important for studying. Like international business, international marketing and global marketing; study of transnational marketing has become essential for class rooms. This shall enable the students and learners to delve into the nitty-gritty of the strategic business expansion; for travelling beyond the country. The subject being taught in business schools and universities; dimension understand shall be eclectic. Relevance to the subject includes premier institutes of India, including Delhi University, Pune University, Amity University, Bangalore University, BPUT University, KIIT University alongwith other numerous universities.

Today through the IT revolution, global customer has become a phenomenon. Transnational as a word is more often associated with the oft quoted terminology, international or global. The word 'transnational' is significant for the current epoch for its application in the case of companies travelling beyond the boundaries of the nation; searching for niche markets. Similarly strategic planning is important for invading the potential pastures of business. In the marketing strategies; positioning of product create opportunities for business and drive the target aspects through communication access. Therefore, this book has the potential to crack the definite market segment and has a unique selling proposition for its indigenous approach. Eventually it shall cater to all segments of students, faculty, scholars and trainees for learning the subtle nuances of business acumen.

This book is categorically designed, for all types of management students, commerce students, communication students and professionals, particularly for the global marketing professionals and practitioners. The instruction laid in the text of the book shall enable them to identify the essential differences that exist between transnational and domestic marketing operations. Issues dealt in the book are in relevance to the attitudes, strategies and operations that are required in this spectrum of today's business, in the face of fierce competition.

Transnational marketing and exports strategy formulations; and necessary functioning have been taken up and discussed vividly, for the purpose of the grooming professionals. It is intended to interface with the centers of trade, commerce and business; for the creation of integrated world order. The present position and status of the current transnational marketing vistas has been analyzed and avenues consolidated for developing professionals. This ideation can shape and design the critical thinking process of persons working in the export regime, too. The export and import policies currently in practice have been included for a detail understanding by the participants.

They include the topics like, export of services, transnational project contracts and agreements for commissioning, designing of industries, maintenance of equipments and machinery, civil constructions, export through third parties, registered exporter, export under duty exemption scheme, import and export passbook schemes, diamond /DTC Imp rest licenses, 100% export oriented schemes, export processing zones /FTZ , Re-exports without processing, exports as free replacement during warranty /guarantee period, substitution of import by indigenous materials and import for assistance to export oriented units based on export performance certificate, so forth. Other specified exports have been dealt with due emphasis on engineering goods and minerals.

In fact, the basics of the names and locations of buyers and sellers, description of goods and quantities to be contracted, unit value and realizations, delivery schedules, turnaround and response times, packaging and payment to the intricacies of the transnational market has also been analyzed. Exploration in this fashion is expected to lead to the discovery of the new there in the business.

Transnational marketing strategy calls for arguments on the following aspects too:

- Means for earning foreign exchange and hedge against domestic currency devaluation and excessive inflation.

- Best means for availing of government concessions.
- Promises a much bigger size of market.
- Promises better than the national average rate of growth.
- Way of reducing risk and hedge against domestic recession.
- Promises a more preferable way of broad basing the product.
- Window to the world.
- It has other preferred spin-off effects like: sticking to delivery schedules, acceptance of more rigorous third party inspection, much improved response and turn-around times, quality and technology gains and growth of transnational management culture, instantaneous marketing, informal flexible systems & styles of management and better government-business relations.

The theme is reflected on the statement of James E. Burke, Chairman, Johnson and Johnson (USA). That is, 'You have to take risks today. Business has become more competitive on a worldwide basis. The answer to that challenge is no different than it's ever been. You've got to get better and better and if you don't you will be left behind. Young people perhaps understand this better than we do. The key is to get the very best people you can, and then provide them with an environment that encourages them to handle these challenges, the way they see fit. There's no great magic to that, if you're not competitive especially in Europe, Japan and the United States and if you are not inter connected from a technological and marketing point of view, competing successfully is going to be increasingly difficult. You must create a system that will enable everyone to move freely and rapidly. There are important synergisms in a world business, overlook them and over the long run you are out of business."

Transnational Marketing Skills

Transnational Marketing Strategy book is crafted in a modular frame; working on the methodology and practical aspect of business. The integrated components are situation based and experience driven. Invariably transnational law, government policy and domestic laws employed in the operations have been analyzed with accuracy. Being imparted, it can make the trainee and participants educated about the trans-national, global and multi-national angles clearly focused. Significant steps of marketing concepts have been perused in a realistic form and style.

It addresses issues of new markets in the global sphere, ascertain products and services, technique to reach customer, pricing plans, snags in managing distribution channels and smooth flow of business abroad. The package shall skill the learning curves in the target readers and shall facilitate unique ideas to let the mind spark with an incessant quest for exploring differentiating transnational marketing from that of domestic marketing.

Innovative Impact

This is designed in response to survey of the professionals of TATA, SAIL, BHEL, Aditya Birla and other companies having transnational operations. The content and structure of the course has been incorporated in accordance to the essence. Based on the thoughtful feed back certain features have been distinguished and inserted.

They are mainly the latest approach and allied issues, entries strategies, transnational potential, market planning logistic, roles of regulatory bodies and deregulating, world experience, marketing decisions, new thoughts, economic analysis, global trade and sales promotion, positioning analogy, condensed and comprehensive connotations. The book shall help the government employees, corporation, companies, industries, groups and individual consumers to learn the changing realities.

Transnational orientation, universal application and recurrent solutions to problem has been elucidated effectively. It essentially communicates to the marketing great guns to understand negotiating with the business environment.

Gist of the Book

Chapter one highlights the core concept of the book and illustrates the essence of the global requirements. It ensues the summary of the entire book comprehensively crystal clear, giving clue to all the chapters that follows.

Here in this chapter the reader shall understand the goal of transnational marketing strategy through business worldviews and strategic orientation of companies. Recognize the modalities of channels of distribution and ascertain the paths of integrated marketing communication employing IT. Describe marketing communication together with the views of Alvin Toffler, John Naisbitt and Theodore Levitt. The ideas are elucidated on the driving forces and retraining forces of the economy, the roles of technology, transportation, driving market needs, cost, free markets and pace in driving, culture, national controls, war, management myopia and nationalism. It conveys ideas regarding access of media communication in creating global customers and relate system approach and trade agreements, basing on transnational check posts.

It preaches about mass market getting classified and need for market expansion, which can effect through market communication via media promotion. Moreover, domestic companies have been believed to be going global identified as ethno-centric companies, poly-centric companies, region-centric companies and geo-centric companies. Role of GATT reformation leading to WTO regime has been crystallized. Cultural universals, invention and innovation are believed to be the source of scaling the economies. The case-lets highlight on the worldviews for understanding. It reflects on the holistic ideas of transnational marketing strategy and the core elements associated in the study of the book as such from its greater perspective.

Chapter two in the book is dealing with the essential differences between transnational marketing and domestic marketing. Accordingly, the following questions have been analyzed and interpreted in details. They are how to distinguish between domestic marketing management and transnational strategic management ? How to distinguish between domestic and trans-national marketing strategy implementation, from a behavioral science point of view? How to distinguish domestic product-positioning strategy from transnational product-design strategy? How to distinguish domestic promotion expenditure strategy from transnational promotion–mix strategy ?

It explains about the ways to discover and harvest business; by invading new markets, innovative strategies to beat competition through acumen in TSM and DMM. It reveals the implication of marketing and strategy for segments in sectors for proper planning. Relate to corporate strategy, mission, objectives, goals and portfolio analysis, besides transnational strategic plan; examining differences and similarities; even for multi-business transnational planning. It succinctly highlights eight aspects which are salient to designing product strategies and positioning strategy, stressing on single brand and multiple brands. This chapter also speaks upon diversification strategy of products and promotional strategies fitting to inclement business environment. Never the less infuse ideas on promotional expenditure, promotional mix approaches in single market, multi-market, market geography, local market and total market strategies.

This chapter two illustrates on the role of transnational domestic and transnational strategic marketing, its application in management. It shall unmask enigmatic ideas beyond borders; unravel treasures of business knowledge. Competitive edge and brisk innovations for market share have been viewed with a perspective and methods stated. Entire domain is dealt along the line of corporate strategy, business mission, portfolio analysis, competition, customer and product strategy etc. It offered a blue print on areas of focus. The text delineated redefining a cutting edge logistics and penetrating communication strategy.

Chapter three titled 'mapping and mobilizing transnational market' of the book refers to transnational market expansion strategy through mapping of prevailing market forces. This study is wanted to graduate new business beyond the frontiers, to mobilize profits on sales. It teaches ideas on the pertinent aspects of product USP; analyzed through accuracy. MBO is given priority for victories. These mobilizing techniques encompass test marketing and its complimentary attributes. It shall lay emphasis on differences that prevail between in cross border approach; barred by constraints of laws. This comprehends the ideas and concepts; including distribution channels.

After going through, the reader shall know the mapping techniques of marketing approach, break-down methods and binding-up methods. It shall estimate the potential of new products against branded products, test-marketing products through scaling the market size, market growth and other building blocks. It shall study through the three dimensions of environmental influences and explain the penetration processes through the rings of entry into market places. Penetration strategy include aspects like product line, types of customers and geographic scope etc.. It will deal with facets of multi-faceted distribution channels for launching new products and enhance deeper knowledge on the field.

It has dealt on aspects like how to design market strategies in the transnational marketing in terms of single market, multi market, total market, local market, regional market, transnational market, first-in, early entry, laggard market entry, market commitment, market dilution, de-marketing pruning of marginal markets, key markets and harvesting? How to formulate transnational product/market strategy, as strategic outline? How to define market boundaries in terms of technology, customer function and customer segment? How to determine the strategic thrust of the core transnational strategies viz. start-up, growth with industry, faster growth, attainment of cost leadership, differentiation, focus, renewal, defending position, harvesting, finding niche, hold niches, catch-ups and withdrawals? How to evaluate transnational new product management? How to delineate governmental constraints on an transnational company's growth, in terms of constraints on corporate growth, corporate governance constraints, constraints on managing the work force, employee relations, problems and opportunities of business-government partnership and politicizing of economic decision making ? What are the distribution differences between domestic and transnational marketing, in terms of additional transnational distribution channels?

In fact, mapping the modus operandi of markets; is the key to strategic plan. The chapter elucidates on the critical facets of judgment and macro market decision making. It highlights the major three methods of test-marking new products like UFM, PUM & A/SM and discuss the five aspects like market size, market growth, profitability, type of buying and customer market structure. In this aspect new product management has been explained measuring score boards to gauge. Influencing environmental issues governing boundaries of business and factors likes adoption, diffusion and acclimatization process have been dealt. It reflects on the aspects like product line, hedging competition, type of customers, geographic scope and distribution channels. It has emphasized on the distribution channels for its utter importance in the subject of study. This chapter has detailed into the dimensions which are important for measuring transnational market potential.

Chapter four deals with the macro aspects of strategic thrust It is to envisage the invisible future. This chapter demonstrates the thrust areas of companies in the macro-perspective. Ambitious companies cross-the-border for utilizing business opportunities; cooking up approaches. They design roadmaps and milestones of the action plan zeroing into the goal. Normal kind of 3-level process undertaken by number of companies are assessment of issues, spotting key variables and selection of strategy for implementation. The major strategic thrust begin with the start-up stage, cost leadership, differentiation, market focus and restoration of product line etc.. It endures to convert market share into higher rate-of-return. At stages holding a slice of product in the market uncontested by rival companies; at times by early bird entry opting with choices from amongst variables. Right sizing company assets have been treated. It analysed on barriers between countries and agreement. It maintained on culture-savvy workforce and public welfare related business. It dealt on strategic factors relating to finance, marketing, operations, management, human resource and similar topics. It associated effectiveness of marketing strategies, score sheet with grades to rate a company's product launch.

The other angles of approach are assessment of issues, spotting key variables and selecting strategy for implementation. It pro-actively related to certain vital areas embracing the entire product life cycle and sectors. It optimized the overall aspects of leveraging transnational markets moving through transition, transportation and transformation of business. It delineated governmental constraints on transnational company's growth, corporate growth, corporate governance, managing employee, employee relations, business-government partnership and politics.

Chapter five aims at developing a new 'maxi-transnational marketing model' for the new 'de-massified' market; which provides a new direction in the field of inter-national marketing. A market situation in which the prospects and potential customers are identified, located, persuaded, motivated, converted and cultivated in a way that maximizes sale and profits. 'Maxi marketing' is a continuum which turn prospectus into long-term (repeat customers) purchase.

Interestingly, each step in this 'nine phase model' is logically linked with the objectives likes maximizing repeat sales, maximizing customer loyalty, maximizing line extension, maximizing cross promotion and maximizing success of new ventures. The approach taken is just the opposite of the old Latin saying "Qui non proficit, deficit". Indeed, in the process if you are not losing customers; you already a potential winner.

Moreover, the chapter begins by tracking the basic objects of marketing, describing the elemental differences between domestic and transnational marketing. Today on the other hand we see that domestic marketing is largely dependent on brand merchandizing, and transnational marketing is fast moving on personal selling. There for a linkage assessment grid of the value of sale and degree of involvement is also provided to assess the relevance of maxi marketing. It is assessed on a particular transnational marketing situation.

Additionally, it described a process for maximizing synergy for transnational marketing, through the double duty strategies of marketing. Primarily by illustrating the emerging era of new transnational marketing modes and codes, empathizing with the customer. Myopic short run strategies are discouraged by the maxim 'No one wins a sales promotion war; specially in a Catch 22 situation'. On the domain of advertising and promotional strategy; upscale educated consumer wants have been highlighted. It says, to learn more about a product and not less. Despite the explosion of information confronted, products have to be bolstered. New developments in the media and marketing methods, channels and practices are also covered systematically.

The models provide routes to trans-nationally maximize the target through personal data banks and data-base. It explains that marketing can be done through media, accountability, awareness, activation, synergy, linkage, sales and distribution. In developing the model a distinction is made between making a sale, reaching the prospect, and developing the relationship between the client and the customer.

Maxi-transnational Marketing (MTM) strategy reinforces convergence of facets of business; for profits optimizing catalogue of efforts. It begins from the nascent phase of business and exceeds beyond consumer delight. This chapter infuses 'learnt efficiency' to foster competencies throttling promotional –mix applied to products, from planning to roadmap to ultimate practice. Increase in market equity, brand image is the intention of MTM. It reflects on the touch points of media impact, advertisements and other promotional mix. Life time customer value (LTV) , Response Marketing (RM) , Total Market Coverage (TMC) and value and life styles (VAL) have been related and elucidated with grids and store boards, enabling the reader replicate and experiment. Few small case lets as company's example give a coverage with newness.

Chapter six has been titled as maxi-transnational promotion and psycho-somatic customer access and dealing on maximized accountability. It is seen that maximized accountability always become ultimate objective of promotional strategy and is intrinsic in nature . The advertisements imagined for a customer segment have been seen to have definite results on sales. Strength of brand image leads to customer loyalty; depending on product quality. Theme of advertisement campaigns have to be sensitive and sensible.

It is the psycho-somatic aspect of the buyer brain which plays a key-role. In fact, left –hemisphere and right-hemisphere of brain respond differently and therefore left –brain and right-brain advertising have been unique. It is also observed that USP of product and advertisement have lasting impression in the mind-tree of the viewer. Moreover the diagrams, tables and provocative assessment questions have provided ideas for scanning the view-points. The chapter has ample open-ended rebounding ideas to reflect.

Maximized accountability is driven through impact of advertisements designed for target segments. It is the effect of buying decisions made effective by advertisements. It relates and estimates the value of expenditure incurred on advertisement vis a vis sales. Advertisement create, promote and build a lasting brand image for influencing decisions for purchasers. It speaks on the concept of USP in every product for creating mind share and identify the mechanical aspect of 'right brain' and creatively of 'left brain'.

This chapter describes the impact of sales promotion associating tools like coupon promotion, min-max marketing , promotion, sampling promotion and sweep stakes promotion etc. for maximising synergy. Assessment based grids approach have been deployed for ultimate customer catch. All aspects have been engaged for attending to the ambit of promotional strategy.

Chapter seven and eight discusses the issues, methods and processes in transnational marketing planning and special roles that corporate strategic planning plays. The most formidable challenge here is commented by Bertrand de Jouvenel in L'art deta conjecture. It quotes 'The great problem of our age is that; we wish things should change more quickly on the one hand and that things to come should be better known on the other" . It deals with the reckoning issues, marshaling operations and combating challenges. Hence, it starts with political risk and governmental action that influence transnational marketing planning. It invites and provides an alluring criteria for the country selection in marketing products and services. It discusses and hints a guideline for transnational investment and business strategy, provides a notional reason for acceptable transnational risk. Preferred antidotes are also clearly endowed.

In launching a marketing strategy of a product abroad, special considerations must be accorded to the stages of development. Stages of development could be dormant, traditional, transitional, pre-take-off, take-off, innovative, rapid growth, technological maturity, high mass consumption and affluence of the country. The transnational company have a bewildering selection of possibilities in terms of resource, market strategies and systematic plans.

Similarly, policy alternatives for new product development, modifications and diversifications are examined exhaustively by a set of alternate situations and options. They are discussed in terms of dependence on product range, marketing potential of product life-cycles , special opportunities, spin-off from R&D, inventions, seasonal balance of products, liquidity and other trigger situations. Options for moving abroad has been elucidated by means of the decision tree and historical strategy. Flow charts portrayed to analyze transnational opportunity for export, sale of knowledge, planning for foreign investment, joint ventures and licensing/franchising. Future developmental aspects by strategic subsidiary, regional centers are described. Thoughts for organizational planning of the transnational marketing firm have been speculated.

Chapter nine reveals an insight into the ways and means to win transnational markets worldwide. Philosophy of the book revolves around the intrinsic evolving character of the market forces, and how to handle these fundamental changes in the market place. The following eight inherent factors have been identified as the characteristics of a winning company . They are leadership, autonomy, control, involvement, market orientation, getting back to basics, innovation and integrity. Out of the above mentioned winning factors, four steps have been earmarked for special attention in the case of transnational companies aspiring to keep on winning. They are autonomy, control, market orientation and innovation.

A company constantly looking over others shoulders, without a strategic perspective, on the above, manned by rudderless bureaucracies, with a complex centralized bureaucratic structures, complex formal procedures of work and communications, little delegation, aversion to risk, functional specialization, financially lackadaisical, in-attentive to last details of transnational business planning, average standards of performance, low brand visibility , insignificant customer relations, average quality control, passive marketing, averse to too much market information, many barriers to change, lack of curiosity for others and non-transnational perspective is not expected in the race.

Chapter ten sums up the 'do's and don'ts' of Transnational marketing. There are '120 suggestions on the do's and 60 on the don'ts' of transnational marketing given. All the suggestions given in the book pertain to image of the company, type of managers , nature of planning and its special impact , packaging, delivery schedules, the product offering, response times, risk, pricing , customer responsiveness, controls, product- market strategies, synergy in promotions, the marketing ethics, commitment, MIS and database marketing, new promotional and advertising tools, culture, personalized factor in selling ,creativity and innovation. Journey into the entrails of marketing and transnational marketing channeled through a mazy motion of organizational performance criteria will be of immense value, curiosity and benefit to the reader.

— Authors

Acknowledgements

"Market is a macabre mockery
An exotic flurry of curry full with puree;

Run for the strawberry and cherry
Run to the global market place; devoid of drudgery"

Our thanks are due to Peter Drucker, Michael Porter, Warren J. Keegan, Kenichi Ohmae, Noam Chomski for their seem less flair in spelling creativity for the global business; obviously with a splendid touch.

We are thankful to all our colleagues, students and philosophers. Our lavish thanks for the friends and foes.

We would like to express our special thanks particularly to Mr. Alok Ghosh-P.A. to Vice Chancellor, KIIT-U, Mr.Ansuman Jena (Research Scholar), Miss Preety Priyambada - Executive Assistant-Chintan, Mr. Niranjan Mishra-Data Entry Operator and Rituparna Mishra MBA- I (2009-2011) for their help and assistance in the right time for preparing the manuscript of the book.

Never the less, our profuse thanks Dr. Achyuta Samanta Founder-KIIT University, KIIT Group of Institutions and social reformer for his motivation, unstinted support and a platform to realize our dreams.

Dr. Biswajit Das
Dr. Ipseeta Satpathy
Dr. Sanjay Saran

Contents

Chapter 1

Transnational Marketing Strategy

LEARNING OBJECTIVES

After going through this chapter; the reader should be able to:

1. Explain the natural and goal of transnational marketing strategy through business worldviews.
2. Understand the strategic orientation of companies in global market environment.
3. Recognize the salient points for creating and expanding the business transnational and ensuring modalities of channels of distribution.
4. Identify the trends of marketing applied to almost all the organizations and managers to all the levels in the organizations; wanting to go transnational or international.
5. Ascertain the paths and patterns of integrated marketing communication leading to globalization; employing IT revolution in the WTO regime.
6. Explain the fundamental ideas of ethnocentric, polycentric, regiocentric and geocentric companies for approaching the globalization, process moving towards global village.

> *'The future is already here. It's just unevenly distributed'.*
>
> — *William Gibson*
>
> *'How did you go bankrupt? Gradually, then suddenly'.*
>
> — *Earnest Hemingway*

7. Describe the vital aspects of marketing communication in creating mass markets; along with the views of Alvin Toffler, John Naisbitt and Theodore Levitt.
8. Describe the multifarious approaches of the driving forces and retraining forces of the economy. Roles of technology, transportation, driving market needs, cost, free markets & peace in driving, and culture, casts, national controls, war, management myopia and nationalism in refraining.
9. Display how the management operational process relates to the theories of management, and it scientifically blends practice into theory and vice-versa. It is emphatically depicted in relation to the access of media communication in creating global melting pots and global customers.
10. Realize that all orientations of management require a systems approach, taking into account situations, incidences, contingencies and complexities of the market places. Market is in a flux; and has to unshackle from the conventional mode, and integrate into the desired forces of markets, which can reinforce through trade agreements.
11. Define into the essence of globalization mode; passing through the transnational check posts, for capitalizing on market share; expecting ROI on R&D for innovation in products and services.
12. Interact on the aspects of leveraging on experience transfer, resources become optimally utilized and scales of economies in the countries integrate and symbiotically develop.
13. Insight in to case-lets on company types replete in the business world and overcome obstacles in the path of progress.
14. Understand into the essence of the book that it intends to portray.

The mass market has splintered into the 'demassified' market. In *The Third Wave,* Alvin Toffler has described how the mass market has split into ever-multiplying, ever-changing sets of mini-markets that demand a continually expanding range of options, models, types, sizes, colours and customizations'. Further, as John Naisbitt concludes in *Megatrends*, 'the multiple option society is a new ball game and marketers know that they must win consumers market by market'. Perhaps, the most dramatic example is General Motor's announced plan for its new Saturn automobile—the car will virtually be designed by its today's wisdom, contrary to the old, that the more products you can go to market with, the more constituencies you will attract. However, it must be reckoned that opportunities are problems in disguise. Is it possible, the question arises, to sell all or most products to all constituencies and keep them sold, with the same old shotgun approach of mass marketing that worked so well in the past?

With expenditures for advertising reaching $100 billion a year in the US alone and sales promotion estimated as high as $60 billion US, transnational businesses must re-examine the advertising, promotional and marketing assumptions and test them against the new realities. The new approach, in essence, needs to use new techniques and technologies including the media to target the most likely marketing prospects, insist on accountability for each advertising expenditure and link the advertising to a public and/or private database used to convert prospects into 'tiers' and transform tiers into heavy users, through multiple distribution channels.

The reasons for it are the following:

- Demassification of the market
- The changing transnational and US household
- The decline of brand loyalty
- Deregulation
- New ways to shop and pay
- The development of database marketing
- The rise of the service economy
- The flowering of the information society
- Proliferation of new products through innovations
- Multiplication of distribution channels
- The explosion of couponing ($20 billion annually)
- The slippage in network television advertising efficiency
- The new playing field—Customers, Marketers and Ground Rules

To sum up, the transnational marketplace is changing dramatically, whether one likes it or not. Demographic and lifestyle changes have delivered a heavy blow to mass marketing and brand loyalty. Today's is a multi-population society, and the individual consumer is (more of a) king. De regulation has splintered the financial, travel and communications sectors into a shopper's paradise of choices.

It has become affordable for any company to keep track of an individual's preference and purchases and respond to them. Thanks to the computer, marketers can reach out to customers and competitor's customers with special products, services and offers tailored to the personal information accumulated in Public and Private Customer databases. The toll-free telephone call, the 6 to 10 credit cards per household, the retail transaction computer terminals and the targeting of direct mail to individual lifestyles and psychographics are all reshaping consumer habits. These are the new considerations on every side—no the service economy, the information society, the flood of 'me too' products. However, in this highly competitive market the innovating companies can still win.

PRELUDE

Transnational marketing is the business process of aptly focusing on the resources and objectives of a company on a transnational marketing opportunities and scope. Almost all the companies, nowadays, pursue global marketing for a couple of reasons. The companies take up the advantage of the available opportunities for growth and expansion and to survive. Those who fail to follow transnational opportunities eventually lose their domestic markets as against the expansion plan of multinationals. They are driven to a side by the competitive competitors launching and operating from overseas. What is important is to apply the 'universal discipline of marketing' to transnational opportunities derived from the markets. Fundamental objective of marketing is to create customer value, innovation integration and competitive advantage. Further, it has to be reinforced with focus and to be maintained properly.

Management of companies is categorized in terms of its orientation toward the global markets. International companies seek marketing opportunities outside the home market by applying the various elements of marketing mix. They are basically called ethnocentric, polycentric, region-centric and geocentric. A polycentric business worldview dominates business as a multinational company. Herein, marketing mix is adopted by the 'country executives' operating autonomously. A polycentric orientation is said to be having worldviews, which are unlike that of the ethnocentric companies (which disallows the company to look abroad) Unlike ethnocentric fanatic – patriotic, polycentric companies wish to expand their business to the other potential foreign centuries. They are essentially the transnational companies already operating in overseas market. But in the case of multinational companies, the companies have operating chief functionaries and executives from the same country or other countries. All polycentric companies may not be multinational companies. Executives at global and transnational companies are either region-centric or geocentric in orientation. They follow both extension and adaptation strategies in the global context of business. Transnational marketing is formed by the dynamic interplay of N-number of driving and restraining forces. They include needs and wants, technology, transportation, costs, quality, economic growth and recognition of opportunities to leverage global business. Similarly, the restraining pressures and forces include market differences, management myopia, organizational culture and national controls. Economies are bound to grow in the virgin markets. Product innovations are bound to happen, and people will always adopt superior products with affordable price tag.

MANAGEMENT ORIENTATION AND BELIEFS

Management is about getting things done through others utilizing man, material and money. Orientations are the factors contributing to the domain of make-believe principles adopted in the environment, across the countries. Make-believes create viewpoints and orient the mind to understand with a perspective, and the perspective is a belief in a matrix.

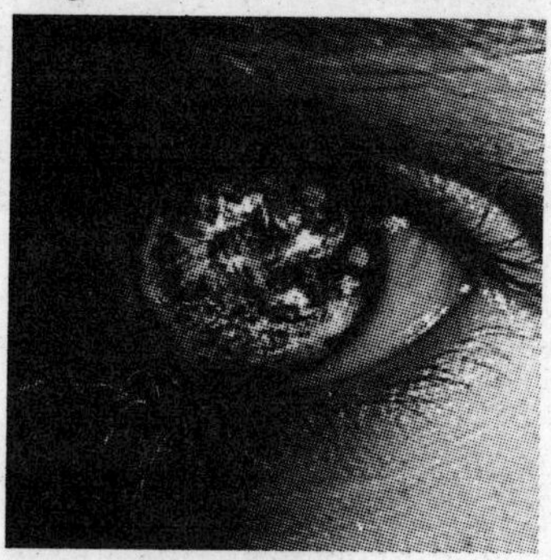

Mind's eyes

All the companies around the globe respond to the transnational market opportunities. It is greatly dependent on the management's assumptions or beliefs. It could be conscious or/ and unconscious. It is about the nature of world of business and its antecedents, interactions and interceptions.

Taking these perspectives into view, the worldview of a company's employee can be described. In fact, these worldviews are pertinently termed as ethnocentric, polycentric, region-centric and geocentric.

As a matter of fact, the management of a company with its prevalent ethnocentric orientation can consciously make a change by adopting a decision to make it geocentric. These are based on the line and length of the companies' ambit of work operations in the business environment. These orientations in its acronym, collectively and continuously are known as EPRG framework. They are:

E: Ethnocentric

P: Polycentric

R: Region-centric

G: Geocentric

Global people

Details of the aspects have been duly summarized in the following figure.

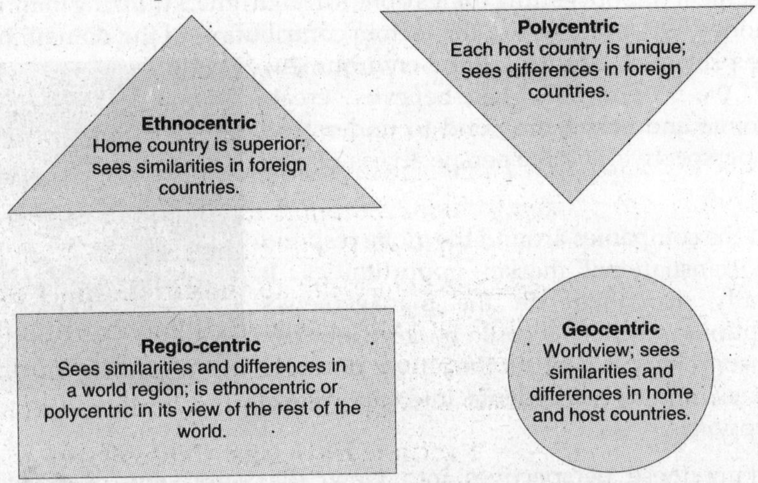

Fig. 1.1 Management Orientation and Assumptions of Companies

Source: *GMM, Warren Keegan*

❑ Ethnocentric Orientation

Ethnocentric orientation has the idiosyncratic characteristics of people. He is said to be ethnocentric person, who assumes that his home country is superior in comparison to the rest of the world. A person with a perception like this is said to have an ethnocentric orientation of the psyche. Ethnocentric orientation means, when an employee sees 'only similarities in all the markets'. It is assumed that the products and practices that are successful in the home country will be successful anywhere in any foreign market due to their demonstrated superiority amongst the competitors.

Spice market in Dubai

Ethnocentric orientation speaks about hegemony of the promoter of the company with respect to product market. A feeling of highhandedness in the marketing of country made products limiting to the own country. These companies being promoted by the native of the country sees no market in other countries. This is a blinding perception of the promoter doing business. In all probability nationals of Germany origin may have such feelings about India, Cambodia, China, Thailand and other similar countries. The aspect of precision in Germany is exceptional and recognized world wide. Middle East companies have perception similarly different on oil and its allied sector. An example of the sale's strategy of pre-engineering products of Zamil Steel and similar products of TATA Blue Scope and Kirby is evident in the Indian market. Zamil Steel does not accommodate customization of small sheds constructed in different parts of the country in India where industrial boom has taken place and do not compromise on price. Moreover, whole of Middle East have a typical ethnocentric regional mindset, and the same is seen in Europe with erstwhile French colonial rule.

Ethnocentric orientation means that in certain companies, opportunities outside the home country are treated as insignificant. These companies are at times called as domestic companies. The ethnocentric companies, which conduct business outside the home country, are said to be international companies. They cling to the notion that the products that do a good market in the home country are superior products. Hence, it can be sold everywhere.

In ethnocentric international companies, foreign operations are seen as secondary and subordinate to domestic markets. Ethnocentric company has an assumption that 'experienced headquarters' knowledge and organizational potentials are important. They can be applied in certain other parts of the world or in major regions. This sometimes works to the company's advantage. The learned valuable core knowledge and core experience in the local markets are honed and encashed.

To a manufacturing company, firm and enterprise, 'ethnocentrism' denotes foreign markets that are 'seen as places for disposal of surplus domestic production'. Overseas market plans are chalked out from the plans, policies and procedures similar to the home country. In fact, herein, no careful and systematic marketing research is conducted for the foreign market expansion, outside the home country. Even it is seen that seldom any major modifications are made on the products/services. Many a time it is seen that consumer needs and wants in international markets differ from that of the home country. However, in ethnocentric markets, the headquarters command control is oblivious and differences are ignored.

Nissan car

An example of Nissan in the given context is noteworthy. Nissan's ethnocentric orientation was apparent during the first few years of exporting cars and trucks to the US. Being born to the mild winters of Japan, these vehicles were difficult to start when exposed to cold winters in many parts of the US. In fact, in some parts of northern Japan, car owners put blankets over the hoods on Nissan cars. Nissan presumed that the US people could do the same.

Similarly till 1980s, Eli Lilly operated as an ethnocentric company from the US. Its activity outside the US was monitored from headquarters. It focused on selling products in the prices originally developed for US markets. Most of the business enterprises 70 years ago, especially located in Triad countries like the US operated with ethnocentric orientation because of their monopoly over the international market. Currently, it is a treat for the company to expand business operations overseas.

❑ Polycentric Orientation

In fact, polycentric orientation is the opposite of ethnocentric orientation which has been defined before. Polycentric, as the term signifies, describes the quintessence of the type. Many boards of management (often unconscious) believe that, each country in which the company does its business is absolutely unique and distinctly different. This kind of belief creates a strong basis for each of the subsidiary company to build its own unique business and marketing strategies. It is ultimately to succeed. Often, the term multinational company is used for the same.

Toyota company

An example can bring clarity to the concept of polycentric company. Citicorp's financial services operated on a polycentric mindset, around the globe. Corp's executives thought that the company climate was like a medieval state, in which there was the king and his court who were incharge of the command.

It was exactly not that. It was indeed more like the 'land barons' who were incharge. The king and his court may ordain, but the land barons went and did their thing. John Reed, the CEO of Citicorp, realizing the spat of globalization of financial services, attempted to integrate between the Citicorp's operating units worldwide. Like Jack Welch, the CEO of GE, John Reed too moved to instil a polycentric orientation to enable the business run smoothly.

❑ Regio-centric Orientation

Regio-centric orientation of a company is otherwise also known as geocentric orientation; but is not the same. In regio-centric orientation, company's viewpoints are unique. Herein, management sees different regions as unique and seeks to knit and develop an 'integrated regional strategy'. Almost all the treaties that are being held between countries with a common agenda or a mutually agreed agenda located in a region are examples.

G-8 Summit

ASEAN is an association of countries combined for mutual interest in the Southeast Asian region. G-8 is a trade agreement made on a perspective of regional interest of the countries that have become members. Companies oriented in this direction are understood to be regio-centric. An US company that lays stress on countries of proximity bracketed within the North American Free Trade Agreement (NAFTA) like that of U.S., Canada and Mexico is said to have a regio-centric orientation. It could be similar with other European companies that focused attention on the European Union or Europe, Oceania or Middle East is said to be a region-centric company.

❑ Geocentric Orientation

Geocentric companies are an extension of the regio-centric companies expanding their market share across the geographical expanse. A company with geocentric orientation sees the entire globe as a potential market. These companies strive to extend an integrated worldview market strategies to capture the market. *Any company that has a board of management whose ideology is region-centric or geocentric in orientation is sometimes called as a global company or transnational company.*

This geocentric orientation represents a perfect synthesis of ethnocentric and polycentric orientation. It is a 'facet' or 'worldview' that envisages a host of similarities and dissimilarities in the marketplaces and in various countries. It, as such, seeks to create and recreate a global strategic move that is fully responsive and fully comply with the local needs and wants.

Microsoft

In a conservative assessment, a regio-centric manager is said to have a 'worldview' on a regional parameter. The world beyond the 'region of interest' is seen with an ethnocentric or a polycentric orientation. They sometimes have a common meeting ground with a thin line of difference. Company managers and promoters carry geocentric pride and mentality; which drives the market and that also bump as a roadblock in the market channels. Globalisation taken for granted is the opinion of the managers who believe in globalization. They are unlike the managers with ethnocentric orientations who prefer to confine themselves and see no prospect outside.

Some company managers having an innate geocentric orientation are inevitable. When we reflect on Jack Welch's quote 'globalization must be taken for granted', it implies that a good number of company managers are geocentric in their taste and likings. Yet, it has also been observed that a number of companies confine their regional competitiveness to niche out the target markets. Rather than moving directly to develop global markets they retain to the regional soil. Competitive environment do not make the company expand the product segment to the global customers.

SUMMARY OF THE FOUR ORIENTATIONS

If we review all the four conspicuous kind of worldview orientations, then apart from the subtle nuances, we see the following situations:

1. Ethnocentric company is seen to centralized, conservative and traditional in its marketing management,
2. Polycentric company is decentralized and delegated,
3. Region-centric companies are integrated in a regional platform in a scale and
4. Geocentric companies are integrated on a global scale.

The crucial differences between all the four orientations are noted above. The ethnocentric orientation is based on a belief of managers who run the business. This belief is about the superiority of one's own home country. However, perception and belief are not the reality. Reality is quite different from belief and perceptions. Ethnocentric orientation is a state of mind which is traditional in essence. Similarly, the underlying belief and assumption of the polycentric approach is on the unity and diversity and on the division of responsibility per territory. Polycentric approach states that there are so many differences in cultural, economic, social, legal and marketing conditions in the world that it is next to impossible and futile to attempt to transfer experience across the national boundaries. Regio-centric parameters are based on the trade relations and consortiums amongst the companies in countries adjoining the geographical distribution. Geocentric or transnational companies are global companies in the true sense of the term. They have seamless flair in penetrating into the global marketplaces. An example could be Coca-Cola's presence across countries.

DRIVING AND RESTRAINING FORCES AFFECTING TRANSNATIONAL INTEGRATION AND MARKETING

Market mobilization, driving and restraining forces affecting global integration and global marketing are important topics to introspect. Over a period of 70 years, since World War-II, there has been a significant and mind-boggling growth and development in the global economy. By virtue of the brisk and dynamic interplay of the innumerable actively surging drivers of the economy, the issues and challenges associated with it have been overcome. These driving forces have contributed to the creation of inclusive capital and wealth of the nations.

During these seven decades, multiple companies from various parts of the globe in different industries achieved great success. This success came by pursuing international targets, multinational targets and global strategies. Marketing pastures were monopoly driven. They formulated strategic agenda to invade new markets and explore the potential customer base. Recent spurt of changes in the companies and WTO norms during the last decade of 20th century have marked a drastic change in the business environment. Numerous crowding confrontations presented countless challenges for establishing corridors for doing business. However, despite these challenges new businesses were created in different ways and kinds. Growing importance of global marketing brought down the barriers of transactions between countries. It stemmed from the fact that driving forces have more momentum, speed and peace than the restraining forces. We can see the forces affecting global integration in the following diagram:

Global Integration

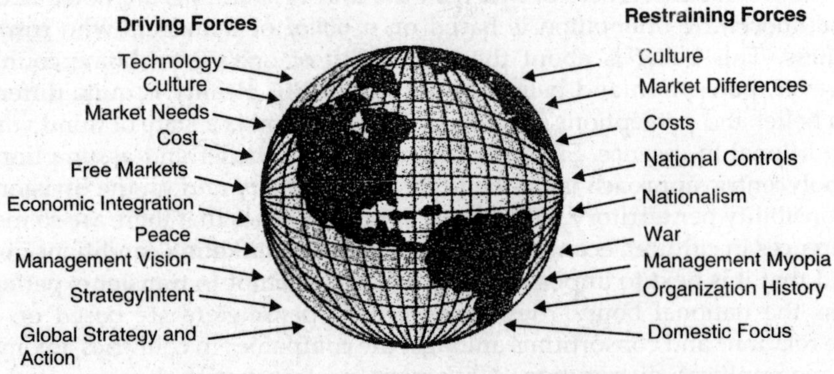

Fig. 1.2 Driving and Restraining Forces Affecting Transnational Integration

DRIVING FORCES OF TRANSNATIONALIZATION

Driving forces are important for transnationalization or globalization. Confluence and convergence of market needs and wants, advances in technology, cost-cutting measures, quality improvement in products, enhanced hi-tech communication network, transportation technology, worldwide economic growth and honing of opportunities, etc., are the key driving forces which leveraged the advancement of the global economy in the past decades. The vital driving forces for the globalization that the industries are generally subjected to, have been discussed as follows.

❑ Penetration of Technology

The accessibility of technology is a significant factor in penetrating foreign market. Technology helps in crossing national and cultural boundaries, which are so peculiarly different. As a matter of fact, technology is 'stateless'. It does not have any cultural boundaries; nothing can limit its entry into the business. It is observed that, once a technology is invented and is found helpful for the mankind, it becomes available everywhere in the world. It moves very fast across cross-cultural bottlenecks. It is the phenomenon which supports Theodore Levitt's citadel of concepts on global village. Levitt's prediction relating to the rise of global markets for standardized products/service is befitting in the context of technology emergence. The much quoted harvard business review article stands as a landmark, wherein Levitt anticipated the flood of communication revolution. Today in the current times, in fact, communication revolution has bolstered and has actively become a driving force for steering the global marketing and its entertainment, information and educational products etc. The mass use of satellite connections globally, disks linking satellites and its global television network connectivity like that of CNN, Geography Channel, BBC and MTV, besides the Internet, are a small list of the technological factors responsible for the emergence of 'global village' concept. In some of the regional markets in Europe, the US and even Asia, the overlapping clash and clamours of the acts of advertising spreading across the national boundaries have resulted in the mobility of consumers. This have eventually opened avenues and opportunities for marketers. Fast-moving customers in the swing have gone pan-continental. Companies and markets have also started pursuing pan-European, Pan-US and Pan-Asian product positioning strategies for exploiting market niches.

CNN

❑ Regional Economic Agreements and Tie-ups

Isolation of a country does not pay to the economical growth of any country; economy gets imprisoned in a cocoon. Establishment of linkages can happen through economic agreements between countries. A good number of multilateral trade agreements (MTA) between countries have accelerated the speed of global integration and market forces to be proactive. Much talked about MTA called NAFTA has been expanding its trading knots among the firms, companies, corporate and governments in the United States, Canada and Mexico. Moreover, it is eventually the General Agreement on Tariffs and Trade (GATT), which ameliorated the market dynamics first, but subsequently, GATT was ratified by more than 120 nations in 1994 and has been christened (or replaced) by the World Trade Organization (WTO) to promote and protect free trade. This has eventually come under lethal attacks by the basket cases, underdeveloped and developing countries due to its parochial and biased views. Launching of Euro in Europe and the growing membership of the European Union have reduced the hindrances/barriers to trade within the region. This has made the European Union looked at by the US with envy and is believed to have been exercising hegemony as commented by certain economists.

❑ Needs and Wants in Transnational Markets

It is important to understand the needs and wants of the global markets. Any marketer analysing the markets from all around the world shall discover two main types of differences. They are 'cultural universals' and 'cultural differences'. The commonality found in the buying nature caters to the criteria of knowing the opportunity. This underlying knowledge of the opportunity is about the global markets. This is to be served and facilitated by 'creating ready products' matching the market demand. Products are created to compliment the requirements of identified people.

Creation is deliberate. Existence of global market is a reality. It is not static but is dynamic. Therefore, no market that claims to have certain definition of global market is constant. These are creation of marketing minds, creating categories of markets and finding a matrix to compare and judge their potentials.

They are invariably created by marketing endeavour. A clever example can make it understandable. Let's say that 'no one needs soft drinks', but currently, in certain countries the per capita soft drink consumption exceeds the water consumption. It has replaced the position of water required for quenching thirst. Even the bottling of water by different brands is an example, so similar. It is the marketing designs that have driven this behavioural change in consumers. Today, we see that both the bottled water industry and soft drink industry are global industry.

Today, the consumer needs and wants around the globe are converging and falling into a symmetry, a pattern and a single segment. It has created global customers with customized mass markets. This situation creates an opportunity for the expansion of global marketing. All multinational companies going for product adaptation are threatened by global competitors. They have the risk of survival if they do not recognize opportunities to serve global customers.

The advertisement style adopted by Marlboro is a paradigm for any premium global brand. Marlboro targeted the urban smokers. Its brand appealed to the spirit of freedom, independence and open space atop a plateau. It was symbolized by the carefree image of a cowboy in a beautiful western setting with black stallions galloping with unbridled passion. The 'need emphasized by Marlboro' is universal. The basic appeal, advertising and positioning are global in nature. The company Philip Morris, which markets Marlboro, is a global company. It has discovered the spirit years ago—the idea of harnessing the same basic market needs meeting the global approach. What is important is the invading ideas needed for brand recall in the mind tree?

❑ Improvements in Communication and Transportation

Over a period, the time taken for travelling a distance and also the cost have fallen a great deal. It has fallen tremendously over the last 70 years of scientific innovations. The inventions of jet planes have revolutionized the world of communication, by means of which people can travel around the world in less than 48 hours. Tourism has enabled people from many countries to visit places. They see and experience the newest products being sold abroad and carry them back home, find them easy to replicate and sell in the local market.

One core characteristic of global business is the possibility of face-to-face communication. It has become possible for the company and its customers to come closer for a marriage of minds. Post 1990, the new communication technologies like e-mail, fax, teleconferencing and videoconferencing have enabled the managers, executives and customers to be linked with each other electronically. Virtual presence has created connectivity that is strong enough. In fact, virtually from any part of the world within a fraction of a second, one can connect with the other to exchange ideas without the cost of travel. Virtual markets have lessened the cost in manifold ways.

Transportation technology has undergone a revolutionary phase in the last few years. The time and cost required for shipment have sufficiently reduced due to implementation of scientific instruments and machines. Couriers, nowadays deliver a letter from London to India in three days and sometimes faster than the domestic mail. The unit cost of shipping automobiles by specially designed auto-transport ships is less than the cost of overland shipping from other ports. Excavators, earthmovers and conveyors do immense work without human labour and have made the life easy and comfortable.

❑ New Product Development and Costs

New product development has become a bare necessity for beating competition. The pressure that is building up for the globalization process is intense. Transnationalization or globalization entails new product development and new products require huge investments and long periods of development time. The pharmaceuticals industry is a glaring example of the driving force. According to the Pharmaceutical Manufacturers Association (PMA), the cost of developing a new drug in 1976 was $54 million and by 1982, the cost increased to $87 million but by 1993, the cost for developing a new drug reached to an astronomical amount of $359 million. These costs involved in

R&D are recovered in the global market place. No single national market is big enough to support the investments as a market to be recovered. A whopping $200 billion pharmaceutical industry of 2003, in eight countries accounted for 75 percent of sales. New products are a key to drive the market forces and are mostly steered through patents.

Quality Standard is the Key

Quality standard is the key. It is the 'global market entry for business' which usually earns the revenue and generates profit margins. In this process, as an outcome of the entry, the company reacts against adverse situations and learns to combat oddities, the result of which supplements an enhancement of product design and manufacturing quality. Both transnational and domestic companies invariably spend 5 percent of sales on R&D. Transnational companies earn a colossus total revenue which is multiple times more than domestic companies. It is because of this reason transnational companies cater to a far greater customer population. Cases of Coco-Cola, Intel, IBM, IKEA, Caterpillar and Toyota can be studied as to how these transnational companies have achieved world-class quality and status.

All transnational companies elevate the quality bar for all the competitors in an industry. When transnational companies acknowledge a benchmark in quality, the competitors in the industry immediately make their own improvements. They strive to come up to the same level at par. Competitions amongst companies have forced all companies to enhance quality standards. Real transnational products drive down the continued research across all business functions. It is the quality, uniformity and cost reduction which are the appropriate driving forces behind successful companies. This is also the strategy behind the 'Nano—small car' of the Tata's in India and Ford's development of their 'World Car', which is sold in US as Ford Contour Mercury Mystique and in Europe 'Mondeo'. Home appliances, pharmaceutical products and personal care products, etc., also have cut-throat competition.

TRENDS OF CHANGES IN THE WORLD ECONOMY

Transnational expansion is possible through growth in the global markets. The driving forces that have contributed in the expansion of international economy are the reasons behind this economic growth. These driving forces can be discussed in this context. Also, the factors of growth can be analysed.

First of all, growth has given birth to market opportunities. These opportunities provided a major incentive for companies to go transnational. On the other hand, slow growth of a company's domestic market can induce it to look beyond the domestic market for better opportunities. It could also be inside the nation or region or beyond.

World Economy

Secondly, economic growth reduces resistance of domestic firms in response to the entry of foreign firms into domestic economies. When countries grow apace, policy makers look favourably at the foreign firms. Growing country means growing markets. They breed plenty of opportunities for all sections of people. They open corridors for the foreign companies to access any domestic economy without taking the business share of the local companies. In the absence of economic growth, transnational companies quit their business from the soil. Government interventions protect domestic businesses to let the position of the local market grow. Global recession of the early 1990, 2006 and 2008 created fiscal pressure in most countries. It limited the access by foreigners to domestic markets.

The third aspect is the global movement for deregulation and privatization. It is another driving force. Trend for privatization is opening up the closed markets. It is creating tremendous opportunities. A suitable example can be as follows. Earlier, in many nations, the telephone communication was a monopolistic business venture. Subsequently, in many privatized economies, it was made easy for companies to buy the telephone communication rights. Private companies are generally interested to search for the best bidding offer to buy. They buy regardless of the nationality of supplier and vendors. Privatization of telephone communication in the world has created tremendous opportunities. They have also created perceptible threats for non-performing companies in the industry. Competition is the utmost driver of change to take place with cost leadership.

LEVERAGING MECHANISM OF TRANSNATIONAL COMPANIES

All transnational companies have the scope to leverage business. They harness opportunities. Leveraging is a type of advantage for a company. Company enjoys it by conducting business in many countries. Each of the **four important 'types of leverage'** is explained below:

- Experience transfers
- Scale economies
- Resource utilization
- Transnational strategy

❑ Experience Transfer by Companies

A transnational company can leverage business through its experience in any part of the market across the globe. It can exploit market through the management practices, strategies, products, advertising appeals, sales and promotional ideas. These aspects have been tried and tested in the actual markets before; their application becomes easy in other comparable markets.

❑ Scale Economies in Companies

A transnational company can take advantage of its huge volume of manufacturing. It can avail better advantage on the scale of volume in comparison to a solitary factory since in case of transnational companies; small products can be assembled for manufacturing the finished products hassle free. A transnational company can afford to produce finished products by combining the components manufactured in size-efficient machines in the plants. They could be located in different countries. All multinational companies are typical of the kind. Japanese giant Matsushita Electricity Company operates in countries like China, America, Europe, India, Korea, Thailand, Indonesia and so forth, producing small parts which are also importantly priced. It does so looking into the availability of man, material and investment they associate themselves. It has branches in almost many countries doing business by collecting and assembling products and, finally by selling a finished product. Companies implement flexible manufacturing techniques and invest in factories outside the home country. Scale economies were a landmark for the success of Japanese companies in 1970s for a decade. A company can achieve leverage in staffing by eliminating duplicate positions post acquisition. It improves staff competence, quality and efficiency.

❑ Resource Utilization by Companies

Transnational companies have the ability to scan the world to spot efficient people, potential currency and quality raw materials that can compete effectively in global markets. In fact, it is not much of a problem for a transnational company to raise equity. It can raise fund from all countries even if the value of the home currency falls dramatically. Rise and fall in the home currency does not affect the company anyway. Almost all countries have their individual currencies to sustain the country business. They have the validity to transact business of profit, except in the situations like inflation or recession when the currency rates fluctuate beyond lower bracket. All transnational companies seek financial support to compete. They can use the resources where there is an urgent need, opportunity and profit.

❑ Transnational or Global Strategy by Companies

Global strategy of the transnational company is its biggest advantage. This kind of strategy is based on precise information network and efficient systems. It is possible after scanning the entire business environment and identifying the opportunities, trends, threats and resources. On noticing the opportunities, a transnational company takes up through the three principles explained before. It can leverage skills, focus on the resources and create superior perceived value for customers to accomplish competitive advantage. Transnational logistics is to create a winner product/service offering on an international scale. What lie at the bottom of it are survival and sustainability in business.

WHAT ARE TRANSNATIONAL/GLOBAL CORPORATIONS?

The transnational corporations or global corporations do business by following transnational goals, honing transnational resources and exploiting transnational market opportunities. They are the kinds who respond to driving, restraining and underlying the forces of business across the globe. Under the global umbrella, transnational corporations have taken full advantage of the extended communication technologies. They resorted to yielding the potential of market opportunities to contribute to and serve the needs and wants of all humankind. These transnational markets have responded to market opportunity and competitive threat and are the reckoning forces driving the world towards the global world order.

RESTRAINING FORCES

In spite of the impact of the aforementioned driving forces, several restraining forces are slowing down the company's drive in creating transnational marketing happen. The three most important restraining forces are as follows:

- Management myopia
- Organizational culture
- National controls

Today, it is seen that the 'driving forces' dominate the 'restraining forces' for which the transnational marketing is galloping ahead and growing at a pace. The discussions on restraining forces are as follows:

❑ Management Myopia and Organizational Culture

It is seen that at times, a company management ignores the opportunities by not taking up the chance of transnational marketing and forging ahead. Ethnocentric and short-sighted companies do not expand across the boundaries. Myopia creates market disaster. It also happens when the headquarters attempt to dictate. Transnational marketing works with a strong local team which furnishes information on the local market conditions. Top-down approaches have failed in case of Parker Pen which ultimately got sold to a former UK subsidiary of Parker Pen. Gillette company as a matter of fact, acquired Parker.

Companies, where the 'subsidiary management, has a 'know it all' attitude have no room for advice from the top management. Where headquarter management is all knowing, there is no scope for 'local initiative'. They cannot make an in-depth study of local needs, wants and conditions. Executives in global companies learn to integrate and are trained to adopt successfully. Integrating global vision and perspective with local market initiative is important in business. The theme of business is strikingly significant—it is to adopt local initiative and get it added by central headquarters ideas and the reverse.

❑ National Controls and Barriers in Business

Nation-states protect local enterprise. They allow and maintain 'control' over the normal market access. They ensure entry by both low and high-tech industries in the market. These controls range from monopoly control to free market enterprise. From free trade of tobacco in the national markets to national government control of broadcast is customary. Tariff barriers have been removed from the high-income countries. Third world countries are scared of the dumping activities of the Triad countries. Advancement in innovations and upgradation of product is attributed to advanced countries. Yet, the World Trade Organization (WTO), NAFTA and other national economic agreements opened corridors for business in the countries. Non-tariff barriers (NTBs) pose far more difficult situations for the lesser countries and small companies where competition is concerned. In this scenario, for transnational companies to succeed in foreign markets is a threat and a prospect. NTB is under protest from many trade unions and the farmer's community. In order to overcome these barriers, all transnational companies have to become 'insiders' in the country of operation or in all countries where business is to start. Some 'utility companies' are notorious for accepting bids from foreign equipment suppliers in their country. It is a ploy favouring national suppliers. They expect the same treatment when they visit their country while bidding later date like a locale. As local companies they can also become an 'insider' in India or any country.

Transnational communication, advertising and promotion undergo screening, checking and filtering through the government regulations, enacted and enforced. Comparative advertisement is illegal in some countries and pornographic erotic advertisement is a crime in Middle East. In countries like Germany, premiums and sweepstakes are illegal. Global advertising industry uses different technical standards in the globe. Americans use Videotape players; NTSC standard is in use in Japan, SECAM is use in Europe (except in France) and France uses PAL system.

Summary

Mass market is being classified into category markets. Demassification is inevitable and ever changing through the continued customization process. Alvin Toffler and John Naisbitt envisaged a posterity market scenario obvious for the transnational business expansion. Market communication and promotional mix shall foster the advent of seamless market access through media. Lifestyle changes shall deregulate the conventional market dynamics and demographic models worldwide. In order to withstand competition, domestic companies have to search for opportunities abroad. The orientation of companies operating business can be classified into ethnocentric companies, polycentric companies, region-centric companies and geocentric companies. They strategically operate with the driving and restraining forces of technology and transformation.

Integration of global markets can happen through transnational aggression and penetration. This facilitating scope for integration has been possible due to the technology, particularly by IT revolution and mobile computing. Regional agreements for economic cooperation have immensely benefited for the globalization process. GATT reformation leading to WTO regime has become a catalyst for market boom. Cultural universals are the changing phenomenon of the current epoch. Invention and innovation have revolutionized the market forces and linked the global community under one umbrella. In the process of development transfer of experience, resource utilization and scaling of economic acts have taken place drastically.

The company types which have been narrated in the given caselets shall highlight on the worldviews and cater to the ideas for the subsequent chapters that follow. Transnational marketing strategy can be understood from the frameworks discussed. In this chapter, one shall find its reflections in the chapters ahead and shall open ideas for thoughts in the desired direction. They have been deliberated in their macro aspects.

CASE STUDY

What is meant by transnational company?

What is a transnational company? Nomenclatures, jargons and platitudes, etc., have dominated the books and a glossary of technical terms has evolved. It has become important for the people to understand the jargons with respect to definitions, to weave their thought process to probe into the dynamics of business. It has become essential to discern and differentiate the nuances of expression to articulate pertinently.

In a given situation we see that, in order to discern the identity of a type of executive and the company's transnational character that is operating in a business environment; many authors have tried to differentiate the companies by citing examples. This has substantially helped the readers in understanding. Therefore, it can also essentially distinguish the kind of executives and the kind of companies by virtue of their operating milieu. In order to dissect and divide the above business milieu, for getting a closer insight, a case-based 'situation analysis' has been given about the 'four executives of companies operating in many countries'. They have been interpreted as 'examples' to critically view the nuances of their character and understand transnational marketing environment. Examples of the four types of companies, their executive activities and operating environment, etc., are given in the following.

Company-1

Company-1 has a typical character. It sells products and services in more than 88 countries and has manufacturing units in 17 countries. In this case, its subsidiaries in the overseas manage business in their respective countries. They take total responsibility for their country operations which includes 'strategy formulations' for the company. Majority of the strategic executives in the subsidiaries are host-country nationals. They rely on the home-country persons for the position of CEO, COO and CFO designates. It could be one or more than one of the designations.

Let us think that the company has divided the world into world regions and the United States is the central hub for being the origin. Each of the world regions reports to its WTOs. It means that WTOs are responsible for all of their business outside the United States. These overseas companies are responsible for adapting the unique market preferences that are existent in their country or regions and are amply autonomous. They are proud of their international reach.

They manufacture not only in the US but also in Europe and the UK, Latin America, Middle East and Australia. They have done very well in overseas markets. They have performed well, especially in the high-income countries or Triad countries with an exception to Japan. They have a plan to enter into

Japanese market, but feel that Japan is a closed and protected country. Japan does not provide any level-playing field for other companies, and Japanese have taken advantage of this protection. They enjoy enhancing the wealth of their home country. They have, on the other hand, diversified into the US market places.

The industry in the given context and the home country US has lost out its market share in the US due to the Japanese market aggression. They are lobbying in US for more protection from Japanese competitions.

Company-2

Company-2 has a unique character. It is a unique transnational media company. It does not dominate in any particular area. It has important presence in three continents. Its business is on magazines, newspapers and television, etc., and it has a global strategy.

Being a global company on information, communications and entertainment business, the company has viewers from across the world. The company is competent to serve the needs of its customers like readers, viewers and advertisers. It transfers people and money across national boundaries. It knows how to acquire properties and start new business. Today, entertainment industry of the media barons has penetrated into villages, through the tools of TV and internet. Entertainment of T20 has the rousing response in the viewers globally who are the customers of the media. Rupert Murdock has access into almost all the countries by virtue of its Star Alliance, striking collaborations with professionals in countries.

It started as an Australian company and then shifted its base to the United Kingdom. Its main target is in the US. It reaches out for grabbing opportunity and are market driven. The company has a good number of Australian personnel at the top management level. Since, it believes that keeping Aussies at the top level would be beneficial as they have been associated with company since its inception and thus know the business well.

However, more and more Americans and British are also taking the top jobs of the company. The company sticks to English as a language of communication because it believes that English is the only language that can invade into other countries. The company believes that it cannot succeed in foreign print, news or broadcast. Aussies know English and the English-speaking world is big enough for its market. The world is shrinking faster than it realizes. To be in communications is to be at the centre of all change.

Company-3

Company-3 has a typical character. It is a transnational company. It is committed to being the number one global company in our industry. It does all of the manufacturing in the home country. It is because of this reason the company has achieved the 'lowest cost and the highest quality' of product line in the world. By keeping all engineering and manufacturing in one location, the company is managing cost leadership.

In the recent years, 'constantly rising value of home currency' has forced this company to invest in overseas manufacturing. This has been done to 'maintain cost advantage' though the company has done this reluctantly. Yet, the company believes to dominate the market it has to go global. It plans to do whatever needs to be done to maintain its position as a market leader.

Moreover, it is seen that all the 'senior positions of managers' in the home turf and in most of their foreign markets, are 'home-country nationals'. The company feels comfortable with own nationals in the key jobs because they speak the same language. Not only the language, they also understand the history and culture of their company and country. It can get very difficult for a foreign national to have the proper knowledge of history, culture and language. This one-country origin is very important for maintaining bonhomie among the parent company and its subsidiaries. In order to have uniformity in the board's decision making, the place of origin is important for the consensus.

Company-4

Company-4 has a typical character. It is also a transnational company of a kind. It has 27 nationalities represented by their headquarters staff; manufactures in 34 countries, markets in 99 countries and is committed to leadership in the industry segment.

It targets to develop business in the Third World and has found it extremely difficult to increase sales and earnings. It has been criticized for its aggressive marketing in these countries. It has only homecountry nationals owning voting shares in the company. Even though the company is global, it does have a home and history, and it respects the traditions and sensibilities of their home country.

The company wants to maintain their number one position in Europe. Over a period of time, they wish to achieve leadership position in North America and Japan, in their target market. So for that they also keep an eye on developing countries. Whenever it finds any country making a move from low income to lower middle or lower middle to upper middle or upper middle to high income, the company gives its best efforts to expand business. It strives to establish a position. Its objective is to achieve leadership position in its own industry. The company does not afford not to restrain from expanding into every growing market in the world.

The company always has a European CEO and will continue to do so in future. European executives of the company tend to serve all over the world. Executives of US, Indian and Japan serve only in their home countries. They

have proved to be able and valuable executives in their home countries. However, they lack necessary perspectives required for the top jobs at the headquarters. Hegemony and fellow feeling have different value systems to combine the workforce of an organization.

QUESTIONS FOR DISCUSSION

Q. 1. How does the transnational market relate to Alvin Toffler's viewpoint? Discuss.

Q. 2. What are the reasons for classifying the advertisements for transnational markets? Elucidate.

Q. 3. What do you mean by EPRG framework? Discuss with examples.

Q. 4. Write short notes on the orientation of company type.

(a) Ethnocentric (b) Polycentric

(c) Regio-centric (d) Geocentric

Q. 5. What are the driving forces of the transnational markets and what are the restraining factors? Discuss citing examples from the contemporaneous business environment of 2009.

Q. 6. Describe each of the vital forces that drives the market. Elucidate with suitable examples from 'The Economic Times' in reference to the contents given in the book.

Q. 7. Illustrate on the forces that restrain the market. Discuss with relevant examples.

Q. 8. How can a company become transnational? Draw assumptions on the ideal aspect of a transnational company.

Q. 9. What kind of company is a transnational company? Elaborate with suitable examples.

Q. 10. What is a transnational marketing? Discuss.

Q. 11. Which characteristic traits and attributes are visible in a transnational company? Illustrate with examples.

Q. 12. How do you differentiate between a domestic, international, multinational, global and transnational company? Discuss with examples.

Q. 13. What is the stage at which India is in? Make an assessment supported with examples.

Chapter 2

Transnational and Domestic Marketing, Transnational Strategy Management and Domestic Marketing Management

LEARNING OBJECTIVES

After going through this chapter; the reader should be able to:

1. Explain about the keys to discover prospects in harvesting business by invading new markets through competitive advantage.
2. Understand innovative strategies for out-beating competition.
3. Recognize the implication of marketing management and strategic marketing for identifying market segments.
4. Identify the strategic sectors candidly for generating comparatively better profit.
5. Explain the corporate strategy, business unit mission, objectives and goals, marketing strategy, portfolio analysis, implementation of strategic plan along with marketing strategy and transnational marketing.
6. Ascertain the transnational strategic plan for marketing; assessing the differences and similarities even in the case of multi-business transnational planning.

> *'Our greatest glory is not in never falling but in rising every time we fall'.*
>
> *— Confucius*
>
> *'In the end, all business operations can be reduced to three words: people, product and profits'.*
>
> *— Lee Iacocca*

7. Describe the transnational implementation and management behaviour and highlights for managing transnational companies succinctly.
8. Comprehend eight aspects which are salient for designing product strategies, including domestic product positioning strategy.
9. Realize the impact of single brand and multiple brands in a marketplace.
10. Define the diversification strategy of products together with promotional strategies befitting all kinds of oddities of market environment.
11. Have an insight into the market-entry strategies together with the issues of strategic commitment.

TRANSNATIONAL STRATEGIC MARKETING (TSM) AND DOMESTIC MARKETING MANAGEMENT (DMM)

Transnational strategic marketing (TSM) is the key to move ahead in business across the globe, discovering innovative pastures and prospects in new businesses. Devoid of this, TSM is a competitive advantage in beating competition, otherwise, without competitive advantage beating rivals in the business is next to impossible. Transnational strategic marketing focuses on picking the appropriate products/services, aptly choosing the right products/services for an accurate and correct market growth in the business at the proper time and space. It believes in sharpness, cutting-edge concepts and precision. All these focal decisions that form the cardinal principles of TSM are essentially not very different from the principles abided by the theory of domestic marketing management (DMM). They are same yet in different hue, shape and size. They are different in their macro and micro dimensions, theory and practice. In fact, they attack, nurture and approach decisions from a different domain, direction and angle. They advent and accomplish from stimulating aspects that have subtle differences.

MARKETING MANAGEMENT AND STRATEGIC MARKETING

A galaxy of instances can be cited on this subject of study, elucidating the colours and shades of differences that exist. For example, in the domain of **'marketing management'**, market segments can be taken up for analysis. Marketing segments actually are redefined by making clusters of customers or grouping customers in accordance with the symmetry and similarity in the marketing variables, available in the marketing mix of the market under observation. Minor differences are overlooked, avoided and ignored for limiting the factors of study leading to the identification of a market segment. But in the case of **'strategic marketing'**, these same market segments, from the horizon of the market mix are constituted, created and formed to differentiate and identify groups, homogeneity and clusters in a broader perspective. It zooms into a wider degree in the sector and the radius of the circle becomes greater. This is obvious in a mass of situation that is greater than the former. It is done to cater to the company as reinforced, calculative and forecasted sustainable economic advantages, enabling the firm to overcome competition prevailing in the avid market environment.

❑ Strategic Sector

If we still lay threadbare the logical reasoning to the extent of our fuzzy sensibilities, we find that each of the segment, cluster and group is a **strategic sector** by themselves. We have to unbundle the stakes and see merit in each of the type of sectors, segments, clusters and groups. In fact, in a given circumstance the 'largest competitor' in an industry can become unprofitable, if it does not review the 'sector specific market forces'. Under the given circumstance, the largest competitor becomes dominated by the collective efforts of the 'individual strategic sectors' and the 'smaller competitors' that are prevalent in the groups, segments and clusters of the business. We have to dismantle and reassemble the business for 'revisited strategic drive' at periodic intervals.

Furthermore, it is seen that in the field of **'marketing management'** the raw materials, resources and objectives of the firms/enterprises are treated as uncontrollable variables. Here, it is viewed that all variables do not converge in tandem creating a collective magic impact and so are beyond control. Variables are invisible like the specks of particles in particle physics. Thus, the objectives are uncontrollable. However, in the field of **'strategic marketing'** all the objectives are defined meticulously and systematically at different levels. These are done after a detailed and thorough scanning and examination of the necessary factors, facets and inputs. They are arrayed in a systematic mode of approach.

STRATEGIC MARKET PLAN AND MARKETING PLAN

A **'strategic market plan'** is not the same as a **'marketing plan'**. Strategic market plan is a plan drawn on the overall aspects of an organization in a market situation and is futuristic in nature. It is forward looking. Essentially, it is an organization's strategy in the marketplace where it is preparing to create business and enhance market equity. A 'marketing plan' on the other hand, relates, handles and deals fundamentally on the product/services, target segments, communication, distribution channels and pricing policies. It deals with the marketing mix of the business milieu. In reference to the above, a model outline of the transnational strategic marketing process has been given in Figure 2.1. Through this, the process details become clear and distinct enough. The major six components are organized systematically and are given below. They are:

- Corporate strategic
- Business unit mission
- Objectives and goals
- Marketing strategy
- Portfolio analysis
- Implementation of the strategic plan

However, due to brevity and the assumed knowledge of the reader, these components in its elements are not elaborated here.

MARKETING STRATEGY

Marketing strategy is based on the 3Cs. They are corporation, customer and competition. In fact, the **corporation** impacts through the business unit's mission, goals and objectives, strengths and weaknesses and products/markets of the unit; **customers** of a corporation are all pervading and omnipresent; and the **competition** affects the business unit mission and strengths and weaknesses. However, the components of domestic marketing management are as follows. All these components are quite different from the marketing strategy elaborated above.

- Marketing strategy
- Short-term marketing plan

- Competition
- Customer
- Product strategy

TRANSNATIONAL MARKETING

In assessment of the marketing management, we can also review the factors associated with transnational marketing. Though they seem to be similar in a way, they have a wider coverage and the canvas is broader. It deals with the global orientation of the market forces interacting in the marketplaces. We see that transnational marketing has mainly the following features. They are:

- Corporate strategy
- Corporate publics
- Value system
- Business unit mission
- Market environment
- Marketing effectiveness (not sales)
- Product market momentum
- Objectives and goals
- Marketing strategy
- Customer
- Competition
- Portfolio analysis
- Business unit strategic plan
- Strategic perspective of other functional areas
- Strategy implementation

All the above angles have subtle nuances and essential gaps between themselves, which require in-depth reading. If we try to understand the manifold angles, we shall have to delve into the quintessential cores, which have been further discussed in this chapter. This has been observed that value creation and integrated innovation are the rudimentary catalysts that can be engaged for introspection. Then the facets will require coordination of the different dimensions that it automatically entails in such situations. Figure 2.1 is empirical and amply clear.

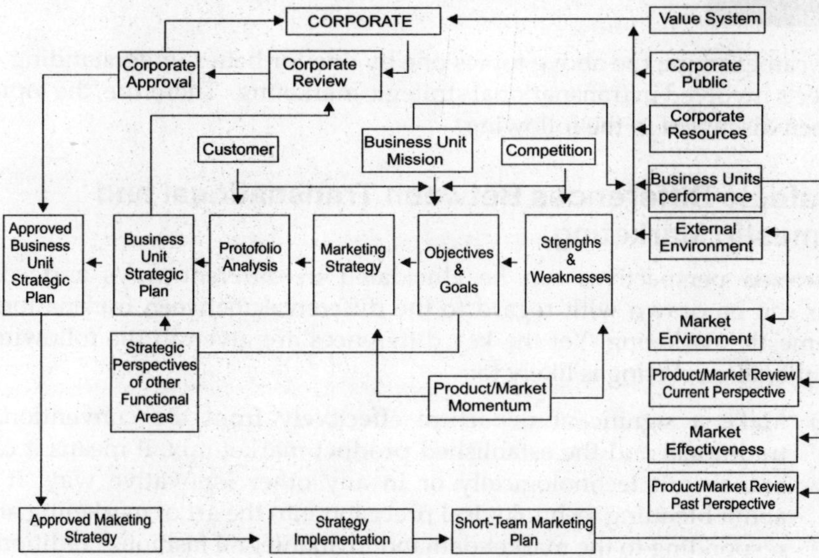

Fig. 2.1 Transnational Strategic Marketing

Nevertheless, the significance of the differences in the components of transnational strategic marketing discussed will be revealed by the end of this chapter. The following points have been examined to crystallize the ideas on the subject. They are:

1. Strategic differences between transnational and domestic marketing.
2. Transnational strategy implementation and management behaviour.
3. Transnational and domestic product strategies.
4. Transnational and domestic promotions strategies.
5. Transnational and domestic market strategy.
6. Transnational market boundaries and market potential measurement.
7. Transnational new product strategies.
8. Transnational product–market strategies.
9. Transnational distribution channels.
10. Transnational strategic thrust.
11. Governmental constraints in transnational marketing.
12. Elements of transnational strategy.
13. Rating the marketing effectiveness of transnational companies.

We can examine the above topics one by one for better understanding of the aspects involved in transnational strategic marketing. Therefore, the topics have been discussed in the following.

❑ Strategic Differences Between Transnational and Domestic Marketing

Multi-faceted perspectives can be elucidated in different ways and conclusions can be drawn with regard to the differences between transnational and domestic marketing. Yet the key differences are given in the following. Transnational marketing is likely to:

(a) Make a significant departure effectively from the conventional, traditional and the established product market mix, it means it can branch out technologically or in any other innovative way. It is about blending technological precision into the art of marketing and responding to the market demand in an integral fashion. Traditional rigidity shall slowly melt into the stimulus of market forces.

(b) Have provisions for undertaking programmes with an unusually high degree of risk. This risk can be in relation to the previous experience too for example, it can be done by 'using untried resources of entering uncertain markets where predictability of success is noticeably limited or low. Higher the risk higher the profit in the ball game.

(c) Include a wide and broad range of available alternatives to cope with a major competitive problem. Scope of these alternatives provides significant differences both in the results and in the resource required. Challenges and alternatives are pivotal.

(d) Engage, involve and impose 'important timing options'. It shall be in both ways, in starting developmental work and for deciding when to make the actual market commitment. It has schedules that are time driven and target oriented.

(e) Promote in favour for major changes to ensure 'competitive equilibrium'. It can do so by creating and inventing a new operating system that has a customer acceptance pattern. It shall be done through greater customer responsiveness.

(f) End with the choice of leading of certain markets. It also can conclude by the competitive advances based on a trade-off between the costs and risks of innovation. Innovations incur investments for R&D; but the innovative products yield competitive advantage though risk to the company for R&D is obvious. Trade-off in the business is lucrative and, therefore, calls for investments. Sensible companies always move ahead of time; pioneering new products creating inroads and equity in the marketplaces. Abstinence from forging innovations in the new products shall trap the identity of the firm into abyss. Propelling market forces are innovation-driven tornados of lasting calibre who make a mark. It is dynamic and is in a flux, propelled by a speed that is expected of the market.

Multi-business Transnational Planning

Transnational market planning (TMP) is considered separately in the chapter ahead in more detail. In this chapter, we would discuss on the relative dimensions and perspectives that are comparatively assessed. It is seen that the impact of 'corporate planning on marketing' is significantly greater in 'transnational marketing' than in 'domestic marketing'. This is because corporate planning is ardent for streamlining a variety of factors that come into play that are both strange and confounding at times. They also revolve around a plethora of components. All these factorial impacts are measurable in the ambit of each of the decisions. Ambit of each of the decisions like market share, pricing of the product, product promotion, existing product lines and new products have been explained in Figure 2.2. Certain strategic policies propounded, enacted and recommended in a general way not hold good in exceptional cases; yet they are of importance. Policies that should be recommended for an emerging transnational company are as follows:

1. Aggressively building up of market share across all segments.
2. Lowering of prices to build share.
3. Investing heavily in promotion to build share.
4. Expanding the volume of existing product line. Adding line extensions to fill out product categories.
5. Expanding product line, through new products by acquisition, self-manufacture or joint venture.

Marketing Decision	Strategy Adopted for Division or Product Line		
	Invest for Future Growth	**Manage for Earnings**	**Manage for Immediate Cash**
Market share	Aggressively build across all segments	Target efforts to high return/high-growth segments, protect current franchises	Forego share development for improved profits
Pricing	Lower to build share	Stabilize for maximum profit contribution	Raise, even at the expense of volume

Promotion	Invest heavily to build share	Invest as market dictates	Avoid
Existing product line	Expand volume, add line extensions to fill out product categories	Shift product mix to higher profit product categories	Eliminate low contribution products/ varieties
New products	Expand product line by acquisition self-manufacture or joint venture	Add products selectively and in controlled stages of commitment	Add only sure winners

Fig. 2.2 Impact of Multi-business Strategic Planning on Transnational Marketing

Similarly, in the case of domestic marketing, 'harvesting' may be a good strategy. The harvesting aspects of domestic marketing have been described subsequently in this chapter under the heading 'product strategies'. Figure 2.3 summarizes the differences between 'transnational strategic marketing' and 'domestic marketing management'. The comparisons and contrasts that it highlights are empirical to the arguments. It says that 'strategic marketing' differs from 'marketing management' in many respects. They differ in their orientation, philosophy, approach and in their relationships with the environment. They differ in their management style. Strategic management requires a manager to forego short-term performance in the greater interest of long-term results. Similarly, strategic marketing deals with the significance of the decision to enter into a business and how to be in it, while marketing management just 'stresses on running a business'. In the domain of marketing management, an array of environmental factors affects the business. However, in the field of strategic management, it derives alternatives and counter options for upsetting the equilibrium of marketplace and re-establishing the business in favour of itself. Marketing management accepts the marketing projections, business set up and competitive positions as have been given. In addition, it seeks to optimize within those constraints the hiatus and bottlenecks. On the contrary, strategic marketing, by contrast, seeks to throw off those constraints wherever possible and stride ahead finding recourse to positive steps. Marketing management is deterministic, whereas strategic marketing is opportunistic. Marketing management is deductive and analytical while strategic marketing is inductive and intuitive. Marketing management is a plain Jane but strategic management is aggressive.

❑ Transnational Strategy Implementation and Management Behaviour

Transnational strategy can be described as a foreseeing business where successful transnational companies focus on customers, competitors and potential marketplaces and are not confined to financial reports. They have a broad-based viewpoint and orchestrated vision.

Strategic planning generates a resistant behaviour among the part of the operating managers, who are mostly short-sighted. Critical observation has identified three types of prevalent resistance behaviours. They are **measurement myopia** (a manager's behaviour that shows comparatively good short-term performance), **measurement invalidation** (managers that furnish the top management with a short-sighted and distorted data, or a biased selected data) and **measurement justification** (managers who adopt excessive justified behaviour and become excessively cautious on specific factors like the identified critical cash flows and determinants of return of investment (ROI).

To solve all these problems, it is important to know that the sophisticated management tools, benchmarked ideas and up-to-minute techniques of business schools, may be of adequate assistance. Generally, these would help in identifying a desirable strategic course. Implementation of the strategy calls for a number of time-honoured simple, plain and straightforward approaches. In fact, these are the vital prerequisites for success of an organization doing business.

Point of Differences	**Strategic Marketing (Transnational)**	**Marketing Management (Domestic)**
On the time frame	Long-range (decisions have long-term implications)	Day-to-day (decisions have relevance in a given financial year)
On the orientation	Inductive and intuitive	Deductive and analytical
On the decision process	Primarily bottom-up	Mostly top down
On the relationship with environment	Environment is considered ever-changing and dynamic	Environment is considered constant with occasional disturbances
On opportunity sensitivity	Ongoing and seeking new opportunities	Ad hoc search for new opportunity

On the organizational behaviour	Achieve synergy between different components of the organization, both horizontally and vertically (with respect to values, merit and response time, etc.)	Pursue interests of decentralized unit National markets and slower response times (more rationalized approach for creating credibility).
On the nature of the job	Requires high degree of creativity and originality	Requires maturity, experience and control orientation
On the leadership style	Requires proactive perspective	Requires reactive perspective
On the mission	Deals with what business to emphasize	Deals with running a delineated business

Fig. 2.3 Major Differences between Strategic Marketing (Transnational) and Marketing Management (Domestic)

Successful Management of Transnational Companies

The points given below are the salient eight basic attributes that contribute to the successful management of transnational companies. They make the transnational company emanate as a success story in the firmament of business. They are as follows:

1. **Biased action to be erased:** To avoid biased actions, introspection, analysis and questioning with regard to products needs to be undertaken. For avoiding cumbersome, intricate and complicated procedures while developing new ideas, it is better to work on a doer's mind set, fixer's mind set and have a relentless trying attitude. Such positive vibes eradicate all biases of the psyche. IT and ITES companies operating in the environment are examples of this kind.

2. **Simple organizational form and lean staff:** What is important is to keep the staffing strength small enough to avoid bureaucracy, multiple tiers in the hierarchy and hurdles that it creates. It should be simple in its structure and form and should have accountable staff functions.

3. **Continuous rapport with the customer base:** Company should establish, ensure and maintain quick contact with the customer kings, to seek positive insights on issues that direct the company. This is carried out by giving autonomy to them. Effective and efficient means should be used to reward them all.

4. **Productivity improvements through people:** Business should motivate, excite and stimulate the employees by giving them autonomy to operate with the designated job definition. It should derive incentive plans to reward the employees for improving their self-confidence and spontaneity. It should be encouraged for better productivity and results of the firm done through its people.

5. **Autonomy in operation yields entrepreneurship:** Company authorities should designate, authorize and encourage different managers at different levels to think, strategize and act like entrepreneurs. An entrepreneur's mind can flourish from freedom to operate in the organization. The Tata group, GM and Toyota are some of the examples of the companies/group of companies who believe in encouraging the spirit of entrepreneurship among employees.

6. **Stress on a single 'key business value':** Authorities have to ensure that each single employee spots, identifies and pursues a 'key business value' based on their priority, with utter zeal, dedication and grit. Priority has to be fixed on the listed work agenda. Wipro, Infosys and IBM's lay stress and emphatically tackle the problems of individual customers. It is also possible in a FMCG market.

7. **Emphasis on doing what they know best:** Under a broader parameter, domain knowledge has to be provided to the people in a single division. Employees, best on the frame, should be advised to deliver what they know best. It has to be reviewed from time to time. Ultimately, it has to assess its employees build on the strengths and competencies, like product modification, product innovation, low-cost manufacturing and channel integration, etc. Employees have to contribute in the key strategic areas.

8. **Control tight and loose little:** Hot and cold method is by far the most commonly chosen model of approach. The carrot and the stick method is well accepted globally for better productivity. The company has to control a few objective variables tightly but allow flexibility and looseness in others.

These eight aspects are important for the company to garner better profits for the company. Not abiding by the aforementioned traits, factors and yardsticks will mean devastation for the company. In the absence of these, all transnational companies doing business in a competitive atmosphere stand to lose their growth rates, vitality and competitiveness. In order to encourage perpetuation of new ideas, concepts and innovation, the **management of all the companies should do the following.** They are:

- Management should emphasize and focus attention on the goals of strategic planning, rather than on its processes. Processes are the offshoot of the goals of strategic planning. They should concentrate on substance and not on the form. Innovation can happen in stages of goals being probed in depth. It can evoke new ideas for leveraging a competitive business.
- Management should ensure to infuse, integrate and inculcate into the business strategy the analysis of recently invented and emerging technologies and technology management. Advanced technological ideas shall prompt the emergence of creative designs to the benefit of the organization. Due to the changing consumer trends, demographic shifts, regulatory impacts and global economies new products are more readily accepted in the market. Perpetuity of company can happen through constant innovations in technology desired by the changing market patterns.
- Management should ensure and look up to design new planning processes, review and revamp applied standards and accept criteria guidelines for the technological advances. It shall generate thrust in new business, which might not conform entirely to the firm's current corporate basis. It happens, in companies, which make the other company products obsolete and outdated.
- Management should adopt a long-term planning horizon. It should be prolonged and long-sighted with a matrix. This is to ensure that a promising business player envisaging the business on a technological development does not cut off prematurely, due to the environmental factors. Long-sighted ideas drive the market longer.
- Management should ensure and pertinently see that very stringent financial requirements are not imposed during the starting phase of a new project. In case of tightened expenditure incurred towards the initial phase of the project development, optional aggressive growth cannot happen. It shall restrict the free flow of employee synergy.
- Management should create special organizational committees and teams. They could operate like 'satellite teams' with think tank groups. There should be new venture groups to invade into new territories of creative concepts. Their mission should be to pursue new ideas, thoughts and replicate existing concepts with a novel taste. They should be free from the day-to-day work pressures that prevail

in operations and regular activities. Freelancing employees need to gallop with unbridled passion, in order to recreate, resurrect and reinvent.

- Management should ensure that the organization's financial incentives, sundry facilities and career rewards, etc., should promote and encourage the people with boldness. It should promote innovative development programmes to be implemented.

❑ Transnational and Domestic Product Strategies

Transnational marketing strategy is macro in nature. Domestic marketing is focus centric. Domestic marketing of most of the products in India, including 'Tata' follows a product positioning strategy for brand merchandizing. However, it is seen that the successful firms in transnational marketing are invariably employing either of the two strategies that follow. They adopt **product design strategy**, where the emphasis is on standardization of customized options. Secondly, they might adopt **diversification strategy** where the emphasis is on product/markets, where maturity has been reached and new attempts have been aimed, either at spreading risk or at capitalizing on gained experience or the both. The vision, mission, objectives, requirements and benefits arising from these domestic and transnational strategies are entirely different. They call for entirely different approaches, capabilities and operations as shown below. The outlines are justified in detail.

Domestic product positioning strategy

Domestic product positioning strategy is 'placing a brand in that part of the market where it will have a favourable reception compared with competing brands'. Its objectives are to:

(a) Position a specific product in the marketplace as if it stands as a separate product from competing brands available in the market.

(b) Position the product as if it tells the customers what it stands for, what it is and how the company would expect the customers to evaluate the product.

However, in the case of positioning multiple brands it seeks business growth by offering varied products in different segments of the market. This is done to avoid competitive threats to a single brand.

Its requirements are to use the marketing-mix variables that are especially designed and that which have the necessary communication efforts. The requirements differ from case to case. They are:

1. Successful management of a **single brand** requires:
   (a) Positioning of the brand in the marketplaces as if it can withstand competition from the toughest rival in the segment;
   (b) Maintaining its unique positioning stance by creating an 'aura of a different product' that is distinct.
2. Successful management of **multiple brands** requires careful positioning in the marketplace, such that they do not compete with each other and create cannibalism. Cannibalization is the biggest threat. Hence, it is pivotal to be quite careful in segmenting the market and to position an individual product through design and promotion. It has to be done to be uniquely suited to a particular segment.

The expected results of the same could to be to meet, as far as possible, the needs of specific segments of the market, limit sudden changes in the sales and make customers faithful to the brands. Try to establish trust and acceptance with genuineness in quality.

Transnational product strategies

Product design strategy: The definition that is befitting to the above is as follows. In fact, the product design strategy essentially deals with the degree of standardization of the product in assessment of the cluster of products in view. The company that is going in for the same has a choice among the strategic options like a standard product, customized product and standard product with customized options as modifications. What is important is the choice to alter, change and modify the product or services in tune with the customer demands.

In order to attain the objectives the following aspects are important:

1. Standard product is needed to increase the economies of scale of the company.
2. Customized product is needed to compete against the mass producers of standardized products. This is done through product design flexibility.
3. Standard product with modifications required to combine and complement the benefits of the two previous strategies.

For doing the above, what is required is a close analysis of the product or the market perspectives, angles and environmental changes. Especially, technological changes become all the more important. By doing this, the expected results are enhanced and an increase in the growth trend, market

share and profit margins becomes more of a possibility. Additionally, the third strategy enables and allows the company to keep close contacts with the market and get further experience in developing new standard products that fulfil and are befitting to the market needs.

Diversification Strategy: The definition of diversification strategy is an essential part of understanding the aspects that it entails. It develops unfamiliar markets and products through concentric diversification, horizontal diversification and conglomerate diversification. They are as follows:

(a) **Concentric** diversification happens where the products that are introduced are related to the existing ones, in terms of marketing of technology.

(b) **Horizontal** diversification happens where the new products are unrelated to the existing ones, but are sold to the same customers all along.

(c) **Conglomerate** diversification happens where the products/markets are entirely new and latest.

Here, in case of diversification strategies, the **objectives** are as follows. Here, the diversification strategies respond to the desire for growth, when the current products/markets attend maturity, attain stability by spreading the risks of fluctuations in earnings, are secured, instead of the company fearing a backward integration from one of its major customers, and have credibility to have more weight in capital markets.

Diversification strategies are required to reduce the risks inherent in a diversification strategy. To do that, a business unit should diversify its activities only if the current product/market opportunities are limited, have some good knowledge of the area in which it diversifies, provide the products introduced with adequate support and forecast the effects of diversification on the existing lines of products. The expected results could result in an increase in sales, greater profitability and greater flexibility.

❑ Domestic and Transnational Promotion Strategies

From studies, it is seen that most of the domestic companies opt for **promotion expenditure strategy** while promoting their products. This includes mostly advertising, personal selling and sales promotion. Here, in this case, the emphasis is fundamentally on allocating a total promotional budget figure, hoping that the job is done somehow. Understanding of the sales process is implicit. It seldom manifests itself in the promotion process because it is largely experimental and intuitive in character.

Transnational marketing is steered and governed by a promotion-mix strategy, involving determinants of the explicit and judicious mix of the three main types and the sub-types of promotional measure. It involves factors like product factors, market factors, customer factors, budget factors, marketing-mix factors and environmental factors in a complex and critical process. Furthermore, it is supplemented by media selection, advertising copy, selling and sales motivation and supervision strategies. However, the main differences between the two approaches are focused in the following lines.

Domestic promotion–expenditure strategy

The above aspects are defined as follows. It is the determination of the amount that a company may spend on its total promotional effort. This includes aspects like advertising, personal selling and sales promotion mostly. Here, the objective is to allocate enough funds essentially to each promotional task. It is done, so that, each is utilized to its fullest potential. To do this what is required are adequate resources to finance the promotion expenditure, understanding the products/services and sales response, estimating duration of the advertising effect, understanding of each product/market situation relative to different forms of promotion and understanding of competitive response to promotion. The expected results are allocation of sufficient funds to the promotional tasks to accomplish the overall marketing objectives.

Transnational promotion-mix strategy

The above aspect is defined as follows. It is the determination of a judicious mix of different types of promotion, which has tangible, measurable and calculable results. This can be quantified essentially. Here, the **objective** is to blend sufficiently the three types of promotions to complement each other for a balanced promotional perspective. The requirements that it attracts are mainly the six factors given below. They are product factors, market factors, customer factors, budget factors, marketing-mix factors and environmental factors. We can explain all the factors one by one.

Product factors: It is about the nature of product, perceived risk, durable and non-durable and typical purchase amount.

Market factors: It is about the position in the life cycle, market share, industry competition, industry concentration and demand perspectives.

Customer factors: It is about the household and business customers, number of customers and concentration of customers.

Budget factors: It is about the financial resources of the organization and traditional promotional perspectives.

Marketing-mix factors: It is about the relative price/relative quantity, distribution strategy, brand life cycle and geographic scope of the market.

Environmental factors: It is about the transnational marketing considerations.

Here, the expected results are to ensure that the 'three types of promotion' are assigned roles, as if they provide the best communication for the entire range of the market.

❑ Transnational Market Strategies

It can be observed that all transnational business strategies should be justified by the availability of transnational market. If a viable market potential is absent, even the best of strategies formulated is susceptible to failure. In fact, framing of configuration of marketing strategies for each business should be realistic and tied along with the target transnational market. Market is necessary for marketing, and market is the focus for successful marketing. Only those strategies aligned to market/markets direct the roadmap for each business. It serves for the overall corporate strategy and gives direction for programming key activities and projects in all functional areas. However, when the corporate resources are scanty and corporate prowess is saturated or limited, it becomes catastrophic to expand them in too many markets. On the contrary, in the above situation, the above critical resources should be concentrated on the key markets. It could be in terms of the type of market, geographic location and time of entry and commitments for the success of business. Namesake allocations of resources similar to the domestic firms yield no competitive edge. Nevertheless, if it could be ascertained as to which markets really hold the potential the target business will lower itself into a position of relative competitive superiority. In the passages given below are the 'market strategies' in terms of definition, objectives, requirements and expected results, as were ascribed before.

Transnational market strategy is the most difficult part of the entry expansion plan of the company business. It is the period in which the company business operates accepting, mutually agreeing and exceeding the barriers of trade agreements. As per the definition, it is all about operating outside national boundaries, in foreign soil, in a strange condition. In this place, the objective is to search, scoop and seek opportunities beyond the domestic business. Search for the volume of business is all about reinventing markets and creating a new customer base. Here, the requirements of the business need top management's commitment to consolidate support to accomplish the target, invest huge capital resources to cover the horizon of customers and detailed and threadbare understanding of the transnational markets. In the given market milieu, the expected results are to ensure an increased and accelerated growth curve, speed up the increased market share and hence increased profits. Different markets behave differently due to the forces and factors, and in this case, it is according to the narration made before.

Transnational marketing strategy is designed to enable a company/firm make an entry expansion plan for travelling beyond the territories of business, confined to the own country, to a foreign soil, jumping the barriers of trade and tariff imposed due to international trade. It is approached in multi pronged ways, seeing the market needs and wants. In order to sustain and survive the market competition, companies have to search business potentials in many markets irrespective of the trade relations, economies of scale, laws, culture and so forth. All transnational business growth and development require an understanding of the marketplaces, scope to business potential and strategies to stride ahead in the direction of the planned scheme of action. We shall, therefore be required to dwell on the pertinent aspects, like market, scope and strategy for a deep insight, introspection and study. The following ideas shall appraise the angles threadbare.

Single market strategy (SMS)

Single market strategy (SMS) is an important approach in a given market situation. It confines the concentration of efforts to a single segment. The objective of this approach is to find a business segment, which is being presently ignored, not attended to by the company or served inadequately. In other words, the company should employ this single market strategy method where the required quantity, quality and types of products are not meeting the market needs.

This single market strategy is required to cater to the market dedicatedly despite the obvious initial difficulties and teething problems, which are bound to be present. It shall avoid competition with established firms doing business in other product segments. This kind of single market business strategy of a firm shall result in the manufacturing, packaging and delivering of the product at a low cost and thereby making business transacted result in higher profits. This kind of sales strategy shall yield maximum output in a given marketplace until the market demand is saturated.

Multi-market strategy (MMS)

Multi-market strategy is another important aspect in the field of business in a given market environment. By definition, multi-market strategy (MMS) is about serving several distinct markets. It, as the name signifies does business through multiples. The object of this type of strategy is to diversify the risk of serving only one market. Staying singularly focused has plenty of risks of being effaced from the market by virtue of competition from rival products entering the market. This MMS essentially has to be refined in its approach and is required to make careful selection of the segments, to serve the market. This kind of strategy avoids competition with companies serving the entire market. By doing this, the expected results shall result in 'higher sales' and higher market share. In case of higher sales and higher market share, it can generate business and profits to the maximum.

Total market strategy (TMS)

Total market strategy is an approach for attacking market requirements. In a specific kind of market demand, this strategy is pertinent to be applied and implemented for doing better business. Definition of TMS is to serve the entire spectrum of the market by selling differentiated products to different segments in the market. The logical objective of this strategic approach is to compete across the board in the entire market. Entire market becomes the focus of the strategic plan and is relevant in a context. In order to launch this TMS model of approach the necessary requirements are as follows. The company implementing this strategy has to employ different combinations and variables of price, product and promotion and distribution strategies in different segments and ensure the top management's commitment to embrace the entire market as the target market and should have a strong financial position over the strategy. In this context, the expected results shall be increased growth and higher market share.

Market geography strategy (MGS)

In the specific geographical regions, depending on the geographical contours, markets are driven differently with a different strategy. Market geography strategy encompasses certain strategies having approaches that have been discussed below. It is about the vicinity, region and countries, which are peculiarly alien and similar.

Local market strategy (LMS)

Local market strategy is an approach that is important in a geographical area. By definition, it is said to be the 'concentration of efforts in the immediate vicinity'. It is about the neighbourhood marketplaces. Here, the objective of the business is to maintain control on the business. For doing this, what is required is a good reputation in the geographical area and a good hold on requirements of the market. This kind of local marketing strategy is mostly possible in big towns, metros and cosmopolitan areas like Mumbai, New Delhi, Kolkata and

Chennai in India, Hong Kong and similar other places in China. In doing this, the expected outcome shall be that of short-term success and ultimately it must expand to other areas. It starts to create a demand for itself, making its market presence felt; it switches over to many markets. It is the starting point of the business, and the long-term objective is to expand ultimately, in search of new pastures.

Regional market strategy (RMS)

Regional market strategy is an important strategic idea nurtured for the market demand, unique to places across the globe. Religious, cultural co-relations, geographical togetherness and a similarity in the social texture are the key traits, which propel the market forces to carry a set of business. As per the definition, regional market strategy is about a business company operating in not more than two or three states, two or three countries or over an exclusive region of the country. For instance in India, the northeastern region (also known as the seven sisters) has identical characteristic behaviour and can be termed as a regional national market.

Here the objectives of the company business are to diversify the risk of dependence and faith on one part of a region and to keep the control centralized. It does not believe in one single marketplace but a cluster of identical places. This strategy is required for the management's commitment to expansion, having adequate resources for the required investment and the company's logistical ability to serve the regional area, etc. It is essential for the company to create an impact for the mass-market mobilization. In the given business, the expected results will be to increase business growth, generate higher market share and give a tough fight to the market rivals and competitors.

National market strategy (NMS)

National market strategy is a strategy usually earmarked by the company for the entire nation to be covered in the comprehensive plan of the business. They look at the symmetrical demeanour of the market behaviour and the patterns of regular sales of products. As per the definition, NMS is all about operating nationally, confined to the boundary of the country. In the said context, the only object that is driving the market forces is too seek growth in the market. In this kind of market, the requirements are top management commitment, capital resources to widen the umbrella of the market and the willingness to undertake risks and fight battles for a market share in the marketplace. Normally, in the above kind of business climate, the expected results are the increased growth rate, increased growth in the market share and enhanced profitability in sales volume. A blanket growth and development-oriented roadmap is drawn to connect the market niches for a seamless access.

Market–entry strategy

Market entry strategy has many models to imitate for cracking into the market. One of the biggest ordeals that is faced is during the period of market entry. Like different companies behaving differently, different countries do have their various twists to accommodate and align to the prevailing strategies. It is based on varied aspects, is a changing phenomenon and is in a mode.

First-in strategy: First-in strategy, by its definition is about entering the market before all others. To become the first mover is to tap the virgin potential of the people to buy products, before they know about the various product types, the company strategies to enter. Here, the objectives are to create a market leadership and a lead over competitors who shall be latecomers. In this case, if the market is captured primarily, it will be difficult for the subsequent market folks to beat and match the inclination of the buyer. In the given market environment, the company should have the following requirements. The first-in company should have the willingness and ability to take risks, should have the technological competence and strive to stay ahead, have heavy promotional measures, create primary demand and carefully evaluate strengths. It is an advantage, and the desired results reduce costs through gaining experience, increased growth, increased market share and increased profits for the company.

Early-entry strategy (EES): Early-entry strategy (EES) is a key advantage for any business—to enter, grow, expand and spread freely, devoid of the hassles. It is said that, early to bed and early to rise keeps a man and company healthy, wealthy and wise. In this type of strategy, gaining ground in the market prior to any other product entering the market gives a monopoly to the company to distribute and penetrate their products in the traditional channels easily. By definition, EES is all about entering the marketplaces in quick succession to the market leader and gaining ground. Here, the objective is to check and prevent the first entrant from creating a stronghold in the market and getting into a free flow distribution, a base network at the ground level getting into the buyers mind. In this strategy, the marketing requirements are a superior and dominant marketing strategy, ample and sufficiency of resources and resolute and strong commitment to challenge the market leaders, if any, with a strong foothold. In this environment, the expected results could be the increased profit margin, increased growth rate and the increased market share. These targets are obvious and inevitable.

Laggard market entry strategy (LMES): A laggard market entry stage is the stage during which there is a decline in the product sales in the market. By definition, it is about the product entering the marketplaces during and towards the tail end of the growth and development phase of the product life cycle graph. It is during the maturity phase and decline of the market in the identified product. It is seen that two modes of entry are feasible in the above context that can be employed. They are 'imitation-entering market', this is to enter with a 'me too' product strategy and the second is 'initiation', i.e., entering the market with unconventional marketing strategies. Either it has to replicate or clone the products circulating in the market or carve out a dramatic and radical market entry, which is entirely different. Here the objective of the company marketing department is to work as an 'imitator'. Imitator to attack and capture those portions of the markets that are not brand loyal and can switch over to any suitable company providing similar products. The second objective could be that of the role of an initiator. This is adopted to serve the needs and wants of the market areas better than the firms that are already doing the rounds in business do.

It has its own requirements, which are unique and ardent. In order to become an 'imitator' the company has to have the ability to market research and the capability for production. For becoming, an 'initiator' the company has to have the ability for market research and generate creative marketing strategies. These are a couple of the superior aspects, which come with the priority of requirement. The expected results could be different in the case of 'imitator'. It is preferable to increase short-item profits. In the second aspect, in the case of an 'initiator', the expected result will be to put the market on a novel growth route, propel increased profits and with some growth opportunities.

❑ Market Commitment Strategy (MCS)

Market commitment strategy is to retain the marketplaces by any means or strategy. It is based on the commitment for fighting a market warfare by employing tactics and techniques, which are in the direction of the 7 P's. It is quite an aggressive approach to business and the market standing, committed to a win by a 360 degree attack.

Strong commitment strategy (SCS): Strong commitment strategy is all about a market strategy for penetration. It is about the conviction and the strength to combat a spectrum of market offensives by competitors. Like a guerrilla attack, it takes all angles in consideration and all forms and facets of warring aggression. The definition that comes up is about 'fighting and out throwing challenges aggressively and firmly by engaging various forms and means of the 7 P measures'. Distribution strategies are of utmost importance for the aggression. The objective is to defend the attacking position at all costs and by all possible means of approach. In order to do this,

it is required to realize the economies of scale in promotion, distribution and manufacturing, etc., and to refuse and reject to be pig-satisfied, accommodating and content with the existing situation or position. It is also required to engage all the simple resources available and have the willingness, conviction and ability to take risks that are lurking in the brink. The expected result targeted is increased growth rate, incessantly increased profit margins and increased market share in the business approach.

Average commitment strategy (ACS): Average commitment strategy (ACS), is about maintaining a steady and comprehensive enthusiasm for the market, for stabilizing the business status by attending to customer delight. Customer is the ultimate king in the context who is significantly pivotal. A definition that comes is to maintain a stable incremental interest in the market, which is driven by the customer focus, having an objective to maintain the status quo of business. This objective call for ideals to keep the customer kings satisfied, happy and gay. The anticipated results are the acceptable profitability in margin.

Long commitment strategy (LCS): Long commitment strategy (LCS) is to maintain marketing expansion through usual drive and normal ways, being in dark by having no long-term strategy, on investments that are forward looking but for shortsighted benefits and profit. The definition for the above could be to 'maintain normal interest in the market focus' having an objective that is to operate 'in the dark'. None of the objectives is forward looking. It avoids any sort of investment for any kind of long-term benefit for the company. The expected outcome is to maintain the status quo and not to increase the growth in the profits and enhance market share and market equity.

Market dilution strategy (MDS)

Market dilution strategy (MDS) is all about maintaining a stance for the product to discourage a certain category of customers from buying by reducing the promotional programmes, to retain the customer base and enabling them to look for the same product line. It generates a sense of feel good for the products, which are scarcely available in the marketplaces. In this process, the company increases its brand image and brand personality for suggesting alternative products of the same brand creating a magnetic pull. A pulling strategy of the company is conspicuously designed and meticulously planned.

The definition of this kind of strategy is not to discourage all customers in general; it can also be for a certain class of customers in particular too. It can also be on either a temporary basis or permanent basis, from looking for the product that the company floated. Here, the objective is to manage and maintain the buyers, purchasers or customer goodwill during the periods of scarcity of the product. It is many a time designed by the company and is at times evolving in nature. The requirement for this strategy is to evaluate and monitor the customer time requirements or the period of absence from the market, it necessarily has to be calculative, in order to ensure a ration-like product supplies for meeting short falls, directing the customer base that has immediate needs. It calls for attending to customers who have a supply of the product but have no immediate need for that specific product and also trace/identify, spot and suggest alternative products for meeting the immediate needs of the customer. The expected outcome is increase in the profits, increase in strong customer goodwill and product image of not being generally available and in loyalty for the brand. It has a scientifically designed plan of action to accomplish.

Pruning of marginal market strategy (PMMS)

Pruning of marginal market strategy (PMMS) is about concentrating in a market, which needs to cut off some of its branches to make the business on investment grow better. It is always better to make certain portions of the market smaller by removing parts that you do not need or want. Hence, firms should essentially target at markets that give them hefty profits on the investments. Many a time, this is implemented in a market where the business is not making good profit due to the presence of competitors entering the fray. These kind of marketing strategies are undertaken in the markets that are growing in nature, those that have a potential. This has been quite alluring for markets to have mostly short-term investment plans. By definition, it is said to be 'weeding out markets that do not provide acceptable rates of return on investments.' The objective is to have direct investments in growth markets, which are lucrative. It is employed to skim business profits in a marketplace. Eventually, the requirement for this begets from the willingness to disturb the status quo of a conventional business continuum. It is to drop out from the non-profit-making traditional markets by shifting to emerging new potential growth markets. The expected results in the vista is for the projection of long-term growth and development, enhanced and improved return on investments made and limiting the customer base to the target by decreasing market share.

Key markets strategy (KMS)

Key markets strategy (KMS) is all about the chosen marketplaces being exclusively identified those that have lasting potential to drive in the customers. It can be like that of a product market which is based on innovations and cannot be replicated easily. It is a very selected focus with sound knowledge of the product. It could be for example, for the surgical instruments per say. Here, the definition of the same is said to be the 'focusing efforts on selected markets' where the objective is to serve an identified selected market that is extremely fine. Focus in the category of business poignantly segmented for the purpose is the bull's eye. The requirements for the same are to obtain, acquire and gain profuse knowledge of the selected or chosen markets, to reinforce, catapult and concentrate all concerted energies on the focal markets and develop unique strategies to serve these markets. In this process, the expected results are to increase and improve on the profits and enhance market share in the selected markets. These kinds of selected business plans for driving the market forces can operate only in the selected markets. An example can be that of the Arabinda Eye Hospital, Chennai targeting eye operations, forging ahead in the country for conducting eye operation at lower costs.

Harvesting strategy (HS)

In harvesting strategy, targeting the revenue to be generated from a useful market is the focus. It is done by dodging antitrust laws and harvesting earnings through short-term means. Focus is the key, and quick cash flow is the end result. By definition, it is said to be a 'deliberate effort to let the market share slide down' the objective is to harvest the additional cash flow, to enhance short-term earnings and profits and is done to dodge antitrust action. The requirements for this are high market share in the product line, and the expected results are decline in sales but having useful revenues still earned. It is quick money model.

CONCLUSIVE IDEAS

As a matter of fact, from the above ideas discussed, it is observed that, domestic marketing largely comprises of local market, national market and harvesting strategies. They are based on a comprehensive total market approach, adhering to the degree of differentiation in the markets, which is not very high. It has similarities and commonalities. In fact, transnational marketing strategies are highly differentiated due to the kaleidoscope of its market vistas. Transnational strategy typically is a multi-market strategy, which include strategies for multiple and myriad types of unique marketplaces. Transnational marketing strategy is seldom feasible in the national market of small nations; national marketing concepts are usually applied. Except in large countries like India, China, Europe and US, etc., transnational strategies are not employed. It is seen that harvesting is a possibility in transnational marketing. It can attack the niches for harvesting in the particular segment of business. Market commitment in transnational marketing is law based and is higher in the case of certain transnational markets abroad. Most of the aspiring transnational companies in such type of markets usually concentrate and exert their full efforts on 'key markets'. Key marketing products are exported from the country of origin of the company or imported from the countries abroad. It is seen that companies with new-patented products, technological products and with innovative quality and first-in strategies are more often adopted for marketing beyond the boundaries. In short, it can be said that domestic and transnational market strategies normally and broadly differ and vary in the degree of differentiation, concentration, time horizons which are longer in transnational marketing. Short-term profits are prevalent mostly in domestic marketing. However, transnational marketing looks for long-term marketing opportunities for generating credibility in the foreign markets. Firms, often play like 'maverick marketers' depending on the customer traits and behaviours of the consumers.

Summary

Transnational domestic marketing and transnational strategic marketing have wide-ranging application in the vista of management. In order to unfold the enigmatic riddles of marketing skills beyond the boundaries, strategic keys to unveil the potential treasures of business are paramount. Competitive advantage, competitive edge and competitive attack for advent into the virgin markets even need acumen. Speedy innovations of plans for conquering market share have become evident in the concepts that have been elucidated. The fundamental aspects of marketing management have been viewed from a novel perspective and parameters of scaling up methods have been advocated.

The scope of reading illuminate on the aspects like strategic market plan, marketing strategy which discussed on sectors like corporate strategy, business mission, portfolio analysis, competition, customer and product strategy, etc. Apart from the above; the sectors of transnational marketing has been amplified with a list of points. Moreover the process of international strategic marketing offers a blue print of linkages with one another.

The chapter highlights on the impact of multi-business strategic planning on transnational marketing and major differences between strategic marketing (transnational) and marketing management (domestic). It also delineates the domain of successful transnational companies along with their salient features. Product positioning in a strategic business environment is the ultimate strategy elucidated for redefining a cutting edge logistic. The ultimate objective of reading this chapter shall be to penetrate into the fabric of designing communication strategy.

QUESTIONS FOR DISCUSSION

Q. 1. What do you mean by transnational strategic marketing and domestic marketing? Illustrate.

Q. 2. What are the major six components of strategic market plan? Discuss.

Q. 3. What are the salient features of transnational marketing? Discuss with points.

Q. 4. Describe the process of international strategic marketing. Elucidate.

Q. 5. Which are the important policies, essential for emerging transnational companies? Explore and enquire into the details.

Q. 6. Which eight attributes are basic to successful management of transnational companies? Enumerate the aspects with suitable examples.

Q. 7. Write short notes on the following:

(a) Single Brand

(b) Multiple Brands

(c) Promotional – mix strategy

(d) Laggard

Q.8. Elucidate the transnational promotion-mix strategy, explaining all factors.

Q.9. Discuss on the transnational market strategies with suitable examples from industries.

Chapter
3

Mapping and Mobilizing Transnational Market

LEARNING OBJECTIVES

After going through this chapter the reader should be able to:

1. Understand the mapping techniques of transnational marketing approach utilizing the tools enumerated.
2. Recognize the 'break-down' methods and 'binding-up' methods for estimating market potential of new products against established products.
3. Identify the method of test-marketing products by measuring the five major factors like market size, market growth, etc.
4. Explain issues revolving around new product management and marketing strategies, including systemic approach and procedures.
5. Ascertain, the competitive product-market boundaries, through the three dimensions, along with the environmental influences.
6. Describe the penetration processes through stages of entry into marketplaces, analysing factors that include aspects like product line, types of customers and geographic scope, etc.

'The best way to appreciate your job is to imagine yourself without it'.

— Oscar Wilde

'It is not strongest of the species that survive, nor the most intelligent, but the one most responsive to change'.

— Charles Darwin

7. Realize the essence of customers through multifaceted distribution channels, relevantly effective in a transnational market milieu.

8. Acquire strategic action plan for probing into the crowded markets for launching new product with success.

9. Enhance deeper knowledge on the measuring methods of an active market situation having oddities.

INTRODUCTION

Transnational market expansion strategy is possible through the mapping of the prevailing market forces and factors. In order to bolster a new business across the border, for mobilizing profit margin on sales, techniques acceptable to the target market have to be implemented. Apart from the all pervading general practice of business strategy, pertinent aspects befitting to the USP of product in the market have to be analyzed for accuracy in accomplishing the objective. MBO should be given a priority for achieving triumphs in targets.

Mobilizing the techniques encompasses the ambit of aspects like, test marketing and its host of complimentary attributes like market size and so forth. Apart from it, it shall lay emphasis on differences that prevail between transnational and domestic markets; to denote the cross border approach; barred by constraints of countries.

The comprehensive details of the ideas and concepts; including the distribution channels have been candidly explained in the chapter.

MEASURING TRANSNATIONAL MARKET POTENTIAL

Measuring transnational market potential is important for understanding the capacity of the approach in a given business environment. It shall differ from place to place, depending on the universe of study.

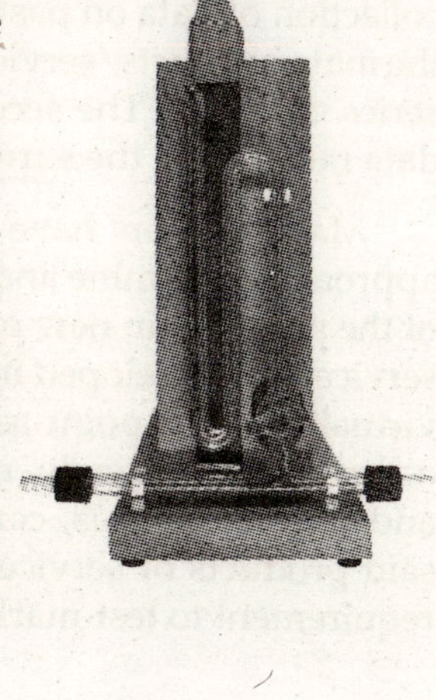

Incidentally, there are various ways and methods to measure transnational market potential. In this case, different methods are required for measuring the market potential of new products as against established products. These methods for understanding, reading and estimating market potentials for the established products may be classified into two broad groups. These are known as breakdown methods and binding-up methods. These groups are based on their contradiction, dissimilarity and contrasting approaches.

The 'breakdown methods' begin with the total industry or market data and the breakdown of the data into 'segments of interest' fitting to the firm with respect to business. The 'binding-up methods' start with individual accounts, like those of the customers and prospects, aggregating the data to the industry or market level until it reaches the level on which it is to be assessed.

❑ Breakdown Methods

In the above, the 'total market measure method' is done by the application of the available aggregate industry data and/or the market data that are available in the transnational transactions. Mainly, it is required to estimate the market activities and the sale potentials. The statistical series method is based on the determination of the observed statistical relationships that exist between the industry, market data and socio-economic variables. These said factors are descriptive of the industry, market and the environment. Critical components are correlated for the accuracy of judgement drawing multiple relations. Reassembling of data is empirical and poised.

❑ Binding-up Methods

The typical 'census method' measures this by making a separate appraisal of each and every individual user or for that matter, all prospective users in a given market under study under the lens. This market survey method (MSM) is often employed and used when the goods and services are in relatively non-concentrated markets or are found in scattered market patches. This method involves the collection of data on past purchases, together with the classification of data on the main products/services, number of employees and other relevant statistical series database. The secondary data method lays stress on the internal sales data rather than the survey database of the product purchases.

Many authors have suggested that test marketing is the best method to approach, determine and measure the potentials of new products. An estimate of the potential in new products is usually required long before the products/services are developed in physical shape, size and in all dimensions. It is made virtually to the point as if they are ready for the test marketing. Hence, in order to obtain timely, relevant and reliable estimates of the market demand and sales potentials, certain objective measures of possible demand for the said products or services are needed. The main three methods that meet the requirement to test-market a product are given below. It narrates the methods

of assessment and estimation. They are usage factor method (UFM), possible use method (PUM) and analogy/substitution method (A/SM).

❑ Usage Factor Method (UFM)

Usage factor method (UFM) is a multi-step process, which estimates the market potential for each of the segments. It is done by multiplying a developed usage factor ratio by the economic activity of the segments in the product.

❑ Possible Use Method (PUM)

Possible use method (PUM) is based on the market survey conducted for the prospective users to ascertain, understand and determine whether a given business can use a specific product or not, if the product in question needs part improvement than to what extent it needs to be customized or made to be customer driven.

❑ Analogy/Substitution Method (A/SM)

Analogy/substitution method (A/SM) is the weakest and the most inefficient of all the three methods of assessment. This method is based on the assumption that the diffusion processes for all similar or related products in the past are analogous and of the same type.

In fact, this method of measurements of market potential is undertaken to gain insights into the five major elements. The elements are **market size, market growth, profitability, type of buying decision** and **customer market structure**. They are the building blocks and the major components to assess and analyse for arriving at the result and the outcome.

To dwell on the aspects of these, we see that the **first element**, market size, is better expressed in both units of measurement and currency denomination. Standard denomination of a currency for example, rupee and its expression in isolation cannot be achieved due to market exchange's distortion and fluctuations that happen due to inflation. It is also volatile and is open, due to currency fluctuations and changing exchange rates in the transnational business, each day. Due to the inflationary upheavals, changing purchasing power parity and commotion, the measuring criteria for new products and product line extensions should specify both, the units and the rupees separately for measurement. Indeed, the market size can be expressed as the total market sales potential or the company market share. However, it is seen that most of the companies, through their customers utilize the figures of market share.

Similarly, the **second element**, market growth, is intended to reflect the secular trend setting of the industry. Here, in addition, the measuring criteria should be specified for new product concepts and product line extensions as before. In fact, the criteria and projections ought to be based on percentage growth in the units. Projections in the industrial settings often are heavily dependent on retro-profit possibilities; it therefore, plans for equipment replacement.

The **third element** in this assessment, evaluation and feedback of strategic potential is profitability. This usually is expressed in terms of the contribution margin. It also happens when the return calculations are done. Evidently, most of the US and the leading Indian companies view profitability in terms of the return-on-investment (ROI) or return-on-sales (ROS) or return-on net-assets (RONA). On the other hand, return on capital employed (ROCE), is often calculated in the multi-national companies. In order to measure the market potential, none of these calculations appears to function better than another does.

Particulars	Items	Potential		
		Low	Medium	High
Market Size	New product concepts; Product line extension or new market segment for existing line.	₹ 10 min. ₹ 2 min. 7 percent 5 percent 45 percent 40 percent	₹ 10 min. ₹ 2–5 Min. 7–10 percent 5–7 percent 45–55 percent 40–50 percent	₹ 20 min. ₹ 5 min. 10 percent 7 percent 55 percent 50 percent
Market Growth	New product concepts; Product line extension or new market segment for existing line.	Straight Rebuy - - - Oligopoly	New Task - - - - - -	Modified Rebuy - - - Monopolistic Rebuy -
Profitability (Contribution margin)	New product concept or product line extension. New market segment for existing line.	- - -		- -
Type of buying decision				
Customer market structure				

Fig. 2.4 Measuring Transnational Market Potential

The **fourth element** is the type of buying decision that it takes. The basis for a buying decision should be predicated. It is like, whether the decision is straight rebuy, modified rebuy or new task.

The **fifth element** is the structure of the customer market. In fact, based on the same measuring criteria as competitive structure, the market can be classified as **monopolistic, oligopolistic, differentiated competition** or **pure competition**. Figure 2.4 summarizes clearly the above elements and shows a **pro forma** of things for measuring the transnational market potential.

❑ Transnational New Product Strategies

Transnational market across the border is sceptic and sensitive for acceptance of new products and brand name of new companies. Strategies laid out for engineering a planned move for launching new products (products new to the market) need to advance on a scheduled programme. The purpose of creating a market space is to create a market share of the intended product in the given market by influencing brand equity. A comprehensive scheme of operation is planned because transnational marketing involves comparatively huge investments due to its inevitable barriers like the cultural, economical, social, technological, political, environmental and legal acceptance. Yet, global products have also in the mean time reached the global customers, of which an example can be TV and mass media. All new products intended for foreign markets have to study the customer psychology, prior to launching of the volume of product types in the alien markets.

❑ New Product Management (NPM)

New product development (NPD) has been the cornerstone of business expansion plans globally. NPD creates a huge market for the business to run for profit. The new product management is a pivotal aspect for the customer responsiveness towards the transnational companies to attract and galvanize business. A global village concept is still far away—presently, mass marketing is on the decline and has become a myth with respect to certain products. Hence, in the given transnational environment, what is important is a customer-specific product creation, marketing mix and marketing. These are the growing phenomenon in the transnational business. In fact, no successful transnational company can reject, ignore and avoid management of new products, in its portfolio of future transnational operations. It is all the more important, if it operates in the places, regions and countries, etc., in different stages of the development process. The scorecard provided below, on which a minimum score of 70 connotes a successful future transnational company (Booz and Allen, 1982).

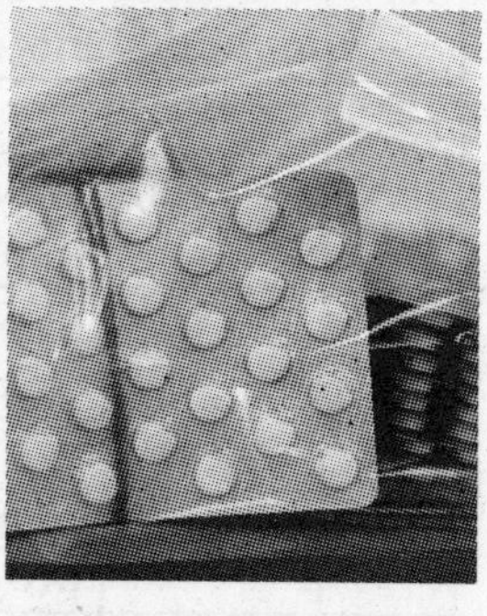

		SCORE
1.	Our corporate growth plan includes an explicit strategic description on the role of internally developed new products over the next five years.	
2.	We have a well-defined new product strategy, which identifies the financial gap and strategic roles that new products must satisfy.	
3.	We establish different hurdle rates, based on associated risk.	
4.	We have had a systematic, yet adaptive, new products process in place for at least five years.	
5.	Idea generation for us begins after we have identified external, domestic and transnational market niches and assessed our internal competitive strengths.	
6.	We have a formalized monitoring and tracking system in place to measure cost per introduction and new product performance against objectives, domestically and transnational.	
7.	We have compensation programmes that encourage entrepreneurship, reward risk-taken and reinforce innovative management.	
8.	We have a clear understanding of who is responsible for new product development.	
9.	Top management provides consistent commitment to new products in terms of funds and requisite managerial know-how.	
10.	We adopt our new products organization to match the requirements of the new products portfolio.	

	SCORE		TOTAL	
	90 – 100	We are one of the best transnational.		
	80 – 89	Improvement areas exist, but we are in good shape.		
	70 – 79	We should consider making changes to our new products programme.		
	70	We better get some assistance in managing new products.		

Fig. 2.5 New Product Management: 1990 and Beyond

To determine how well your business unit manages new products, rate your business from 1-10 points for each question. 10 = 'Fully Meets', 5 = 'Partially Meets', 1 = 'Does not Meet'

TRANSNATIONAL PRODUCT-MARKET STRATEGY: THE PROCESS

Transnational product/market strategy process is the most important formulae in order to make an access into the mystic market. In order to do that several required methods are essential. To formulate transnational business unit strategy, the basic input is the strategy of different products/markets. It compels the business unit to make business and profit. This angle to a great deal is missing in the domestic companies.

Therefore, the first step in formulating a transnational business unit strategy needs a framework for developing the product and market strategy. It should happen in both ways, adhering to the top-down process and bottom-up process. Following is a systematic approach for formulating product/market strategy in consonance to the inevitable factors. They are:

1. Begin with the business going transnational strategically. Speculate, predict and estimate the momentum of business. It should be spread over the planning period, if no other significant changes in the policies and the methods of operations are not made to be implemented. Prediction will be based on the historical performance of last three years or more, along with the scientific basis for good judgment.

2. Precision in forecasting shall be made on the future business environment. It shall be made to ascertain as to what changes will happen to the market environment of the posterity, spanning over the postulated planned period. This aspect will include the overall marketing environment and the product/market environment of the transnational company.

3. It should ensure that modifications to the prediction are made in line with the steps of progress in the light of the forecasted shifts in the business environments, which were discussed in the step 2 above.

4. Company should progress ahead, if the predicted performance, as per the yardstick, is fully satisfactory vis-à-vis the objective. Continue operating, if the prediction is not fully satisfying and meanwhile seek to change the course in accordance to the desired objective.

5. Analyse the significant strengths and weaknesses, opportunities and threats of the business. Comparison should be made with those important competitors of the company along with the products under the scanner. This appraisal should include the required factors

that shall apparently become important at a later date. It should be appraised, both in the marketing, particularly in the areas like market, product, price, promotion and distribution, etc., and in the functional areas like finance, R&D, costs, morale, image and smooth management of the organization.

6. The company R&D has to evaluate the difference between its marketing strategies with those of at least three major competitors in the market. Three is a standard number for comparison.
7. Company has to take up an analysis to invent certain variations in the marketing strategy, which could offer a better and favourable relationship for a competitive stand in the future. Self-assessment is the key to the growth.
8. Company has to assess, evaluate and identify the proposed alternate strategies in terms of possible risks in the market, competitive response to changes and potential competitive advancement.
9. Company has to stop if the alternate strategy appears to be unsatisfactory in terms of the attainment of objectives.
10. Company has to widen the definition of the present business and reiterate the points 7, 8 and 9 together. These shall be reviewed if there is a gap noticed between the objective and alternate strategy. Redefining the business is like looking at the other products that can be supplied to a market that is known and understood. At times, this may seem like supplying existing products to a different market. Similarly, it may mean applying technical and financial acumen to the new products and new markets, at a time.

The usual process of widening the very definition of the business by broadening the windows can be done. It can broaden when either of the following events occur. It is never constant and stable; the dynamics of business is perennial and is in a flux. Chance to select is significant.

(a) When the knowledge domain of a merging area becomes so slim that choice of the sector to be studied is determined by intuition. It has scope for inadequate judgment;

(b) When the cost of studying the new area becomes prohibitively expensive because of the lack of related experience;

(c) When it becomes crystal clear that the scope of finding a competitive opportunity is rare.

If the existing business is not satisfactory, the management has to lower and reduce the number of objectives. This can also happen if the broadening of the business gives unsatisfactory results.

The three most important tasks involved in the 'strategy procedures' that are highlighted above are information analysis (IA), strategy formulation (SF) and implementation. At the product/market level, the product/market managers perform these above tasks. The SBU executive of a transnational company also performs these tasks. In fact, sometimes, these are also performed by both of them together. It is the warranted situation of the business, which calls for a decision making.

MARKET BOUNDARIES—THE DEFINITION

The crux of any strategy formulation is dependent on the market definition. Market is the key. The problem is of identifying the 'competitive product-market boundaries' that pervade and supersede all levels and types of marketing decisions. Such strategic issues of identifying market boundaries unveil the basic definition of the business. Boundaries enable the assessment of opportunities that are seen through the gaps visible in the market; boundaries enable visibility of threats posed by competitive actions. Similarly, decision making on major strategic resource allocations is strongly influenced by these boundaries. Moreover, the assessment of market share for evaluating the performance of the company's product, for making territorial advertising, steering the sales force and other budget allocations, identification of boundary is important. The 'antitrust prosecutions' that bolstered in a spree was also known as defensible definitions of product-market boundaries. The most complex task is to define the market alone. It is critical, ambiguous and complex when we look into the manifold ways and angles in which it can be defined and redefined.

All along, it has been observed that the 'traditional market boundaries' have been defined in terms of **product place/market space**. A 'market' is defined as a 'group of firms producing identical and similar or closely related products'. However, to be more specific, a preferable approach is to 'define the market in terms of products'. What is important is a close relationship in between the products types. Goods and services could be closely related, as if they are eligible to be substituted by the consumers in a market. They are many a times close, because the methods, factors and the ways of the production used in each of the product are more or less similar. A 'market is usually identified with a generic class of products', for instance, we hear of the flower market, detergent market, automobile market, garment market and cigarette market. Nonetheless, we have many more markets of the kind. Eventually, all these are 'product markets'. It refers to customers having purchased a given class of products. In order to manufacture the desired products in massive quantities, products are currently considered as a manifestation of the application of a particular technology, for a particular customer function and for a particular customer segment. Based on the given logic, it is said that 'market boundaries' should be determined around the three dimensions given below:

❑ Technological Application

A specific 'customer function' can be done by different technologies. Alternative technologies can also be applied to satisfy a 'customer need'. What is important is to attend to the 'customer satisfaction' by executing the desired 'customer function'.

❑ Customer Function

Each of the 'products' is identified and considered in terms of the functions they serve and the ways they are being used. Different 'functions' provide different customer benefits. What is important is the 'customer function'.

❑ Customer Segment

Each 'customer segment' refers to a homogenous set of customers with similar needs and same characteristics. They are typecast and identified as a separate segment in the market. Moreover, it is seen that almost all the transnational markets evolve five sets of **'environmental influences'**, which essentially affect product-market boundaries. These main environmental influences are identified as:

1. **Technological change:** Changes in the technology are inevitable in a techno-savvy market. GPRS technology of mobile phones was replaced by 3G technology. It is a paradigm change and shift in the facility to affect the product-market boundaries. Technology helps in reaching the customer king beyond the market boundary by environmental influence.
2. **Market-oriented product development:** Multi-facility products that are developed combining features of several products into one multipurpose offering are very important for reaching beyond the market boundaries. An example can be that of a multi-purpose portable music system (Gadget) with camera facility. An example can be I-pod, software and sophisticated washing machine, etc.
3. **Price changes and supply constraints:** Price changes and constraints in supply influence the perceived set of substitutes. In case of difference in the exchange rates of currency from one country to another or in case of required quality standards of the products, it creates problem in the supply and the pricing of products. It is the summation of business environment which relates to the purchasing power of customers. Countries with economic agreement normally have purchasing power parity. Product price tags given in the case

of INR, USD, Euro and Yen are different, for which products are manufactured with the country version of the quality too. These become factors for environmental influence to access ahead of the defined market boundary. Due to the environmental influence, the small Indian manufacturing firms replaced the Chinese toy market and Chinese-made fengsui artefacts by 2000. Taiwan and Korean products substituted the Japanese watches and electronic gadgets available in 1985.

4. **Social, legal and government trends:** Social, legal and government trends are very important, due to the trade barriers, traditions and social customs. Bindis that are very common in India are not used in the Middle East. Use of 'burqa' is not accepted in some European countries. Similarly, common law, codal law and Islamic law are quite different to each other. A country like India does not believe in the principle of eye for an eye applied in Islamic law in some of the countries. The philosophy of Indian law proclaims 'Let 100 criminals get acquitted; one innocent should not be punished'.

   Government trends are peculiar to countries, of which the polity of India, Indonesia, Thailand, etc., like other countries are quite unique for their changes over the recent past. Mandate of the political party in power, enforce the charter of demands and ensure the countryman to abide by. Barrack Obama's enforcement of social security net at the cost of federal exchange of the government of the United States of America is a glaring example. Golden quadrilateral of BJP regime in India during Atal Bihari Vajpayee as the prime minister of India is an offshoot of the tendency of the government in power.

5. Transnational trade competition changes geographic boundaries. Mittlestand products of Germany influence environments beyond the frontiers for high-end industrial products of SMEs mostly.

These changes are caused by three fundamentally different phenomena, which are seen in Fig. 2.6. They are transferred by virtue of **adoption, diffusion and acclimatization process**. Their penetration results in creating new customer groups. The process of systemization of products results in the sale, absorption and utilization of products for serving a set of combinations of functions. **Technology substitution** process underlies the changes on a technology dimension.

As shown in Fig. 2.6, the task of market boundary definition amounts to grouping together of a set of market cells. Each 'unit of grouping together of a set of market cell' is defined in terms of mainly three dimensions. They are customer groups, customer functions and technologies. In other words, a 'product market' may comprise of any of the holy combination of these cells. A business firm/unit can cater to the total transnational market or can contextually limit itself to serve just a part of it. Many a time a business expansion plan of a transnational company may decide to serve the entire market. It becomes easy to serve the smaller and narrower markets. Transnational companies enter the foreign soil looking into the scope, shape and size of the total market. On which market a decision has to be taken for transnational approach is based on certain factors. The salient decisions and factors are:

- To adjudge, sniff and perceive from the market surveillance, scanning and mapping, which 'product function' and 'technology groupings' can best be penetrated, protected and dominated in a foreign soil.
- To assess the internal resource limitations of the foreign country, which enable, propel and force a narrow focus.
- To read, understand and adjudge, which trial-and-error experience has resolved in reacting to threats and opportunities of the proposed business.
- To ascertain, which unusual competencies are stemming from access to scarce resources or protected markets. Threat perceptions are to be made because transnational aggression involves comparatively a huge amount of money.

❑ Technical Substitution–Extension to New Technologies

What is important is the pertinent strategy to identify a transnational pocket for entering and expanding. Strategically, accuracy of choice of a market where a business unit/product is served is presumably based on the following means of approach. They encompass various aspects like:

❑ Length and Breadth of the Product Line

Specialization is the key for edging out competition with a product line. It is based on the users' capacity and market potential. They can be:

1. Specialized in terms of technological edge and broad range of the product usages;
2. Specialized in terms of product usages and multiple technologies;

3. Specialized in a single unique technology and a narrow range of product usages;
4. Specialized in broad range of related and allied technologies and usages;
5. Specialized in the broad and narrow range of quality, volume and price in the required levels.

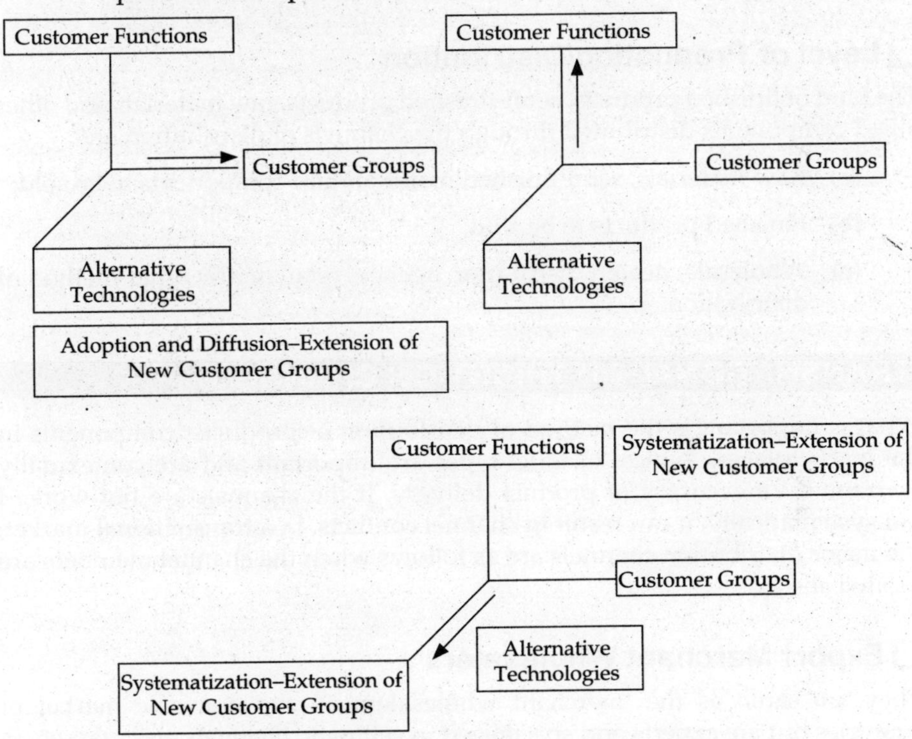

Fig. 2.6 Market Boundaries in Three Dimensions

❑ Types of Customer Kings

The customer type and segment have to be identified before entering into the plan and programme. They can be:

1. Single customer segment
2. Multiple customer segment
   (a) Undifferentiated treatment
   (b) Differentiated treatment

❑ Geographic Scope

What is important is a geographical approach, meeting the scope to business. It is dependent on the scope to market expansion across places.

(a) Local or regional

(b) National

(c) Multinational

❑ Level of Production/Distribution

The kind of finished products, semi-finished products, raw materials and other allied components distributed through the channels of distribution are:

(a) Raw materials, semi-finished materials and components to be sold;

(b) Finished products to be sold;

(c) Wholesale, dealer, distributor, agency, retail or any other method of distribution.

TRANSNATIONAL DISTRIBUTION CHANNELS

What is important is the method of distribution of products/components in the marketplaces. Typical channel types are important and are contextually warranted for accuracy of product delivery. If the channels are not worked out systematically, it can result in channel conflicts. In a transnational market, the major distribution channels are as follows when the channel members are located abroad—

❑ Export Merchant Wholesalers

They are same as the 'merchant wholesalers' in the domestic market of countries but are experts and specialized in selling to channels and markets in the export trade. They are available in all countries.

Cargo Ship Carrying Consignment

❑ Export Agents or Brokers

They are same as the agents and brokers in the domestic market, but specialize in selling to export channels and markets. They have a definite role to play across countries.

❑ Commission Agents or Foreign Buying Agents

They are the 'finders' of foreign firms wanting to purchase domestic products. By doing the job of finding and enabling a transaction, a commission is paid to them by their foreign clients. They negotiate for the business to happen.

❑ Buying Representatives of Foreign Company

They are the direct representatives of foreign companies. They are the people who are sent abroad by trading companies. They could be from Japan, US, India and other countries.

❑ Export Management Companies (EMCs)

They eventually act as export departments for the several manufacturers of non-competitive products. Cannibalized export marketing is not encouraged by these companies. This is done to avoid competition. They in fact, solicit and transact business in the name of the manufactures, searching for the market at their behest. They represent the products before the buyer for a commission, salary and/or retainer fees plus commission. Some also like to take title to the goods and carry financing for export sales.

❑ Agents

They represent the domestic exporters in the important foreign ports for the business to run. They develop sales with the foreign importers, like the merchant wholesalers or industrial users. They do not take title to the goods but instead receive a commission. Agents have a great role to play in the business.

❑ Manufacturer's Sales Representatives

They take responsibility for a manufacturer's goods exported to a particular country or market area and receive a commission. They are more under the control of the manufacturer and or exporter than the most of the categories of agents.

❑ Merchant Distributors

Merchant distributors, unlike agents, take title to the goods, which they purchase from exporters of their channels. They sell the goods either directly or through the wholesalers or the retailers to the end-user markets abroad. They are also known as **'importer distributors'** for the function they do.

❑ Manufacturer's Distribution Branches

These people have their own shipping terminals and storage facilities in foreign ports, from which they sell their own factory's/company's/mills' production, as well as, that of the other domestic manufacturers. They sell the products to foreign wholesalers, retailers or end users. They have a huge role to play on behalf of the company.

❑ State Controlled Trading Companies

They are found in countries, which have state trading monopolies. These are the countries where business is conducted by a few government-sanctioned and government-controlled trading entities. Gaibatsu and Kairetsu models of business have been the forte for Japanese for churning the market opportunities and have been reckoned the world over. Similarly, **private trading companies** are privately owned merchant importers and exporters handling transnational business. In some countries, they may exercise considerable control over both, in the importation of goods and their distribution within the country. Glaring examples of both the types can be seen in Japan, US and some states of divided Russia.

❑ Merchant Wholesalers

They essentially take title to the goods purchased and 'may' act as stocking wholesalers or drop shippers and sell the goods/services either to retailers or directly to end markets. Merchant wholesalers have all the liberty to do business with the goods under their purview, in the style called for by the

❑ Retailers

They typically buy from distributors, wholesalers and sell the products to contractors, industrial users and/or end customers. They retail to end customers based on a margin of profit.

Shopping Mall

❑ Merchant Wholesaler Retailers

They are the firms that are involved in both wholesaling and retailing. They may own retail chains, whose targets are contractors, the do-it-yourself market or other end users. They have the flexibility of choice. Pantaloon, Mustafa and Planet M are some of the examples.

CONCLUSION

The world of domestic market and transnational market is amazing, flexible and business driven. In domestic marketing, distribution channels could be complex and extensive, but the channel structure is not as complex as in the transnational marketing. In transnational marketing, the numbers of channel members are comparatively larger than domestic marketing. Evidently, state-controlled trading companies, foreign company buying representatives, foreign buying agents and export management companies, etc., are exclusive to the transnational markets. Conventionally, the domestic distribution structure comprises of merchant distributors, local sales agents, retailers and commission agents only. In the transnational marketing, the strategy that is involved requires competency to operate the business. It requires certain cross-country rules and regulations to be understood, interpreted and acted upon in favour of the business transactions made globally. It also calls for a detailed understanding of the trade relations amongst countries, market players and products.

Summary

Mapping the modus operandi of transnational markets to know about the engaged tools and techniques employed is the key to strategic planning and implementation. What is therefore significant to the study is measuring the market potential of the current business. It examines the potential of new products, with respect to already accepted products by using 'breakdown method' and 'binding-up method'.

The chapter elucidates on the critical facets of statistical components for accuracy of judgement and macro market surveys to resolve at a decision making. It highlights the main three methods of test-marking of new products and discusses the five important aspects that it entails like market size, market growth, profitability, type of buying and customer market structure.

New product management has been candidly explained with measuring score boards to gauge potential and design market strategies laying necessary process in place. The subtle approaches which are not required for domestic market have been compared for clarity. It identified product/market boundaries reading into the traditional and the breakthrough new products. Elaborate analysis have been offered on technological application, customer function and customer segment. Influencing environmental issues governing business boundaries and factors likes adoption, diffusion and acclimatization process have also been given.

Contd....

Besides the diagrams that are significant to the given description, it reflects all other aspects like product line, hedging competition, type of customers, geographic scope and distribution channels. It emphasizes on the distribution channels for its utter importance in the subject of study.

QUESTIONS FOR DISCUSSION

Q.1. What do you mean by measuring trans-national market potential? Discuss on the 'breakdown method' and 'binding-up method'.

Q.2. What are the main three methods employed to test market a product? Explain on each of them giving examples.

Q.3. Narrate the particulars of the grid for measuring transnational market potential. Describe on each of the component.

Q.4. Describe the importance of new product management in the field of transnational marketing environment. Elucidate with relevant examples of companies and products.

Q.5. Examine the new product management scoring format in your business environment, make a mock test on the score sheet and tabulate the results. Understand the significant areas of emphasis required for the market place surveyed and submit a detail analysis of the concerns.

Q.6. Illustrate the salient factors of transnational market-product strategy.

Q.7. What do you mean by market boundaries? How are the market boundaries determined? Discuss.

Q.8. How are changes caused in market places by virtue of adoption, diffusion and acclimatization process? Illustrate giving suitable examples from market.

Q.9. Deliberate on the methods of transnational distribution channels normally deployed for better business. Elucidate with examples.

Q.10. Write short notes on:

(a) Break down method

(b) Binding-up method

(c) Usage factor method (UFM)

(d) Possible use method (PUM)

(e) Analogy/Substitution method (A/SM)

(f) Market size

(g) Market growth

(h) Profitability

(i) Baying type of buying decision

(j) Customer market structure

(k) Technological change

(l) Market-oriented product development

(m) Price changes and supply constraints

(n) Social, legal and government trends

(o) Trade competition changes geographic boundaries

(p) Length and Breadth of product line

(q) Types of customer kings

(r) Geographic scope

(s) Level of production/distribution

Chapter 4

Macro Aspects of Strategic Thrust on Transnational Marketing

LEARNING OBJECTIVES

After going through the chapter, the reader shall be able to:

1. Identify the strategic thrust areas for pushing the new products to target market by a company.
2. Recognize the processes adopted by emerging companies for moving to transnational markets.
3. Realize the essence of assessment of issues, spotting key variables and selecting strategy for implementation.
4. Define major strategic thrusts from 'start-up stage' to 'restore and revenue product line' by companies for traversing beyond the frontiers of the parent country.
5. Explain the strategic thrust areas for defending relative competitive market position by employing variety of strategic designs.
6. Show the governmental barriers and roadblocks for the business journey beyond the boarders.
7. Understand the role of corporations, public offices and their areas of concern.

> *'Vision is the art of seeing things invisible'.*
>
> *— Jonathan Swift*
>
> *'Change is the law of life, and those who look only to the past or present are certain to miss the future'.*
>
> *— J F Kennedy*

8. Know the strategic thrust factors of business with respect to areas of operations in a company.
9. Analyse and assess the effectiveness of marketing thrust of companies and rating them on a scale.

STRATEGIC THRUSTS IN TRANSNATIONAL MARKETING: FACETS

Strategic thrust for accelerating the pace of business; pro-actively require certain vital areas of transnational marketing. Stand points of the strategy embrace the entire product life cycle and sectors of business, beginning from initial starting stage of the new product/services. Efforts are needed for overcoming the industry distributions reaching to the customers and retailers. It is the achievement of lowest cost of product which is amounting to ultimately aggressive fast growth. It can also be through differentiation, market focus and by positioning of products identifying specific niche markets; evidently profitable on investments. Interestingly it is believed that the approach to exert strategic thrust require total mobilisation of efforts from all quarters; optimizing the overall aspects of leveraging means. Transnational is about transition, transportation and transformation of business in its essence.

Strategic thrust is pivotal in the domain of transnational marketing. It is to push the product into the target market destination. In fact, the strategy development for the identified product/market, in the field of transnational marketing, for any enterprise/firm/company/business unit requires predicting the momentum of current operations into the future market. It has to design a road map for phasing the marketing processes in a timeline and drawing up a plan of action. Moderating and modifying the momentum of negotiation for transactions, in the light of environmental changes is urgent in transnational business. Reviewing the adjusted momentum against goals is all the more important. Evidently, if no gap between the set goals and the predictions is noticed, then the present strategy is said to be steady and well continued. It has to be monitored as per the strategic plan of action. However, if a gap is traced, which is inevitable in the action plan chalked out, the following three-stepped process is adopted by companies, apart from the nuances inherent.

❑ Assessment of Issues

A deliberate attempt to raise issues for questioning the delicate aspects of business shall provoke proactive thinking. It shall awaken one from the monotony and dullard temperament towards the completion that is intrinsic to marketing. It is oriented with the status quo of the business vis-à-vis the future prospect of business.

❑ Spotting the Key Variables

The identification of the main variables that play a significant role in generating the business is important. Variables have to be adapted for improving the business and bring forth value in the supply chain process of the business. Identifying the key variables can be the harbinger for a turnaround success in the industry.

❑ Selection of Strategy for Implementation

Key to success is dependent on the choice of the right kind of strategy adopted. Choosing the preferred strategy will make or mar the business. The thrust of business is bolstered from the preferred core strategy. It distributes weights on the selected strategy. When the strategic framework is designed, the tactics of attacking the available resources for ensuring the optimal output shall come up. Strategy for transnational marketing should be selected through any of the following methods:

- Identify the most susceptible, volatile and vulnerable non-domestic market segment for strategic projection.
- Identify the products/markets that have/need response rates more than a competitor's ability to overcome.
- Identify products/markets that require capital investment, which a competitor is unwilling to commit for the target business.
- Identify the commercial demand, viability and potential of the new technology, particularly for the new user's acceptance in the marketplaces.
- Identify, read and exploit the available managerial style, method or system. Handling overhead rates at par, optimizing distribution channels, using market image profitably and with flexibility is important.

The major strategic thrust options that are important for the transnational markets have been delineated below for detailed study. They have been assessed, analysed and evaluated on their manifold perspectives.

TRANSNATIONAL STRATEGIC THRUST AREAS: AN APPROACH

Strategic thrust for accelerating the pace of business, proactively require certain vital areas of transnational marketing. Standpoints of the strategy embrace the entire project life cycle and sectors of business from initial starting stage of the new product/services. Efforts are needed for overcoming the industry distributions reaching to the customers and retailers. It is the achievement of lowest cost of product which is amounting to ultimately aggressive fast growth. It can also be through differentiation, market focus and by positioning of products identifying specific niche markets evidently profitable on investments. Interestingly, it is believed that the approach to exert strategic thrust require total mobilization of efforts from all quarters optimizing the overall aspects of leveraging means. 'Transnational' is about transition, transportation and transformation of business in its essence.

❑ Start-up Stage

Start-up stage by definition is all about the introduction of new product or service, with clear significant technology breakthrough. Innovation of product with technological glitz is an advantage for the market for deriving monopoly. It creates an indomitable space for itself in the market notwithstanding the competitions. The ultimate objective is to develop a totally new industry to create and satisfy new demand, where none existed before. Product innovation is the key. The requirements of the organization and management are to undertake risk and engage capital investments in R&D. Risk-taking attitude of management, capital expenditure and expenses in the R&D is the ultimate. In this kind of approach, the expected results are based on the negative cash flow, low-to-negative results and leadership position in the identified new industry. Infosys in software industry, Biocon in pharma industry and TATA in steel manufacturing and campus car like Nano manufacturing are few of the examples of Indian companies.

❑ To Grow with the Pace of the Industry

By definition, transnational strategic thrust urges to limit the efforts to those aspects that are necessary to maintain the market share of a specific product that is delivered to the market, as keeping pace with the speed of the industry in business. The company has to catch up with the tempo and temper required for success. Eventually, the objective is to let the product be distributed and make the resources free to the correct markets, by virtue of better quality product management and trace the production weaknesses in order to plug the intervals. The requirement of the company is all about maintaining management restraint, market intelligence, capital investments and a time-driven strategy. The expected results that the definition yields shall be a stable market share, reasonable profits and cash flow. This strategic thrust shall at best sustain the market fluctuations at the speed of industry averages. It is a steady way of attaining the business prospects.

❑ Aggressive Fast Growth

As per the definition, an aggressive fast growth approach is the speed that the company/product aggressively grows for a larger share in the market. It is also for a large market share and/or for a strong base and firm position in the market, in relation to the competition and competitors. Overcoming the contender, the opponent and market enemy is calls for an ultimate strategic thrust. The objective is to grow by volume of sales, enhance the market share more than competitors and grow faster than the general industry growth rate prevailing. In order to achieve these thrust target what is required is the available need-based resources for proper investment and follow-up, risk-taking attitude and stance of the management and an appropriate investment strategy to wage war, invade and thereby conquer markets. By doing this, the company is likely to obtain certain expected results. These expected results could be a higher market share, short-term access to markets that give a low rate of return and above-average returns in the longer term. It can give the firebrand players a competitive retaliation and retain the belligerent style of market access.

❑ Attainment of Cost Leadership

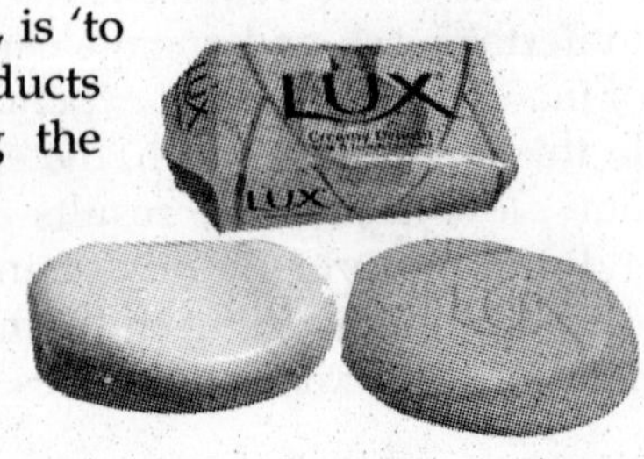

Attainment of cost leadership, as a definition, is 'to achieve the lowest delivered costs of the products in relation to the competitors, by meeting the acceptable quality levels. Quality, costs and competition are priorities of the business thrust. The main objective of this strategy is to increase the level of 'freedom'. It creates a defence against blocks and helps to penetrate in the market. It also defends against the powerful market entries and simultaneously also creates strong customer blocs, provoke cut-throat competitors and produce potential substitute products. Cost leadership is the mantra here. The requirements of the strategy are relatively high market share, disciplined business transactions, management efforts to encourage the employees, access to raw materials, substantial capital expenditures and an aggressive pricing strategy. The expected results in the early stages may yield start-up losses and subsequently with volume of sales that helps to create and build a market share. It ultimately has high margins with relatively low capital turnover rates. It is a competition killer strategy for quashing die-hard competitions.

❑ Art of Differentiation

Art of differentiation by definition is to achieve the highest degree of product or quality or service difference in the industry with acceptable costs. Differentiation has been like the art of lambda dance, which is employed for cracking a market competition. This maverick artistry with its objective reality insulates the company from switching, substitution, price competition and creates strong blocs of customers or suppliers. Art of differentiation is applicable in all sectors of business. The requirements of the company are willingness to sacrifice high market share, careful target marketing, focused technological and market research and a strong brand loyalty. The expected results of the effect of the above strategy could be a possibly lowered market share, high margins, above average earnings and highly defensible position. This is a strategic advantage for market penetration.

❑ Market Focus and Poignancy

The definition of the above strategic thrust is to select a specific and particular segment of the market/product line. It should be slim, narrower in scope than the competing firms. What is important is to assert with a concentrated effort on the pertinently designed goal. The objective is to serve the strategic target areas like that of the specific geographic regions, specific product horizon or specific market universe more efficiently, accurately and more profitably, than it can be served by the 'broader competitors'. These aspects of accurate focus require a disciplined management style of functioning, persistent craving for well-defined ideas, chiselled scope and mission, premium pricing for being pertinent and careful target selection above all. The expected results could be above average earnings, the company business could be a low-cost producer in its area of business because of being a specialist and could attain high differentiation. Slim focus can slam competitors and competition in the category of products, which essentially want accuracy and precision.

❑ Restoring and Renewing Product Line

This thrust area as a strategy is defined as, to restore, renew and revive competitiveness of a product line, in anticipation of the future 'industry demand in sales'. The objective of the strategy is to out beat and overcome loopholes, discrepancies and weakness in the product/market mix. This is done to improve shareholdings in future to continue unabated, to prepare for a new generation of demand, to counter competition and to substitute products. The essential requirements of the strategy are to have strong competition on the product line, to ignite, spark and generate alternative resources for the renewal efforts. It furthermore requires capital investment, expenses for future markets, a management capable of taking risks and the intelligence to recognize potential threats in future on the existing product line. The expected results could see a short-term decline in sales, then after that, a sudden or gradual downfall of the existing volume of sales and thereby the pattern of profit. Cherry-picking model of marketing contributes to the understanding of the above type of business model and its demand for the posterity.

DEFENDING RELATIVE MARKET POSITION

The above thrust area as a strategic move can be defined 'to ensure that the relative competitive market position should be defended, which can, at a point stabilize and/or improve the marketing forces'. The objective is to create obstacles and barriers, which could make it difficult, costlier and riskier for the competitors, suppliers, customer groups and or new entries to downgrade and erode the firm's market position, share profitability and growth. The requirements are establishment of one or more of proprietary technology, a strong brand, projected sources and favourable locations, economies of scale, government protection, exclusive distribution or customer loyalty. The expected results could be to stablize or increase the market share. Defending the comparative STP becomes important to expand the market potential.

Art of Fencing is about Sharpness
or
Fencing sharpens.

❑ Harvesting the Competitive Position

The strategic thrust here can be defined as 'to convert the market share and/or the competitive position into higher rate of returns'. Having a competitive position, the objective is to bring returns up to industry averages by trading, leasing, selling technology, distribution rights, patents, brands, production capacity, locations and/or exclusive sources to the customers. It is targeted for opening avenues for harvesting profits and maximizing them. The requirements are that it looks for: a better-than-average market share, rights to entry and mobility that the industry values as pertinent and alterative investment opportunities in the pipeline. In this connection, the expected results are the immediate surge in the profitability and on return on investments, a gradual decline of position leading to a withdrawal strategy. This provides a huge benefit for the enterprise to run ahead in the market.

❑ Identifying and Finding Niche Markets

Niche market is an important aspect to attack a market in the crowded competitive environment. Strategic thrust here is defined as, 'to opt for retaining a small market, in order to advent into a defensive position in the available marketplaces abroad, instead of withdrawing from it'. The objective it looks for is, to define the opportunity narrowly, so that the large competitors with a broad market share do not find it attractive enough for them to dislodge these small pockets of opportunity. This camouflages and thus escapes the attacking stance of the big players allowing one to carve an identified niche. The vital requirement for this is a 'think tiny' management style. It furthermore, requires an alternative use of the surplus production capacity of the firm and delves into the reliable sources for the supplies and materials. It gets into superior quality and/or service in the selected sector of the marketplaces. The expected results are the pronounced decline in the product volume and share, improved return on investments in the medium-term and long-term business.

Finding the niche market can make the above difference.

❑ Holding into the Niche Market

Being hooked to the niche market and to hold on to it are matters of supreme importance. The definition proclaims 'to protect a narrow position in the larger product/market area from the larger competitors, who have the background and widespread business'. Here, the objective is to create barriers, which make it unattractive for competitors, suppliers and/or customers to enter into this segment or switch to alternative products. The requirements are like designing, building and promoting 'switching costs' into the product. The expected result that it yields is a lower return than the industry average but is steady and reasonable, therefore acceptable. Niche marketing is a typical method of strategic expansion beyond the boundaries.

❑ Catching up the Market Share

For a late entrant in the market, the strategic thrust has to be aggressive in order to catch up with the market share of the first entrants. The objective is to overcome the early gains made by the first entrants by careful choice of the optimum products, productions, distributions, promotions and marketing tactics. The definition could be 'to make up for the poor presence and or late entry into the market'. The requirements of this type of strategic thrust call for a typical situation. It happens when the management is capable of taking risk in the flexible environment due to the possession of resources to make high investments of capital and spend the required money and when it has corporate understanding of the short-term low returns. It is perhaps necessary to dislodge weak competitors from the scene. The expected results are usually in-between 'low and negative returns'. It usually results in strengthening the strong position. It results in the 'belated growth stage of the industry'. Peculiarities and performance are subject to the context of the market scenario; to catch up the market, is to initiate with a target.

❑ Anticipating Specific Market Change

Changes are inevitable. The only thing that is constant is change. Managing change is of utmost importance for a business to run. It overcomes oddities and graduates from a strange environment. As definition, it can be said 'to prolong the existence of the firm/enterprise in anticipation of certain specifically desired, expected and a favourable change in the environment'. The objective is to continue funding a better unit long enough that is waiting to take advantage of the unusual opportunity known to be at hand. This might and could take the form of a patent expiration, management change, government action, technology breakthrough and/or socio-economic shift due to trade relations. It can happen and bring forth a turnaround experience for the firm to harvest a business prospect. WTO reformation has made a paradigm change in the market life of the companies, based on the trade-offs and mark-ups visualized long ago. The requirements are a clear view of the expected environment shift, the willingness of a company's top management and the ability to sustain poor performance. Moreover, it requires an opportunity, scope and resource to capitalize on the new environment with a time limit and the final time. In this context, the expected results that are obvious are less than the average performance—presumably, losses. However, later on, it could make

a substantial growth and suck in high returns for the business. Instances are many in the line. Many companies have made millions based on the changes in the policy decisions of the countries during their reformations in the late 1990s and early 2000s.

❑ Turnaround Changes

Turnaround changes happen in organizations. Within a limited time, the company can resort to a lucrative business, emerging from the ashes like a phoenix. Life of the company transforms radically. The definition is 'to overcome inherent and severe weaknesses in performance in a limited time'. Inherent poor performance of the mining sector in Orissa, since the 1950s, has become a boon for the state, with the emerging boom in the steel industry.

The objective is simple, viz., to halt is to ensure decline in the share and/ or volume. It is devoid of alternative recourse to shift in the profit. In order to bring about a tolerable stability or small improvement in the status, the company has to strive hard to turnaround with a profit. It should protect the firm from competition and substitute products. It can protect it from alternative marketing networks. The requirements are pace of action to prevent disaster, which is likely for the cataclysmic change. It shall reduce and redirect losses and make changes in the morale. The expected results are stable and steady conditions and an average performance in the business.

❑ Retrenchment—A Strategic Move

Retrenchments are all about downsizing the citadel of business, looking into the margin of sales, profits and carrying capacity. The definition of retrenchment entails 'cutting off and downsizing of investments in the on-going business and reduction in the level of risk'. Retrenchments can happen due to the company's exposure to losses. In these types of situations, the top brass of the company redesign the company objective. The drive is take a handful of steps to stop the unacceptable losses or risks. It consequently wants to prepare for the progress of business for divestments and diversifications. It eventually strides to check losses in operations, in the hope of making substantial profits by exposing 'something good'. In order to do this, it requires a highly disciplined management system in place, good rapport with the employees to prevent mass boycott from work, transparent strategic objective and a timeline approach. In this process, the expected results are reduced losses and modestly improved performance. To curb losses and accelerate performance is the ideal way to handle a business.

❑ Divestiture of Assets

Divesting assets for switching into other areas of profiteering is a normal business phenomenon. Most of the PSUs globally have played this role in tandem. According to definition, divestiture of assets means is 'to horn the existing business of some or all of its assets through sale of the product line entirely or in parts, brand value tag, channelizing distribution facilities and the production capacity of the firm'. This is done essentially, to revamp re-architecture and re-organize the dimensions of business to overcome obsolescence and harmonize the company with the latest market trends. Market competitions with a state-of-the-art model of production, begets a quality orientation in the company to achieve excellence. Here, in this case, the objective is 'to fully recover the accrued losses sustained through the previous strategic errors. In order to do this it has to give automatic feeds to raise funds for alternative corporate investments by abandoning pieces and parts, or major parts of the business to withstand the market competition. The requirements that the company looks for in this case, is to create generate and recreate assets that are desirable for fighting the market competition and rekindle an incessant desire to compete in the industry. It must recognize the futility of further investments if any and reorganize its business domain. In doing such kind of restructurization, the expected results are increased cash flows, reduction of the old-asset base and of reducing poor performance by managing no losses. These measures are natural to the emerging economies and the advanced countries to adopt and deliver to competition. Precision perfect approach is the ultimate of all business companies.

❑ Withdraw to Emerge Afresh, Anew with Viva

Taking the company business away from competition is an important method to work. After withdrawing from business, it can again resurrect with novel ideology, intent and advent with a transnational expansion, in an emerging sector. To define this, 'it is said to remove the business from the competition, by even closing the shutters. It is done to emerge with a new economy company'. Bloomsbury reviving in Germany is an example. The objective of the company, in the given situation, will be to take back from the business the remaining corporate assets and expenses that can be recovered through either a shut-down, sale, auction and/or scrapping the operations. It can wind up the business and look for a better and greener pasture to do business in and not in the hackneyed state in which it was earlier. In this case, the firmness of decision that it requires is a stern decision to abandon the existing business, a caretaker management to cut down, a phasing out timetable and a public relations plan to convince the stakeholders. It can at a later date take to, acquisition and mergers strategy to develop a new company. The expected outcomes of this kind of approach are in existence, having made losses and therefore it has to shut down and write-off its assets. Different strategies are employed for different companies at different periods. The company's top management has to get into the process of decision making as they are essentially the market makers for going transnational.

In business, what is important is to develop business, not just to help the business to grow. Business should become better—not bigger only. People's opinions are the key to decision making. In fact, in the domestic market environment, growth and development in the industry are achieved by harvesting profits, and maximizing through promotional actions, making unprecedented losses and resorting to withdrawal are typical strategies. All companies adopt such tactics all the time. These are major decisions that matter the most.

However, in the case of transnational marketing, these typical strategies are at the 'start-up phase'. We see that the 'new products' developed are generated through customer responsiveness. In the absence of a demand-based study, the established data cannot be generated and in the absence of a response database, fast-moving products cannot be conceived with attributes. In this case, the company would wish to find and focus on niches, hold on to a niche for making it exemplary and gradually grow faster having a strong base in the niche to do so. Customers in the niche market endorse the product quality and create a storyline for propaganda. Press people capture them for creating news item for better circulation. Failure stories are not hyped.

❑ Conclusion

From the above it is seen that, implications of all the different strategic thrusts are defined, perquisites chalked out and the expected outcomes are traced deeply from the core. However, considering all the angles of study and research, it is resolved that for a transitional company operating for transnational marketing, a niche strategy is pivotal. All the companies who have transnational success stories have done so. The market also expects the company to adhere to a differentiated product range. These are the irreplaceable strategies that comprehensively reach stages of success in the ladder. Businesses develop by strategies, stepping up in the stages of success in the ladder of progress. It is a journey.

GOVERNMENTAL BARRIERS AND CONSTRAINS ON TRANSNATIONAL GROWTH

Different governments across the world have different rules. They have trade barriers and freedom for exchanges. They have trade agreements, stringent rules for specific hostile countries, enabling free trade opportunity for friendly countries and have mixed rules in place, for certain countries. Eventually, a company can be said to be a transnational company when it transacts businesses with at least two or more of the governments. Usually, it is done with several countries. It can be through either buying and supplying, or being in the trade groups. The multiplicity of rules and regulations and complexity of governmental concerns that they normally encounter are much greater. There are transnational forums to enable the companies to associate themselves. Governmental concessions are normally seen between neighbouring countries. They have natural trade relations. The constraints are that they have to deal with cross-cultural employee relations, problems in business, government-to-government relationships, politicizing of economic decision making and unfair trade practices. It is more important for a company trying to go transnational strive for a niche in the foreign market. Think for instance, about a company wanting to go transnational, e.g., to China, Nepal, Bangladesh and Bhutan. Different issues shall evolve in different countries on different products. These concerns and factors are dealt further in other chapters. The patterns of these issues are given below in details.

❑ Constraints on Corporate Growth

Constraints on the corporate growth are quite natural. It deals on a spectrum of issues ranging from questions of an anti-monopoly policy to the existing industrial structure, national growth policy to economic controls, environmental protection measures and so forth. Relationship of India with Pakistan is a glaring example of hostility.

❑ Constraints on Corporate Governance

Corporate governance constraints are all about the disability of the bigwigs of a company to maintain a proper business climate in the company. It mainly includes the matters of accountability of employees, personal liability of managers and directors. In fact, after the Union Carbide disaster, the fall of Arthur Anderson, the recent collapse of companies like ADB, Lehman Brothers, Freddie May and Freddie Mac due to recession, the board of management and

representatives abroad have become emphatic on pertinence of 'disclosure of information'. This is like a tip of an iceberg.

Enforcement agencies in government are staffed with some employees who are lenient towards their job responsibility besides being callous and try and avoid legal confrontations.

❑ Managing the 'New' Transnational Workforce

Management of the new transnational recruitment and training, for making the employees acquire the requisite knowledge to help them execute their job responsibilities has become all the more important. Knowing cross-country skill sets are extremely important. It has to deal with the growing demands for job enlargement, qualified employment, flexible scheduling, promote equality of opportunity, allow greater participation and individualization. They have to multi-task and have to be multi-lingual and multi-skilled to operate under any business environment. Survival in strange climate is important for the new transnational employees.

❑ External Constraints on Employee Relations

Issues relating to employee relationships might face the external constraints. It could be the 'new pressures' building from the foreign governments on the scopes of employment. Aspects of health and safety, environment and job opportunities are few of the areas that are pivotal. It could all be for the federalization of benefits for the worker, the old communistic ways. Through the unions coalition bargaining and collective bargaining have vanished, human rights activists are entering the fray to safeguard their interests instead. It faces the problem of class action suites 'whistle blowing'. These constraints are obvious for anyone leaving their motherland.

❑ Problems and Opportunities of Business and Government Partnership

Where there are problems, there are opportunities. Business is all about looking at things differently, for converting liability into assets. An example can be the role of private sector, especially the multinational corporations in public problem solving. For instance, Infosys handling the issues governing NREGS for issuing a multi-purpose identity card to all the citizens of India. It is on the ethos of corporate citizenship behaviour. This could be done in the case of a foreign country too.

❑ Politicizing of Economic Decision Making

Decision making is important for organization to run the business, travel beyond boarders, make the products marketed in a boarder less market. The growing government involvement in corporate decisions, like that of the involvement of Chinese government in SEZ projects after FDI investments by foreign companies are due to peculiar and obvious reasons. Governments of many countries encourage an economic balancing act through consumerism, consumer protection rights, anti-monopoly and other legislations. They also make additional moves and mobilize protest laterally in the domain of environment, etc. Countries have political parties with the right to speak in a democratic governance system. Politicizing the economic decision making is right in a democratic country, for it shall counterbalance the process and create a level-playing ground.

❑ Corporate Limitation: Response to Public Welfare

Corporations have limitations in contributing for the public welfare. The purpose being profit and progress, companies do not restrict from making profit and abide by the rules of charity. Philanthropy by exemption is a design of the government to drive the corporate earnings for general well-being.

Historically, it is seen that any business organization per se has considered its sole purpose to make economic gains against all odds. It is observed that it has displayed concern with the other spheres of society, only when the laws require the company to do so. Laws to exemptions have motivated philanthropy, charity and corporate social responsibility. However, a certain chunk of the fund is spent for the purpose of charity. This looks like a celebration of a corporation's good fortune and profits, which was desired to be shared with outsiders . It reflects and displays concerns for the unfortunate masses with pity. Whatever be it, it indirectly bestowed a good name for the company. It also served the public relations function of the corporation. Warren Buffet, Bill Gates, Rockefeller have donated for charity, a huge sum of dollars, like their Indian counterparts, doing charity in different ways. The role of Dr Achyuta Samanta, founder KIIT Group of Institutions, Bhubaneswar, Orissa, in providing 10,000 tribal children free-residential education, is a one-of-its-kind example. The personal touch that he gives to the school is important and is a solitary case in India.

Apparently, many companies and transnational companies are not performing their corporate social responsibilities righteously. Most companies generally serve only the short-term needs of its stakeholders looking into the market fluctuations and managing their position of profit. The disgruntled and aggrieved customer groups constitute the public stakeholders. Transnational business organizations often do not address the grievances of the stakeholders. They make a fiasco of their stakeholders not considering that it is due to latter that any corporate grows and flourishes. The owners, employees, customers, suppliers, bankers, community lenders, government, community and society are links in the vicious chain that unequally distribute the facilities. Each group has its own 'areas of concern', as shown below, 'within which expectations may vary' drastically 'from one time period to another'. In fact, the task of a transnational company becomes very large, almost gargantuan, for the domestic companies. They develop peculiarly, with unique patterns of activities.

There are inevitable 'conflicts of interest' within different interest groups operating in a transnational environment. It could be between the 'national society and the transnational society'. The society's expectation on a transnational corporation grows sizeably. They imagine the corporation as an agent of the transnational social responsibility. Thus, the society emerges with the corporation, emerging as a large entity in the process. It emerges ultimately for a social change. The macro aspects of business attributes can be dealt in detail. The role and responsibility of the corporation and its public and their concerns are presented in a tabular form in Figure 4.1.

Public	**Areas of Concern**
Owners	Payout of company Equity of company Stock prices of company Non-monetary desires of company
Customers	Reliability of business Reliability product Improvement in product Product price Product continuity Marketing efficiency
Employees of all ranks	Monetary reward Recognition with award Reward of price Working environment Job challenges Continuity of employment Advancement ranks
Suppliers	Price fluctuations Stability in supply Continuity in supply Growth

Banking community and other lenders	Sound risk of business Interest payment on borrowings Repayment of principal amount
Government (central, state and local)	Taxes and duties Security law and law enforcement Management expertise in handling Democratic government process Capitalist system Programme implementation
Immediate community	Economic growth and efficiency Education growth Employment and training
Transnational society at large	Societal development Transnationalism acceptance Civil rights and equal opportunities Pollution abatement Conservation of all Recreation facilities Arts and culture Safety and security Health and medical care

Fig. 2.7 Transnational Corporate Public and their Concerns

The salient attributes in the right-hand side have been identified with respect to the concern as against the category of transnational corporate public. However, subsequently the strategic factors of the transnational business have been delineated through the outlines.

❑ Strategic Factors in Transnational Business

The outline of strategic factors in transnational business is traced below with respect to general management, finance, marketing, personnel, engineering, competitive rivalry, production and products, etc. The vital outlines of the strategic factors are:

❑ General Management Strategy

1. Ability to draw, attract and maintain the top management of outstanding quality to lead the organization against susceptible barriers of going transnational.
2. Develop future managers for the smooth overseas operations against crosscurrents.
3. Develop future managers for domestic operations to support the transnational roadmap and advancement.

4. Develop a superior and better organizational structure to design and implement growth.

5. Develop a better type of long-range planning programme with a futuristic outlook and foresight.

6. Achieve a better comprehensive and overall control of the company operations and activities.

7. Use of more of new and innovative quantitative tools and techniques in decision making at the:

   (a) Top levels of management

   (b) Middle levels of management

   (c) Lower levels of management

8. Assure a better kind of judgement, creativity and imagination in the decision making levels at:

   (a) Top management levels

   (b) Middle management levels

   (c) Lower management levels

9. Ability to use computers, software and Internet for the problem-solving, implementation and planning processes.

10. Ability to use computers for information handling, marketing, execution and financial control processes.

11. Ability to divest the non-profitable enterprises and reinvest the earnings in appropriate parts of the business.

12. Ability to excite, motivate and gear sufficient managerial impetus and drive for profits and gains.

❑ Financial Management Strategy

1. Ability to raise long-term capital at low-cost for further investments:

   (a) In terms of debt;

   (b) In terms of equity.

2. Ability to raise short-term capital for immediate investments

3. Ability to maximize the value of stockholder investment by better reliable investments in the risk-free sectors of business.

4. Ability to provide a comparatively competitive rate of return to the stockholders which should be better than that of the competitor companies.
5. A willingness to take risks, which shall be commensurate with a better rate of return; it could be regarding some business types that have the scope to capitalize on excellent new business opportunities to achieve growth objectives.
6. Ability to apply ROI criteria to R&D investments and ensure a steady pace of development in multiples.
7. Ability to finance diversifications by means of:
   (a) Acquisitions of companies or business.
   (b) In-house research and development for innovations and patents.

❑ Marketing Management Strategy

1. Ability to know, acquire and accumulate better knowledge about markets and the market forces abroad.
2. Establish a wide customer base to create a higher market share in terms of the volumes of sales.
3. Establish a selective consumer base that is based on the market segment befitting to the price tag of the product line.
4. Establish an efficient product distribution system, which is comparatively better, swift and dereliction free.
5. Ability to get good business contracts from the government agencies, associate with business houses and create new markets thereby creating a niche for itself.
6. Assured access to the prospective customers through the imaginative advertising and sales promotion campaigns.
7. Effective use of the pricing technique more effectively by including the tools of discounts, customer credit, product service, guarantees and delivery, etc. These tools give an edge over the competing brands sold in the markets.
8. Customization of the market to establish a better relationship between the customer, marketing, new product development and production.
9. Establish a competent and energetic sales team.

❑ Engineering and Production Management Strategy

1. Develop effective machinery and equipment replacement policy to combat obsolesces like a business trap. Tools and machinery have to be up-to-date and calibrated to the strategic intent.

2. Provide more effective, efficient and apt plant layout for the optimization of business in different dimensions. Strategic layout with precision can do well in all spheres of operations.

3. Develop sufficient capacity for expansion, the project layout should have the provision and scope to enlarge, widen and expand in all the likely strategic directions.

4. Develop, manufacture and produce a comparatively better quality of materials and products and an efficient inventory control system.

5. Improve product quality control and products with less of rejections by quality control.

6. Improve in-house product engineering and shaping of proactive intelligent knowhow for application in the given atmosphere.

7. Improve in-house basic product research capabilities for improvising the quality of products, with a think tank mechanism for in-house brainstorming.

8. Develop a more effective and efficient profit-improvement (cost-reduction) programmes, by striving to achieve cost leadership; profits can be maximized in each iota of the aspects of the supply chain.

9. Develop a better ability for mass production at a low per unit cost. Minimizing the cost by maximizing the quantity of products can happen.

10. Develop and relocate present product facilities in different places. Same products can be required in another location.

11. Automate production facilities for hassle free mass production of quality products.

12. Manage the products better. To ensure better results from the research and development expenditures that has been incurred.

13. Establish foreign production facilities for meeting the dearth of the product type.

14. Develop more flexibility in using facilities for different products, flexibility is a process of adoption to all facilities.

15. Products and processes should be extremely advanced and scientifically creative to be in the forefront of technology. Technologically embellished products are creative, durable and competent.

❑ Products Management Strategy

1. Improve the existing products and enhance the quality standards. It is a continuous process.
2. Develop more efficient and effective product line selection for domestic and transnational markets. Befitting market requirements of products drives the market apace.
3. Develop new products to replace old ones, which are becoming old and hackneyed. Updating your products is important for successful competition.
4. Develop new products in new markets. It shall keep up with the race for sales.
5. Develop sales volumes for the present products in the new markets, searching for the niche.
6. Diversify production by acquisition of ideas and firms.
7. Enhance sub-contracting for products to be supplied as OEM.
8. Get a bigger share of the product market by finding new markets.

❑ Personnel Management Strategy

1. Attract quality professionals, scientists, highly technical qualified employees and skilled employees.
2. Establish better relationships with employees to motivate for better productivity.
3. Establish a good relationship with labour unions to negotiate better and enhance the employee morals.
4. Utilize the skills of employees to the optimal.
5. Motivate more employees to remain abreast of developments in their fields by training, both in-house and in-company programmes.

6. Manage the employment requirements as per the need and eradicate any envious climate from developing.
7. Stimulate creativity in employees for evolving innovative ideas.
8. Optimize employee turnover for incorporating new ideas.
9. Retain quality employees from being head hunted by other companies.

❑ Materials Management Strategy

1. Get geographically closer to raw material sources, for avoiding transportation problems and delivery of the same in time.
2. Assure continuity of raw-material supplies as per the quality of requirement.
3. Find new sources of raw materials at a lower cost with better quality.
4. Control the sources of raw materials for obtaining them in requisite bulks.
5. Bridge the 'in-house' purchased materials, components with the market requirements.
6. Reduce the costs of raw materials for reducing the product cost.

❑ Competitive Rivalry

1. To tap the opportunity potential for betterment.
2. To relax the ease of entry into the market.
3. To procure the nature of products suitable for the business.
4. To maintain the exit barriers for a smooth flow of products to the destination.
5. To ensure a homogeneity of the market for reducing the cost of transportation and flow in the right time.
6. To ensure a proper industry structure for maintaining the competitive positioning of the firm.
7. To ensure commitment to the industry and deliver the consignments in time.
8. To ensure feasibility of the technological innovations made for the purpose.

9. To see to the scale economies for pricing.
10. To understand the economic climate befitting to the market.
11. To know about the diversity of firms and nations with respect to the business.

We can see from the above discussions that there are 76 elements in the transnational management strategy. Let us suppose that there are only two possible states, viz., 'present' and 'absent'. We assume that for each element delineated above both the 'present and 'absent' states are available in the strategic mix. If we designate the total number of elements numbering 76 by **'n'**, then the total number of 'strategic combinations' in transnational strategy can be given by $(2^n)^n = (2^{76})^{76}$. It is a large figure. Hence, we see that the transnational strategy process is incalculably more complex, than the domestic strategy process. It can also be seen that, the 'range of choices' or 'strategic combinations' or 'strategic mix' are still measurable to predetermined strategic estimations. Therefore, it can be seen that the 'degree of flexibility' and the degree of organizational permutations required for transnational marketing are incredibly massive. Yet the yardstick to calculate can be drawn scientifically to the mathematical extent.

RATING THE MARKETING EFFECTIVENESS OF TRANSNATIONAL COMPANIES

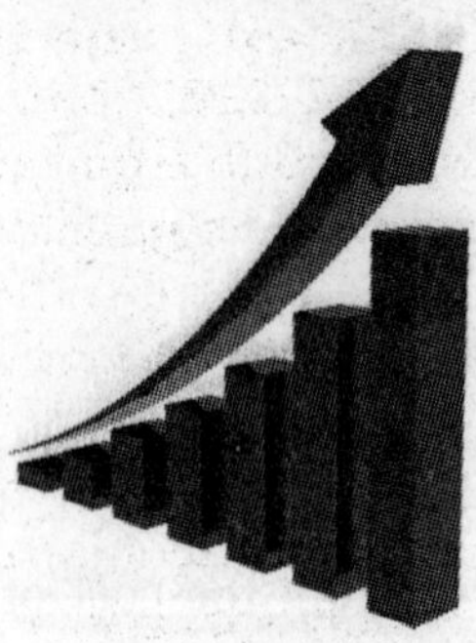

Marketing effectiveness of the transnational companies can be rated by virtue of the criteria of assessment. In order to evaluate, the factors have to be judged with respect to the character of the company. Some of the requisite aspects have been discussed to obtain an overview of the strategic idea. It has deliberated on the intricacies of the issues and challenges that are obvious. In order to elucidate and simplify the angularities, certain questions have been put up with options to facilitate an understanding and scores have been awarded to rate the company. This is a simple kind of test for the companies to be evaluated.

❑ Customer Philosophy

1. Does the company management recognize the significance of the 'designing of company' to cater to the needs and wants of chosen markets?

    (a) The management primarily thinks in terms of selling the 'current and new products' to whom-so-ever who will buy the products.

(b) The management thinks in terms of catering to a wide range of markets and needs, with equal effectiveness and efficiency.

(c) The management thinks in terms of catering to the needs and wants of well-defined markets, chosen for their long-term growth and profits for the company.

2. Does the company management develop different offerings and marketing plans for different segments of the market?

   (a) No

   (b) Somewhat okay

   (c) To a good extent

3. Does the company management take the 'holistic marketing system' in planning the business? It could be suppliers, channels, competitors, customers and environment, etc.

   (a) No, the management focus is on selling and servicing the immediate customers.

   (b) Somewhat okay, the management takes a long-term view of the channels, although the bulk of efforts are dedicated to selling and servicing of the immediate customers.

   (c) Yes, the management takes to 'holistic marketing system' for recognizing threats and opportunities of the company and adopt by changes in the requisite part of the system deficiency.

❑ Integrated Marketing Organization

1. Is there a higher level of marketing integration and control of the major marketing functions?

   (a) No, the sales and marketing functions are not integrated at the top. There are some unproductive conflicts unresolved.

   (b) Somewhat okay, there is a formal integration and control of major marketing functions, but satisfactory coordination and cooperation do not exist.

   (c) Yes, the major marketing functions are both integrated efficiently and effectively integrated.

2. Does the marketing management work in tandem with the management in the field of R&D, manufacturing, purchasing, physical distribution and finance?

(a) No, there are complaints on the marketing to be unreasonable on spending made for mitigating demands and the costs it fixes on the developments.

(b) Somewhat okay, the relations are there, although each of the departments pretty much acts to serve its own power interests in order to take a share.

(c) Yes, all the departments cooperate effectively and unanimously resolve issues in the best interest of the company and they work as a team.

3. How well organized is the new product development process?

(a) The process is ill organized and poorly handled.

(b) The process exists formally but lacks sophistication in approach.

(c) The process is well structured and professionally staffed for the output.

❑ Adequate Marketing Information

1. When were the latest market research on customers, buying influences, channels of distribution and competitor's choice conducted?

(a) Three or more years ago

(b) One to three years ago

(c) Very recently

2. How well does the management know the analysis regarding the sales potential and profitability of different market segments, customers, territories, products, channels and order sizes?

(a) Not at all

(b) Somewhat to an extent

(c) Very well

3. What amount of effort is extended for measuring the cost effectiveness of different marketing expenditures?

(a) Little or no efforts

(b) Some efforts

(c) Substantial efforts

❑ Strategic Orientation

1. What is the degree and extent of formal marketing planning done?
   - (a) Management does little or no formal marketing planning.
   - (b) Management develops an annual marketing plan
   - (c) Management develops a detailed annual plan and a careful long-term plan that is updated annually.
2. What is the quality standard of the current marketing strategy, if any?
   - (a) Current strategy is not clear.
   - (b) Current strategy is clear and represents a continuation of traditional strategy.
   - (c) Current strategy is clear, innovative, database driven and well reasoned.
3. What is the extent of contingency thinking and planning?
   - (a) Management does little or no contingency thinking.
   - (b) Management does some contingency thinking but does very little formal contingency planning.
   - (c) Management formally identifies the most important contingencies and develops them from time to time.

❑ Operational Efficiency

1. How well is the 'top brass marketing thought at the top' communicated and implemented down the line, in the other levels?
   - (a) Poorly
   - (b) Fairly well
   - (c) Successfully
2. Is management doing an effective transnational job with the marketing resources?
   - (a) No, the marketing resources are inadequate for the job to be done.
   - (b) Somewhat okay, the marketing resources are adequate but they are not employed fully.
   - (c) Yes, the marketing resources are adequate and are deployed efficiently and effectively.

3. Does management display a standard capability to react quickly and effectively to 'on-the-spot' developments?

   (a) No, sales and market information is not very current, management reaction time is slow.

   (b) Somewhat okay, management receives fairly up-to-date sales and market information, but the management reaction time varies from time to time.

   (c) Yes, the management has installed systems which yield higher current information and has a brisk reaction time.

The outline of the auditing displayed above can be used in the following ways. As a matter of fact, the auditor's collect information from the given 15 questions. From among the questions, checking is done one by one for each question with the appropriate answer. The scores are added and the total median calculated, which will be somewhere between 0 and 30. The standard scale given below shows the equivalent transnational marketing effectiveness of companies. This scale is designed to the aspects under study.

Scores	Grades
0 – 5	None
6 – 10	Poor
11 – 15	Fair
16 – 20	Good
21 – 25	Very Good
26 – 30	Superior

(Find out the range of the total scores (low–high). Find out the median score. Look at the above score sheet to get the average median score and the qualitative rating for marketing effectiveness. In practice, where the responses are genuine, few transnational companies would score above 20.)

Summary

This chapter demonstrates comprehensive spectrum of strategic thrust areas of companies in the macro-level. Companies are ambitions enough to cross the border for exploiting business opportunities, by launching new products cooking up innovative methods of approach. They formulate roadmaps laying milestones to map out the action plan zeroing into the final goal. The three-stepped process adopted by most of the companies is (a) Assessment of issues (b) Spotting key variables (c) Selection of strategy for implem-entation.

Contd....

Besides, the sundry methods employed, the major strategic thrust is start-up stage to grow with the pace of industry, aggressive fast growth, attainment of cost leadership, art of differentiation, market focus and restoring product line, etc. Moreover, companies deploy other techniques of defending an uninterrupted competitive market positioning strategy. They strive to convert market share into higher rate-of-return finding niche markets, even holding a slice of product in the market uncontested by rival companies. Capturing a market share is possible through early-bird entry (as the proverb goes—early bird catches the moth), but changing fluidity of choices is a must and is natural due to impacting variables of the market. Retrenchment or right sizing divesture of company assets and withdrawal to enter anew are a handful of other ideas which matter.

Yet the barriers of governments in between countries are quite obvious. There might be situations where the companies from two different countries have friendly agreement but the countries have hostile relation with each other. Apart from that, managing culture-savvy workforce is paramount. Bonhomie with public involving in public welfare business and associating with government's interest on the subjects of government shortfalls or concerns is preferable.

All strategic factors rotate on 360° issues relating areas like finance, marketing operations, management, human resource management and other similar topics that are primordial. These sectoral aspects are vividly introspected and solved. Nonetheless, effective marketing measure is quintessential to all business. Therefore, it is quite important to rate the effectiveness of marketing strategies implemented in the markets abroad. The score sheet with grades provided allows the marketing researcher/executive to rate a company's product launch based on the chosen criteria's in which the question is framed.

This chapter illustrates on the canvass of company's approach to business entry in the wider range.

QUESTIONS FOR DISCUSSION

Q. 1. What do you mean by strategic thrusts in transnational marketing? What is the usual three stepped process adopted by companies? Discuss.

Q. 2. Which are the major strategic thrust options for transnational marketing? Illustrate with suitable examples.

Q. 3. How can a company defend its relative market position? Discuss.

Q. 4. Discuss the aspects of anticipating specific market change and turn around change in the case of a transnational company.

Q. 5. What are the usual government barriers and constraints? How to overcome them? Explain with suitable examples from the new papers and news bulletins in the media.

Q. 6. Discuss on the figure titled transnational corporate publics and their concerns.

Q. 7. Illustrate the aspects dealt in the questions on 'rating the marketing effectiveness of transnational companies' as criteria.

Q. 8. Re-configure a questionnaire for a company you work with or by developing a questionnaire assuming yourself as a company executive. Than collect the answers to the questionnaire from the company folks. Discuss.

Q. 9. Write short notes:

(a) Assessment of issues

(b) Spotting key variables

(c) Selection of strategy for implementation

(d) Start-up stage

(e) Attainment of cost leadership

(f) Art of differentiation

(g) Market focus and poignancy

(h) Market position

(i) Competitive position

(j) Niche markets

(k) Market share

(l) Divestiture of assets

(m) Retrenchment

(n) Resurrecting afresh and anew

(o) Constraints on corporate governance.

(p) Managing 'new workforce'

(q) Politicizing economic decision making

(r) Response to corporate publics

(s) General Management strategy

(t) Financial management strategy

(u) Marketing management strategy

(v) Personnel Management strategy

(w) Competitive management strategy.

Chapter 5

Maxi-transnational Marketing (MTM): A Model Approach

LEARNING OBJECTIVES

After going through this chapter, the reader should be able to:

1. Identify the meaning of maxi-transnational marketing (MTM) and the series of efforts involved in the process of business, ultimately for maximizing profits.
2. Recognize the steps starting from the early stages of visualizing the prospects to the point of after-sales care of customer/end user for relationship marketing.
3. Define the ability of executives to gauge and enhance the efficiency of advertising, promotion and marketing practices.
4. Appreciate marketing promotions for making lifetime customers of a company.
5. Realize marketing strategies, planning and approaches reinventing models to create market share.

'Even if there is only one possible unified theory, it is just a set of rules and equations. What is it that breathes fire into the equations and makes a universe for them to describe?'

— Stephen Hawking

'Advertisement is an environmental striptease for a world of abundance'.

— Herbert Marshall Mcluhan (1911–80)

6. Explain modern domestic marketing vis-à-vis transnational marketing.
7. Understand the values and life styles for deploying tools and techniques to exploit and contrive profiteering business transactions.
8. Describe the cases that are being encountered in business and calculate prospective designs for mock practice and implementation in reality.
9. Introspect the value of data mining , fishing the prospects, telemarketing, TV commercials, info-commercials, magazines, direct mail , electronic shopping and sky-tray etc.

MAXI-TRANSNATIONAL MARKETING (MTM)

Maxi-transnational marketing (MTM) is a series of continuous effort for optimizing the dimensions of business. It is to maximize all and sundry aspects of business. MTM never ever advocates the idea of giving up what the company is already doing. It believes in the continuance of it. MTM means examining, reviewing and scanning each step of the selling process that is distributed transnationally. It starts from the early stages of visualizing the prospects to the point of after-sales care of the customer king. In fact, it is more about how the customer is treated after the sale is made. It is done to maximize profits. Profit is at the butt of all the targets of business. It means to 'add on powerful new capabilities' to ameliorate the activity what the competent company is already doing for travelling transnationally. It travels from the forerunner to the end user. In doing this, the marketing efficiency can network like a spider web, finding a niche in any corner of the marketplace.

Maxi-marketing (MM) puts all things on a one-to-one relationship with the customer. The response one gets from the likely prospects and the contacts with end users of the products add a reality check to the decision making. It infuses a new ability to measure and enhance the effectiveness of advertising, promotion and marketing practices. It enables one to enter the new world of 'responsive advertising' and focus attention for obtaining measurable responses from the people–customer, for whom the company developed the advertising message.

Maxi-marketing has immensely tangible estimating provisions. It can calculate the multi dimensional aspects of the intricate aspects of business domain. Maxi-marketing can enlighten the readers to appreciate and to fathom the subtle nuances and difference between marking promotions, striking a sale and getting a long-term customer. A company should spend a definite amount of money for implementing a study for the purpose. Maxi-marketing calls for an expenditure, which is three-fourth of the amount of sale for getting a long-term customer. If we consider the amount of money spent on the lifetime customer concept of transnational marketing and also consider its gains, then we would understand that it would be worth the price incurred on maxi-marketing

Maxi-transnational marketing (MTM) is a novel direction in the horizon of transnational marketing. It replaces the 'industrial concept of standardization' by the emerging 'post-industrial concept of customization'. There by the customer prospects, who are the potential customers, are identified, located, persuaded, motivated, converted and cultivated in a way that maximizes sales and profits. It is to tap the customers by scanning the customer base. In order to examine this, as to how this is done let us look at the basic selling process. It is the selling process, which is the key to introspect. It mainly deals with satisfying the customer needs and wants, a prospect for sale being converted to a purchase, lifetime customer by building a relationship with the customer and by creation of loyalty. The points given below enumerate the aspects in a nutshell.

❑ Selling Process is the Key

1. All marketing planning, strategies and actions should reach out to satisfy the needs and wants of the prospects. This is the be-all and end-all of the customer king.

2. In all marketing approaches, converting the prospective customer's interest into a buying intention and striking an actual purchase succinctly is important and penultimate.
3. All marketing approaches should seek to develop an ongoing relationship with the customer. It should always be after the sales, by encouraging further purchases for continuing loyalty of the product and the retail counter. Creating repeat purchaser is to create a lifetime customer.

All these above broad principles are taken into consideration in the maxi-transnational marketing model that is given below in Fig. 5.1. It shall highlight the aspects of reaching the desired customers—innovate ways to reach them in a new route, convince the customers that the product is worthy and appealing to the mind, meet the inquiry and sales promotion, prompt the enthusiastic prospects by creating market share, mindshare and heart share and also by adding new channels of distribution and finally establishing a relationship with the customer. What is ardent for the market response to drive the products to the customer is based on maximizing and optimizing each of the links in the supply chain leading to the customer.

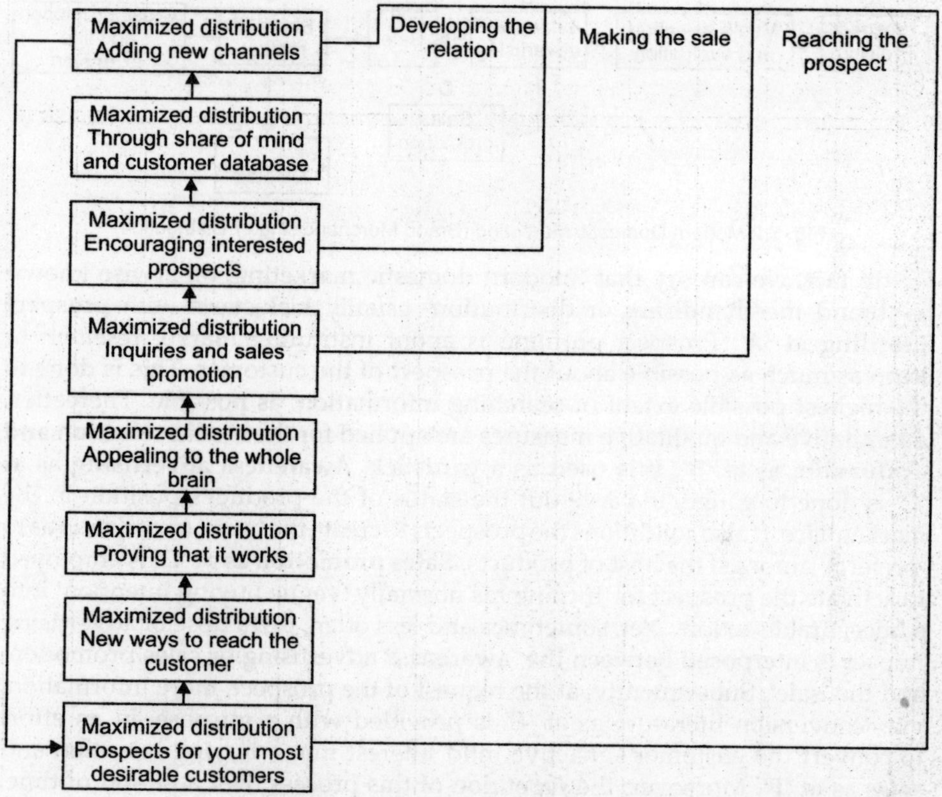

Fig. 5.1: Maxi-transnational Marketing Model

The aforementioned maxi-transnational model is constituted by the following nine components. They are maximized targeting, maximized media, maximized accountability, maximized awareness, maximized activation, maximized synergy, maximized linkage, maximized sales and maximized distribution. Through these nine components, MTM also distinguishes between reaching to the prospect, making the sale happen and developing a relationship with the customer.

❑ Modern Domestic Marketing

It relates to the aspects concerning brand merchandising and distribution, which encompass and entail the facets of prospect profiling, media selection, advertising and awareness building, sales promotion, sales and gross sales

and so forth. The Fig. 5.2 gives a view of the aspects that have been narrated just below Fig.5.2.

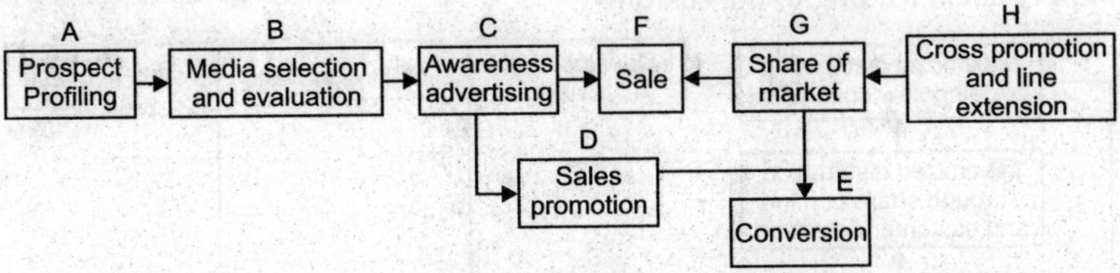

Fig. 5.2 Modern Domestic Marketing (Brand Merchandising or Distribution)

In fact, we can say that 'modern domestic marketing, otherwise known as 'brand merchandising or distribution' usually kick-starts with **prospect profiling at 'A'**. Prospect profiling is about instituting market research to learn as much as possible about the prospect of the customer. This is done to the highest possible extent of searching information, as possible. Thereafter, quantitative and qualitative measures are applied for the **media selection and evaluation, as at 'B'**. It is used as a yardstick. **Awareness advertising as at 'C'** is done to gauge, to carve out the status of the product's position in the marketplace. It also conditions the prospects to create the 'want factor' or so as to 'prefer it' amongst the host of products. **Sales promotion as at 'D'** is employed to activate the prospect for turning his normally 'vague buying intention' into a 'measurable action'. Yet, sometimes and less often, extra dose of advertising impact is interposed between the 'awareness advertising or sales promotion' and the 'sale'. Subsequently, at the request of the prospect, more information, viz., conversion literature as at 'E' is provided with a purpose, in an effort to convert the customer's inactive mild interest into a buying intention and **sales as at 'F'**. Moreover, the repetition of this process over a period of time, results in a **share of market as at 'G' or consumer brand franchise,** however large or small. As a matter of fact, this 'share of market' is a corporate asset. This creates the possibility of **cross-promotion and line extension as at 'H'. A** company (say TISCON), with a steady line of successful products, can use one of them for cross-promotion by any variety of joint promotions. The built-up popularity of this brand name can sometimes (not always) positively rub off onto the introduction of new products with the same brand or company name. These are the sequences, which are played into the game of MDM.

❑ Transnational Marketing

Similarly, in Fig. 5.3, transnational marketing has been enumerated with the phases of developmental actions that relates to prospect profiling or prospect data, selection of identified media choice, awareness advertising, sales force converting sales and sales to customer buddies. Retail sales, direct sales and sales through marketing all foster to the customer requirement. These are placed in A, B, C, D, E, F and G below.

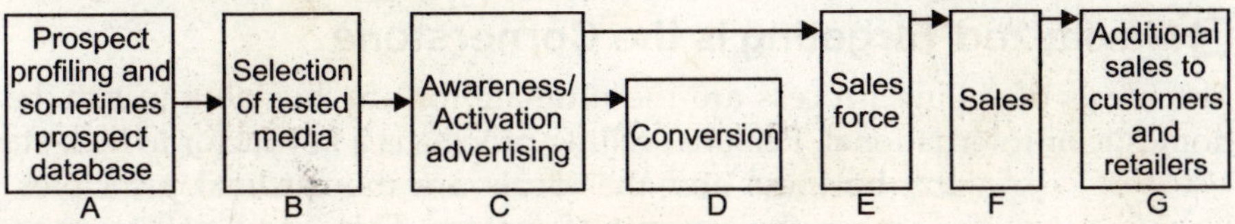

Fig.5.3 Transnational Marketing

❑ Personalized Selling Modalities

It is seen that personal selling has conventionally taken one of the following two routes. The first route is cold canvass selling to consumers by the agents. Here, the company is providing no names to the sales agent. The second route is selling by agents to a list of sales prospects generated by advertising.

The advertising that is designed to collect, generate and provide the identified list of persons for personnel selling, obviously begins with careful targeting. Careful targeting or prospect profiling is at 'A' in the above figure. When this is responded, reflected and promoted through advertising, portraying the products or the product line, it creates, converts and provides 'sales leads'. They eventually can provide an 'index of the efficiency of various media sources'. Advertisements could be made for different regions by different media agencies, depending on their competency. Hence, the 'selection of media' as mentioned at 'B' comes into play in the link. Many companies are normally quite careless about measuring the media responses for studying the tangible impact of advertising that has been made. The company should also estimate the cost per response, estimate success rates and the conversion rates of the media sources. This stimulation, activation and ignition by the help of 'awareness and activation' as at 'C', are usually the terms of 'awareness' (only). This is also called 'advertising'. They laterally as well as cryptically instigate the dormant cells of the mind for initiating the process of activation and for taking decisions. They make it occur in the customer prospect. On an enquiry to ascertain more information regarding the product, the inquirer is replenished with sufficiency of 'conversion literature' as at 'D'. It is either done prior to the execution of contact or during the contact and is done by a member of the 'sales force' as at 'E', who seeks to complete the sale (F). This is subsequently has a sequel and is followed by 'additional sales to customers and retailers'.

In the context of a simple personal selling method, the supply chain process of the channels in the flow of decision making is quite natural. They pass through these ways and gain access to the buyer's decision-making process.

It is a usual phenomenon in the selling process, which should be kept in mind for understanding transnational marketing in its threadbare details.

❑ Maximized Targeting is the Cornerstone

The ideals of selling process are the ultimate for any business to run, be it domestic or international. Personal selling process is a key factor to kick-start, any business and the ideals are the cardinal principles to reach the summit of success. This 'ideal' selling process begins with the 'traditional step of learning' as much as possible about the 'market prospect'. Knowing the scope of the business prospect is ardent and is a priority. This is unquestionable and it includes the prospects at all places, wherever possible. This is the selling-process desire, a compilation of database on the prospect. This shall magnetize the marketer to approach his/her target prospects strategically, across nations. It can also be implemented for individual products chasing the prospect, case by case individually. Products could as varied as the selling of paintings, designer sports cars or sophisticated hi-tech houses/offices for global customers. This intelligent database ideally carries not only the names and addresses of likely prospects but also a host of other revealing information about each prospect. It could be garnered from innumerable sources; it could be from the public database of a state, region or nation that can be referred with for the information needed to create a private database. This private database generated might also have been constructed from the responses to the company advertising and sales promotion. Both of them could be mutually helping. Database becomes sacrosanct and is a composite status for influencing the selling decision.

The ultimate effective object of a company decision is the ultimate customer prospect. The advertisements and promotion expenditures are poised for the individual target customer, who needs or wants the company products/services. It is intended for the person who is ready and is able to buy it with a price paid. In order to single out that 'targeted person' from amongst the mass consumer market is getting easily accomplished, at a lower cost, with the onslaught of computer networks reaching people and places. This era of digitization has made the Herculean task of reaching the prospect easier, convenient and comfortable. It can tap the data bank with the click of a mouse or may be through a finger touch. Transnational companies prying to enter into an unknown foreign market are striding for the database polled by the agencies and are buying the required data. This, by itself, has become a business of the type. Automated data generation processes are installed for the purpose.

❑ Maximized Media Impact

A company wanting to head for any market expansion plan might require to examine and explore the budget needed for the media promotion. It eventually shall carefully cross-examine the allocated budget versus the permitted media coverage. The company shall have to pick and choose from an array of bewildering new media options. These numerous options could be either available currently with the media agencies or could be available in future. Company media cell always wants to keep the data exploration process continuous and under the radar.

In case of a media assignment being given to an advertising agency, the company has to study the feasibility beforehand and the media's impact on sales should be tested afterwards. The advertising agency should be held directly accountable and made to prove their value. The agency should generate a table of responses tabulated for evaluation, helpful in optimizing the media impact. With such evaluation, testing the media effectiveness is easy. When the company uses these tools perfected by the marketers in measuring responses, they estimate each advertisement in the print in the newspaper or magazine, each direct mailing campaign, each audiovisual aid or each television commercial. Each of the components is adjudged against the expenses incurred. These are different in different countries and are guarded against the taboos, beliefs and traditions prevalent for their derogatory effects.

Maximized accountability in advertisements

Authority, responsibility and accountability are important for the company to forge ahead maximizing profits. Maximizing accountability is a weighing assessment of the money spent for the job done. In fact, the proliferation of media options and choices and the escalation of media costs and expenditures have catapulted the need for 'accountability' in expenditure incurred.

The typical style and perspectives for accountability are changing from time to time. The 'conventional wisdom' in general, on the 'advertising made' was simple. It dictated that 'media' should be evaluated by the 'advertising cost per impression and readership', by virtue of an audience opinion poll and recollections/recapitulations or by the study undertaken through artificial simulations of the marketplace.

It is becoming pertinent, poignant and precise. In the ever-increasing competition of the companies for captivating customers, the winner companies will be those who shall make their advertising expenditures more accountable. Companies willing to spend money for brand building exercises evaluate and rank media houses. They rank the 'media buys' by the proven advertising cost per prospect response or purchase. Moreover, the companies compare as to how 'two different promises or treatments' in the real advertising environment actually affect consumers. Nerd and geek companies have no space in the firebrand markets.

Maximized awareness in advertisements

The essential age old styles, vistas and views of approaches for maximizing awareness in ads are yet the same and similar except for the radical changes. It has been so over a period of time. Basics are the bedrock principles on which the concepts of advertisement demonstrates to the target audience. Awareness building exercise is always intended for the unaware persons, who could be prospective customers. In fact, stimulating the target audience through the favourable awareness campaign is, more or less common to all advertising designs. Even the 'response advertising method' is used by the mail order merchants. It happens because the prospects cannot buy the company product/ service without having awareness on it. They are, therefore, made aware about the products/services, to entice the need.

The bullets fired might miss the mark due to various reasons. A good amount of 'awareness advertising propaganda' suffers due to a high degree of misguided, misdirected and misfired creativity.

Hence, maxi-marketing strategy addresses the need to maximize the impact of awareness building advertising, by giving extra attention to the 'left hemisphere and right hemisphere of the human brain'. It tries to impact the left brain, right brain and the whole brain. Novel methods of sophisticated awareness-building advertising campaigns are designed to appeal and impact equally to the left and right brain, more often. They are a set of psychosomatic advertising modules specially crafted to leverage on both sides of the brain, the rational right side and the emotional or non-rational left side. Neural marketing concepts propounded by the psychologists speak volumes on the aspects. Indeed, the highest of the creative challenge will be always to appeal to the 'whole brain of the prospect'.

Marketing maestros have been working on the concepts relating to the 'particles of impact on the prospects'. This awareness campaign becomes complex, critical and intricate in a transnational market environment, wherein the platform is having a population size, which is dramatically different in their taste and preferences.

Maximized activation through induction

Stimulating, activating and igniting a 'customer prospect' is a critical job. Activation is quite broader than 'sales promotion strategy' and also, is inclusive of the sale promotion strategy. Activation literally and simply means, making 'something happen' by means of the company advertising, be it in the print or electronic medium. That 'happening of something' could be a purchase made; it could simply also be by inducing the prospect a step closer to the purchase, by prompting him for asking for some specific action. It could be a 'step or steps' initiated in, between the prospect and the purchase. Examples on the subject can be seen below.

Example on 'Activation'

Big Bazaar in Bhubaneswar is offering retailer advertisements at the counter putting up festoons, displays and making announcements like **'products on sale today: today only'**. This is typical of an activation process of advertising. This kind of advertisement is a way of getting 'activation' from the customer visiting the retail counters, for striking a sale. Similarly, when a direct marketer of Readers Digest sends a **'reply coupon which must be returned by 30 June 2009'** or in a context where the marketer has affixed a 'token-for-sale to the reply card', it is termed as 'activation'.

These kinds of 'inducements or activations' are also made in the e-bay.com, Amazon.com and other selling dotcom companies operating in the cyberspace/Internet, for enabling e-marketing to happen. Activations are a popular way of selling in the M-marketing too. It is making transnational access easy through the Internet.

The above example reveals the idea that, maxi-marketing essentially stimulate for implementing, launching and applying the response instantly. It could be on the return of the coupon, in case of Reader's Digest. Secondly, it could be like subjecting the visitor in a Big Bazaar retail for a 'situation to purchase or not'. The same yardstick of efficiency and accountability in promoting 'activation' in advertising is important everywhere. It is to communicate and make aware the folks around through advertising and target the prospect for a purchase transaction to commence. It believes in a situation that enables the prospect to boil down to a positive buying decision in a given point of time, at a fine moment.

Maximized synergy by advertisement

Maximizing synergy in creating a deluge of impression is a milestone in advertising. It is done by making the company or product advertised two or more things/jobs at a time, together. This style of advertising can reduce costs and can achieve a synergistic explosion. It can throttle the customer to identify few products simultaneously. It creates an energetic momentum or bombardment for gaining profitability. This kind of advertisement might candidly mix new ideas, with a twist and turn, to galvanize by virtue of a pull strategy. This is a familiar concept of combining awareness advertising and sales promotion. Here, it mostly combines the message with that of a compatible fellow advertiser to share the cost. It could be 'co-branding' for co-creating a propelling situation to draw the customers to consume the products.

This maximizing synergy might involve advertising as a separate profit centre in a way. This method might promote the brand name, promoting the two or more channels of distribution simultaneously. It steals a space and/or time from the advertising made and promotes an event or a cause, in a way that is helpful to both the companies. Due to the escalation in media costs, it becomes increasingly exigent to review the modes of advertising plans. The earmarked cost of advertising should be spread over more than one purpose. Due to the transnational aggression of market forces, this style of advertising has become quite popular to cut costs and advent more into the global market places. In this kind of advertisement, the company has to look for a pattern, cluster and symmetry in the target prospects.

Maximized linkage and perpetual markets

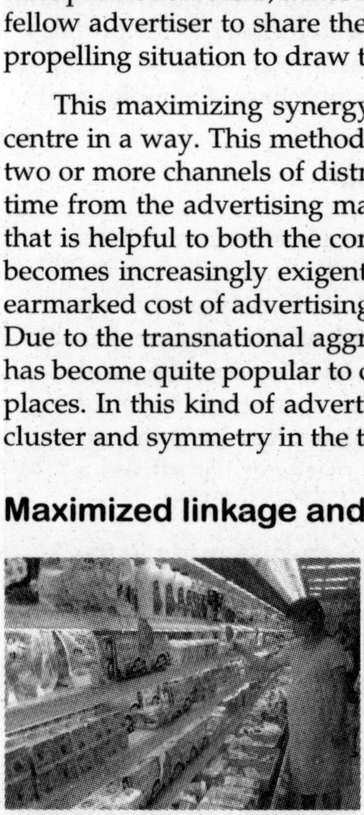

Connecting people for creating prospects and maximizing the linkage perpetually for handling the customer life cycle has become a buzz concept. It is observed that more often than not, most of the awareness advertising leaves the prospect dangling in a catch-22 situation. It makes them indecisive, wandering in a state of a dilly-dally mood. They are left with no idea of what to do next, where to buy and how to obtain more information. However, an ideal advertising and marketing process always bridges this gap. It bridges the gulf or the hiatus between the 'advertising made and the sales' by providing additional information and ensuring that the distribution happens. It cement the gap between the 'advertisement that is made and the sales that has taken place'. It happens due to the additional information flowing through the methods of promotional mix that has been employed. This consequently yields a hassle-free distribution process mitigating the gaps in communication channels. This bridging is called 'linkage'. Linkage means more than just plugging a gap, in the advertising continuum. It focuses more on the most desirable and interested prospects.

Max-marketing uses mass advertising to locate the interest groups and get a positive response from the strongest prospects. It spends the marketing

budget to turn these prospects into customers and loyal customers into lifetime customers. It links the prospects through pertinent advertisements honing the innate desire in the individual.

Maximized sales and profit with satisfaction

Sales and profit are the ultimate of any business, so are the mantra of maxi-marketing. It has its formulations, chemistry and compositions for configuring a citadel to climb the ladder step by step. To reach the zenith of optimization, astute efforts and utter perfection is warranted.

Similarly, all the above rungs of maxi-marketing, when well chiselled, planned and effectively executed, yield substantial tangible results in their significant increase in sales and profits. Maxi-marketing, as such, does not end with the 'first sale made to a new customer'. It probes into the factors of 'what happens after the sales'. What happens after sales can also have a profound effect on the subsequent sales. A company should invent, design and work out long-term strategies to sell lots of products to the public, over and over again and achieve a sustainable share of market, share of mind and share of heart.

As matter of fact, maxi-marketing blends, infuses and aids certain new aspects to the customer database that is generated. Newness is the cutting-edge concept for devising tactics to combat obstacles offing in the market. When the portal platform for updating the database is created and once the automated systems of the company starts, things become smoother for the company. It is because the installed systems start recording and saving the names and address from the enquiries, guarantee/warranty cards on returns, applicants for rebate, coupon redeemers, sample requesters for issues, charge account and credit customers, etc. It can also use, apply and try the latest tools and techniques of segmentation, targeting and positing (STP) to add and subtract other identifiable characters to each of the names and addresses. In this process, it shall virtually construct, design and employ an intelligent and powerful new marketing medium, which can be engaged to promote repeat sales, forecasting sales and introspect simultaneously the futures market. An efficient database system in place can trigger integrated innovations to happen. It can open avenues for the beginning of application of the magical concept of lifetime-

customer value, to enable potentially each and every sale leading to two, three or four additional sales. This aspect might not have been realized earlier by the company management. Any company per se can use mindshare and customer database for the following bullet points:

- To activate and stimulate repeat sales and consolidate market share.
- To enhance and increase the chance for success of the line extensions.
- To cross-promote different products in the line of distribution network.
- To construct, build and create lasting loyalty of potential customers.
- To help open new channels of distribution matching to the demand.

In fact, market share alone, exclusively and unilaterally can help achieve all these goals. Similarly, 'market share plus database marketing' can increase the chances of success immensely for the company. The chemistry of the two in tango can effect, double or triple the LTV of each new buyer, to the company's enhancement.

Customer database is paramount and a paragon for the business to take off. Data drives and drills into the market movers. Ultimately, customer database help/assist the company in manifold ways which the 'market share' alone cannot facilitate. In the case of launching a new product in the domain of services or business, it is essential. However, trying it in a 'regional test market' might be quite costly and might tip-off the competitors. This could well happen due to the occurrence of 'disclosures of the intention to study for the expansion plans'.

Evidently, database marketing can quietly test the ideas, reading into the market psyche, based on the epoch, trends and fads. The company, if compelled, can change, make shift and transform its scheme of operation, in response to the novel database compiled. It statistically, qualitatively and transparently finds out the ideal prospects, who can serve as clues to lead the other likely prospects in the wanted direction. The direction could be of a new product or business that the company can think of switching over. It can also squash the company biases and conspicuously position the loopholes before the management to emanate from it's overconfidence on the quality of product. It can rescue the company from their mental mousetrap with respect to the corridors of business proposals, prospects and panacea.

Maximized distribution with intensity

Maximizing distribution with intensity is essential for the business to prosper and progress. Networking potentially in the channels of distribution, for

ensuring sales is of utmost importance for extracting profit from the business transactions. A company cannot grow and continue to develop when retailers refuse to offer any more shelf space for stacking goods and articles. In this case, personal selling agents cannot find scope and get enough appointments with new prospects. It cannot prosper if the company 'mail order catalogue' is dirty and soiled.

Channel opening for market penetration, making prior reconnaissance observation has been found to be critical from the pragmatic point of view. Down-to-earth reality check of the doctrine of implementation has been astounding and astonishing. Many companies have found out the answer to be in opening up a new channel of distribution. It encounters strange situations and ordeals, like extending business activities to another continent having confronting cultures. High-text culture contradicts a low-text culture in a number of ways. The new transnational companies often do it, without knowing about the complication in offing and criticalities of foreign language, customs, traditions and distribution methods. Japanese businesses adopt front-attack strategy, unlike other Asian countries that have their independent strategies.

In order to overcome this bottleneck, it may seek essential study of the context, for using a database built upon the present customers. It might seek through using a study to ascertain the mindshare. It could build up in one channel to support another channel. It could also be by using some other advertiser's database on the similar kind of dashboard. Very often, they create a synergetic reaction, which is unpredictable. It could be between two or more distribution methods combined for a cacophony instead of symphony. They could be the best of the types in the genre of distribution. In a typical situation, the company can invent or establish a new form of distribution. This new distribution channel propounded could be the old way of handling product. Times change, approaches differ, bunch of new ideas creep in mounted with a new flavour. Everything is in a flux; nothing is static and at a standstill. Old methods seem anew when the background changes with the business canvass.

❑ All the Steps of Maxi-marketing Work Together

Convergence is the art of philharmonic rhythm. In the absence of orchestrating approaches of the parts, the parts remain as isolated wholes. Being together, they become an entity to reckon with as an instrument for extraordinary measures.

The most significant aspect of maxi-marketing approach to transnational marketing is about how the 'various parts' fit into each other and work together in tandem. The 'common thread' is a measurable response from the 'individual consumer' to the person to whom the company wants to sell or has already sold. The wavelength that becomes the 'response' is ultimately important. It is ultimately the 'response' that is desirable. But first let us know, what are these responses?

These 'responses' can tell the company, if the advertising is correctly targeted or not. All 'responses' can provide an 'index' or a 'measure' to the comparative efficiency of different media, different product images, benefits and different offerings. The technique of allocating extra advertising budget for a self-identified prospect depends on getting a 'response' from the products. Responses are the basis of an in-house prospective customer database. These responses are an indicator of the improving performance or changes seen in the face of the emerging new marketing realities. These new marketing realities are termed as **'responsive advertising or response marketing (RA or RM)'**. It as a subject of study is beginning to get special attention, which was earlier bestowed on **'creative advertising or creative marketing (CA or CM)'**. They are more or less the same and similar, but are different in their own rights.

❑ Maximized Targeting is about Targeting Prospects

Target is all about hitting the bull's eye. In order to repeat the process of performance to achieve a zero defect, it has to be error free and accurate. Maverick markets are peculiarly competitive. Individual products have importance, as nothing is a universal product. In the contemporary market place, what is important are the 'who, where, why, when, which and wherever, of the 'prospects'. If the individual target fails, the company loses to the competition. There is nothing called as a 'universal product', i.e., one for which each and everyone is a prospective buyer. As long as there has been advertising, there has been targeting. All kinds of product proliferation in the marketplaces do squarely mean prospect proliferation. With different kinds of prospects brewing in the marketplaces, more of waste in the field of advertising will ooze. This has been a practice since the days of competitive advertising was born.

❑ Five Ways to Find 'Best Customers or Best Prospects'

In the crowded market places, shelled with advertising jargons, surrogate advertisements and deceptive denotes it has become abundantly cumbersome to discern the right choice. Customers are getting confused, cornered and become confounded. They are in an utter dismay to locate the best of the lot. Therefore, in order locating the prospect has become a challenge for the companies. Deriving a technical plan for spotting the right customer base has called for certain focus. The focus here is essentially on 'five potential ways' to find out and talk to the 'best customers or best prospects'. These five ways are:

- Fishing: Targeted messages
- Mining: Target media
- Panning: Listing segmentation
- Building: In-house database
- Spelunking: Niche marketing

Out of the given five ways of angling prospects or finding best of the prospects, the 'first two' ways have been prevalent for a long time. The 'second two' ways aptly represent the powerful new marketing force and strategy. They are based on the magic of database marketing, working as an elixir for all the market ailments to be doctored. The 'last one' is a traditional marketing form, which is reinforced by a computer database. They all have their own indigenous method of handling issues governing customer prospects. Moreover, based on the prima facie elucidation of the five ways of 'netting prospects' for marketing the target products, each of the five ways shall be analysed one by one. Each of the aspects shall be elaborated for crystallizing the ways and means deriving the intricate leeways. They are as follows:

Fishing for the prospect

Fishing for prospects or customers is as age-old as the origin of 'advertising'. This technique involves the galvanization of the individuals from amongst the mass of audience. It gets into the psyche of the prospective customer by 'delivering a message' that is highly meaningful only to that prospect. It is similar to the way of angling fishes (customers), through fishing rods.

Besides the multi pronged ways that it employs, fishing is usually done with words, graphics and normally for the users of competitive products. It has a technique, which snatches away the customer prospects from rival brands in the given niche. Even in a situation, like that of a 'mature market', with little room to expand and encourage marketers, this fishing technique steals from the existing customer base of competitors, in a watertight market, wresting the competitor out with fierce competition, enabling a space for itself. Creating a slit hole of opportunity for building equity later is important. One fiendish and aggressive way of fishing for customers is to offer 'a reward' to a prospect, who submits a 'proof of purchase' of the competitor's product.

Additionally, VALS (values and life styles) is another method of segregating the demand factors from the pool of customer base that the market has for the brand. It is seen that sometimes, within a product category, it becomes desirable to know what motivates some prospects to choose one brand from the other and what motivates others to choose one another. It can introspect into certain psychic predilection, if any, based on the prospects preference for the value system. These lacunae can be uncovered, exposed and targeted.

VALS is the answer for delving into the market requirements. It is a way of classifying people in different places in accordance to their values, life styles and by virtue of identifying their geographic distribution in the neighbourhoods. VALS as a technique can be used for fishing the prospects and panning for prospects.

Mining the prospect

Mining of minerals is a prevalent notion. In the act of mining, one has to dig into the surface of the soil for exploiting ores. The same act of digging process is involved but the context is different. Here, it is the art of finding customer prospects.

'Mining the prospect' is the art and science of digging in places, where there is a probability of rich customer prospect. This prospect base can substantially contribute to the advancement of the business and can better float/sell yachts (ideas) in the 'yachting world'. In order to navigate into the turbulent market places, it is essential to sail small yachts to conquer niches, trace places and invade market territories is essential. In addition, for that definite idea about the wind speed and climatic variance in the case of yacht sailing, prospect data is quintessential. This mechanics can make marketing invasion a reality. Brand new marketplaces call for public database assessment for a market entry. These look for and identify the name, address and all contact details on every prospect category. It goes in for prospect search, which does not use the brand for focal attention.

Mining by telemarketing

Products or services also call for telemarketing, yet one another method. It conducts 'telephone surveys of localities', particular areas around an identified store or manufacturer that wants to build its customer database. All the respondents are asked as to 'what companies they patronize' and what the 'brands they use' are. From this survey, they locate the non-customer. Then only the non-customers are selected in a list, and then mails are sent to them. These are may be mailings of coupons or catalogues designed to woo the non-customers, to make them visit your company or agent. In US, in the year 1995, a drive for data collection was made. Data collectors paid approximately USD 1 for each name of a competitor's customer and for the manufacturers about 10 cents to 12 cents. This drive for database expanded to a collection of 20 million people in the USA.

The study of marketing for expansion essentially looks for knowledge of the users in competing brands. The assessment is mostly made through direct mail. Figure 5.4 depicts a structured idea of the same. It offers a visual forecast of the possible result of a mailing plan, for the promotion of an expensive brand of engineering goods.

An Assumptive Study on Possible Outcome of Mailing to Customers of Competitive Brand

In a given canvas of the market, let us assume that a brand sells for ₹ 20for a unit of the product. The advertiser has secured data through a media agency—names of 1,00,000 users, who have been using two leading competing brands, selling for around ₹ 12 a unit. In the given situation, a mailing list is prepared inviting the users to try the brand and see the difference. In this, let us say, that a gift certificate of ₹ 8 is attached. The fee options are offered to pay the difference, to make it ₹ 20. In this study in view, Fig. 5.4 depicts the working assumption, to be 5 per cent of the recipients of mailing having accepted the offer and used the gift certificate. Let us assume the difference to be a conservative estimate, an assumption. In the given context, a 5 per cent response or a sale of 5000 units, calculated in proportion to 1,00,000 names does not seem to be much. However, it could be more that it involves.

At the extreme right of Fig. 5.4, it is seen that 95 percent of the customer base did not respond. Of these, we assume that 30 percent of the customer base who did not bother to open the mailing. Out of that, let us say that remaining 65 percent opened the envelope and glanced through the mailing. All these did not use the mailing, but 5000 of them, i.e., 1 out of every 20 received a favourable impression of the brand from the mailing and circumstantially purchased one unit anyway. It is learnt that in this aspect of direct mail, the advertising

Contd....

impression made on non-responders is receiving increasing attention in the market. Out of the 5000, who respond, the forecast predicts that, 2000 merely use the certificate and then return to their old brand, 1000 respondents could be sufficiently pleased by their trial to buy one more unit and out of the remaining 2000 respondents, just 2 percent will become converted enthusiasts. After their trial, each is expected to buy at least four more units. Furthermore, because of their enthusiasm, let us think that their word-of-mouth advertising will be quite effective and 1 enthusiast out of 100 mail recipients will influence 1 friend to buy 31 units. That is just the impact in first year.

In the second year, the enthusiasm converts each of the prospects buy five more units. Let us assume that each buys one more unit and half of the positively impressed non respondents who had purchased one unit each, now buy one additional unit. In the given speculative assumption, we end up with a projected grand total of 37,500 units sold in the first two years, as a direct result of mailing to 1,00,000 product consumers. It is quite a different picture from the calculated 5000 units assumed to have been sold to be the total sales return.

Here, four factors are traced from the assumptions, on the hypothetical engineering goods mailing. They are set apart from the routine sales-promotion-driven direct mails and they seem to be cost-effective.

We see that there is waste in circulation. Here, we are mailing only to prime prospects, known users of competing brands. In addition to the gift certificate, the mailer contains a three to four page letter with a dose of potent and persuasive brand advertising. This is known to have influenced the buying attitude of many respondents. The total sales effect of mailing on the respondents, friends and non respondents, over a period of two years is estimated and factored in post research. Moreover, names and addresses of respondents are captured by their entry into a customer database, where they can be used in the future, for reinforcing direct advertising, research, marketing, special offers and other uses.

	5 percent Respond			95 percent do not Respond	
For each two converts one friend tries it and becomes occasional user.	Two percent of the known users of the competitor's brand become regular users and recommends it to.	One percent becomes occasional users.	Two percent tries it without repeat purchase.	Sixty-five percent of the users of competition brand read the mailing and are influenced favourably towards the brand. 5 per cent decide later on to try it.	Thirty percent of the users of competition brand discard the mailing without opening it.
1000 Units	2000 Units	1000 Units	2000 Units		
1000 Units	8000 Units	1000 Units		5000 Units	**Total Year One** 21,000 Units
3000 Units	10,000 Units	1000 Units	2500 Units		**Year Two** 16,500 Units
					Total of two years 37,500 Units

Figure 5.4 Possible Outcome of Mailing to 1,00,000 Known Users of the Competitor's Brand of Product

Panning the prospect

Panning the prospect is important. To reach the targeted prospects through panning, involves a proper scheme of action that is scheduled scientifically for

accomplishing the desired objective. It is like processing through the stages of the plan of action, getting ever-finer screens, until the nuggets of pure gold remain in the pan.

Visualize a Scene

Let us visualize and suppose that a retail counter is interested for marketing expensive high-style jeans for a definite segment of petite blondes. As a matter of fact, market research and/or past sales trends reveal that only in Texas and California, are females interested in high-style jeans. It was thought that, striving to reach them with mass advertisement would be wasteful and prohibitive. Moreover, there is no existing list of affluent, petite and female jeans wearers, living in Texas or California.

In the given situation, what to do is the billion-dollar question? The detailed information regarding the prospect can be sought from a professional data collector. They might have located from the 'lists of mail order customers' of petite fashions. The agency for data provider might collect only those 'names and addresses' available on the lists, of all those who are in Texas and California. Against this list of prospects, the data provider could lay or merge the computerized lists of the mail order of the purchasers of jeans of all sizes, a pertinent list of females staying in the affluent neighbourhoods.

In the given process of identifying a list of prospects, the data collector might contact two or more competitors for a comparative evaluation. It could be Clairol and L'Oréal, two of the competitors, to work out a reciprocal exchange method for identifying the blondes. From the above planning, the final list of prospects could be compiled of the blondes who closely fit into the description of the required prospect. It sounds like 'merge purge'. This nomenclature—merge purge—is befitting to justify because the data collector has merged the two computer files of names and addresses into one and then purged from the combined list. Here duplicates names appear twice. These purged duplicates or 'multi hit' names, form a separate list of people who have the characteristics of both the lists. In a candid form, they are identified.

Prospecting database

Prospecting database is important for the strategic transnational markets. The ultimate purpose in database prospecting is to construct and maintain a sophisticated 'prospect database'. As it adds the names, addresses and other information to each name, the company learns more about the prospect. It learns about who, what, when, which and where of the prime prospects. From this database, the company can build a subgroup of prospects, for any specific marketing target.

In the current epoch, direct mail is no longer a costly affair. This medium relatively has a low response rate in the domain of transnational marketing. The rates of prospect responses are best suited for high-margin direct marketing. While targeting the capabilities of public and private databases, it makes the possible response rates of direct mail a cost-effective medium. It is same for low-cost and low-margin products.

Spelunking for prospects

Spelunking for prospects is another name for niche marketing, about which we are quite familiar in some ways. Spelunking is the exploration of cares, and this care is a deep niche. In spelunking, two kinds of niche marketing are seen. They are:

- Finding a new niche for the product;
- Finding products for a niche, waiting to be explored.

This approach is a nice method to earn business in a competitive environment. Niche marketing is particularly effective for opening up market avenues in the new areas of transnational marketing.

❑ Maximized Media

Media innovations happen in flick of seconds. They grind creativity and emanate with creativity and newness in the media modes. None of the weeks are devoid of any media innovation or proved news making in the arena of communication. 'The advertising industry, whether it likes it or not', will have to come to grips with a whole new way of advertising, says Stuart Young, the English business executive and accountant who became the chairman of BBC Board of Governors in 1983 and stayed in the position till his death in 1986. It is true of the changing lifestyles.

As an example, it could be the ambient video or the video wallpaper with its moving images displayed continuously in the discos, bars, restaurants, cruise ships and transnational flights. Video wallpapers could be interwoven with the advertising message or absence of it. This is a sample illustration. The common denominator in all media choices is their measurability. Vivacious advertisements of the modern era have undergone a sea change and are heading towards a global village. The following are the examples of the kind of measurability employed in different types of tools and time slots for their optimal delivery.

TMC and SMC

As a matter of fact, the total market coverage (TMC) and its selective market coverage (SMC) are the biggest developments in the domain of newspaper advertising. In comparison to the TV viewers, newspaper readers were much more educated and had/have higher income levels. A 'TMC vehicle' is an 'alternative distribution system', which consists of an 'expanded special edition', oneday of the week, delivered free to the non-subscribers. An SMS user covers the paper's market area and supplements it with SMC-shared mail to non subscribers, within its immediate or specified area. It is intended to deliver a concentrated punch at a manageable cost.

Freestanding inserts

FSIs have been introduced since 1968. It offers an aggressive retailer an opportunity to use quality colour printing to display his entire catalogue of merchandise, price-off coupons and mail order ads, etc., providing all additional allurement at the cheapest cost, with guaranteed large-scale coverage. It becomes cost effective and easy for the agency to do propaganda of the offerings.

TV for information society

Rates affect viewers. As rates escalate, audiences continue to dwindle. Maximum equity, need-based projection and competition reduce the individual tariffs of customers. People become lured by the Cable TV, VCRs, hi-tech gadgets, Internet and other hi-fi network commercials in the scales of economy. Slowly, it is seen that advertisements are getting shorter, specialized, intense and fewer. In the US, instead of the previous 30-second spot for a 'stand alone ad', a 15-second spot has become official. Commercial programmes could sound repellent, but a tasteful 'infomercial' can be entertaining and appealing. Prospects are always hungry for information and entertaining presentation. Infotising and infomercials of 15–30 minutes duration are a revolution that is about to happen. This medium range timing and amusing packaging is fascinating for the products or services that need multi dimensional explaining.

Radio

As per the standard, less than 7 percent of all advertisement is done by radio, though FM radio is gaining momentum. In radio, three-fourth of the advertisements is done by the retailers, small and medium mostly. It is mostly used for the FMCG goods and not industrial products. Companies like Campbell

Soup, Taco Bell, Ciba and Ford in the US and Hindustan lever, P&G, Colgate and Nirma in India are still able to get a lot of mileage out of it. A prospective medium is the new call-in 24-hour programme. Ciba vision scheduled radio slots for ads' finding women aged 18 to 34 as prime prospects for their new products. Soft-tinted contact lens-users category being the target group are identified to have been listening to radio during the morning hours and evening hours as frequently and especially, in between the rock and soft rock tunes.

Magazines

The big question of the survival of magazine was haunting the media czars during the harbinger of e-revolution. The question was could magazines survive the video revolution? Revolutions in the past in the annals of communication have suggested that the magazine can withstand and fortify its stand. Today, the public is buying more magazines than ever before. Population boom and inclinations are changing day by day. This is because of the following:

- **Specialization:** These are now over 1700 consumer magazines in the US alone; the great majority of them are highly specialized. They have an exorbitant price tag for each single magazine. Per-page cost becomes quite high for each of the magazine and the readership is then quite less. **Regionalization:** By 1984, there were 147 city and regional magazines in the US, many in India too. In many cities the ambitious publishers are attempting to 'slice the pie' even finer. They created magazines designed for special interest segments within the city.
- **A big splash for a few bucks:** Bigsplash is not a bad proposition. An occasional/one-time full-page splash in TV Guide, Newsweek, Business Week, Business India, Sports Week, Readers Digest, etc., for just local or regional circulation at affordable cost is a fabulous proposition.
- **New technology:** In 1985, the leading newsweekly in France – 'Le Point' published the first electronic print ad. It was a four-page IBM ad that lit up and played music. That revolutionized the process of advertisements.

- **The customized magazine:** R R Donnelly & Sons, a printing firm developed a process called **Selectronic**, which harnessed the computer to the printing press, to print tailor-made individual copies carrying a named ad/message for each subscriber. Farm Journal, Games, Education, Reality, etc., are effectively using this process.

Cable TV

Around the year 1986, most of the major cities were still about to be wired for connectivity. Over 46 percent of United States' TV-owning households had cable, and wiring had begun in all of the top 20 TV markets that did not have cable. However, despite a number of brave experiments, Cable TV advertising had been viewed by sponsors as a way to provide 'cheap way of conveying message and advertisements'. Eventually exposures for commercials were prepared for the TV mediums.

Direct mail

Some of the major developments regarding direct mail are mentioned below.

- **Shared mail:** This is a direct answer to the daily newspaper's TMC. Assorted advertising by participating marketers is bundled together and mailed to selected households, customer groups or customers.
- **Direct mail co-op. packages:** Advertisers participate for splitting the costs. Direct mail co-op. packages are precise, concerted and economic targeting tools. Different kinds of co-ops, are available from the leading suppliers, with their annual frequencies of advertisements. It could include three Hispanics, six coloured, eight preschool, five children aged five to twelve, seven teens, five seniors, three upper-income adults, four sports, three colleges, fourteen newly weds, fourteen expectant mothers, ten new mothers.
- **Card decks:** These are probably the fastest growing form of co-op. mail designed for advertisers looking for direct response. In the US, more than 88,000 businesses participated in 1983. They began as card stock booklets, affording each advertiser a business reply card. Subsequently, they evolved into a plastic bag containing a stack of loose cards, each with an advertising message, fill-out reply portion and a business reply face on the other.
- **Local names from national lists:** They are a productive source, especially from the subscribers of *Business Week, Metal Bulletin, News Week*, etc.
- **Driving customers to your retailers:** This is a surprisingly underutilized form of direct mail, with mailings sent to target prospects to get them to buy the product at the nearest outlet.

Video cassettes

By 1986 VCR's reached into over 38 percent of TV households in Western Europe and USA and 66 percent were expected by 1990. This catapulted into taking up video cassettes seriously as an advertising medium. It offered all the impact, power and influence of the TV's hypnotic visual communications, without TV time limitations. This medium can be tried and tested anytime, especially when the company is to sell a matching product or service, which could benefit from a deluge of demonstration, visualization and audio-impression. This can also be an alternate medium for retail selling. This has been in use rampantly.

Boom in telephone marketing

The telephone has become the third largest national advertising medium, in the biggest and the most important markets in the USA. However, in 1985, the number of people involved in the telemarketing was around 3, 00,000. US News & World Report predicted that by 2000, this number was to rise to 8 million. Today, the number has gone up much more than that. In 1983, direct marketing association research pointed to a total telemarketing sales in 1984 to be of $100 billion. In telemarketing, it is possible to succeed. There is no limit to the future of inbound telemarketing, because the public wants it and likes it. M-commerce has boomed over a period of time. Outbound telemarketing is different, and the government legislation is restricting unwanted invention into public privacy. Use of the automated dialling and recorded message player's (ADRMP's) has been restricted and banned in many places.

Outbound telemarketing

If the company is thinking of using telemarketing to contact prospects or customers here are some considerations:

- Each call was costing about ten times as much as direct mail solicitation, but being successful, it is producing ten times more results. It shall be quite less.
- Do not institute it yourself. Use professional services.
- Lower the expected response rate, higher the unit of sale.
- Company/firm can install a machine called 'automated dialling and recorded message player (ADRMP) to automatically dial a list of prospects and deliver your taped message.

Inbound telemarketing

Many companies may think that simply answering the phone is not marketing at all, but it is that. However, in this process many opportunities are overlooked. These features include:

- Referring customers to dealers and vice versa;
- List building;
- Adding a service to your product;
- Line extension;
- Call-in sweepstakes;
- Up-sell: If the company has operators taking orders on the phone, good training and/or a good script will enable them to increase the size;
- Sell during 'hold': A company, Audicom, prepares tapes to company specifications, so the company can give the caller a sales message, when they are on 'hold';
- When callers paid 50 cents on their phone bills and get a recorded message, the sponsor paid a $250 set up charge and $25 a call, if the number falls below 2000. Above 2000, the sponsor is paid a few cents on a sliding scale.

Electronic shopping

Electronic shopping is easy to deal with. Due to this reason, literature on electronic shopping has become obsolete in many places. One such example of electronic shopping medium is video machine. Video machines of the size of a video arcade game were placed in shopping malls, airports and other high traffic areas. They were useful in finding new customers those who had not been reached by current sales force. Videodiscs were used on which 54,000 frames could be stored, and through computer technology it could display stills or move in high resolution colour, or could convey complex product information. These machines

could also collect valuable data, even when no purchase was made. They recorded everything as long as the user stayed at the machine for examining product catalogues or products. Other media choices are as follows:

- **Floppy disks** for the home computer.
- **Tele conferencing:** Making live presentations for marketing to the prospective clients or dealers. It is done simultaneously at various locations for different segments.
- **Sponsorships:** Sponsored entertainment and sports have been quite popular media for marketing. A massive funding is involved in sports sponsorship and this creates a huge earning for the sports celebrities and games or events conducted.
- **Sky tray:** These are found in international sky liners and planes in the advanced countries. A computer, built into the seat back or tray table of commercial passenger planes, provide enjoyable two-way communications.
- **Street selling:** Street selling is a particularly done for holding major campaigns. The basics of marketing white goods, FMCG and household consumables are made through street selling. Almost all products are marketed this way.

- **Door hangers:** These are hung on doorknobs of homes and offices. Marketing of many household products are done this way.
- **Billboards:** Marketing of products through billboards reaches million of households. An army of trained parttime employees place them on the ends of shopping carts, put on the vehicles like autos, taxis and pick-up vans.

- **On pack/in pack advertising:** This is the most neglected promising medium. As a pack, it is present in every household in the developed countries. It is done in an exclusive kind of population and geographical situation.
- **Movie theatres:** Movie theatres were successfully used by Apple for marketing of their products. They used the theatres for promoting

Macintosh in the late 1984s. They were expensive and required a month's continuous exposure. Yet, it remains a good way to reach younger upscale people, who would rather go to the movies than watch TV.

- **Mail-order catalogues:** This contains its usual wider circulation and presence in the prospective customers.
- **Shipping cartons:** Shipping cartons are more often seen to have been stacked in store aisles. These 'shipping cartons, used for shifting products nicely packed have become an important and economical point of purchase advertising medium. It is all due to the dramatic improvement in the scale of printing methods and designs.
- **Lamp posts:** Lamp posts attached with tear-off coupons or messages, giving name of companies, stockists, product and contact addresses and phone numbers are good media of marketing. This has been a practice since the early times, because light posts were places of activities. It can also be a mode for the exclusive kind of places installed with fancy streetlights and visited by people like places like the Darjeeling marketplace, Connaught Place in New Delhi and so forth.
- **Match box:** Match box with 20 matchsticks in the box does a lot of hype to position the product advertisement. The advertisers get exposure of a message that lasts longer than a 30-second commercial. During uuage it is imprinted in the mind of the user and helps for brand recall.

Summary

Maxi-transnational marketing (MTM) is an excellent strategy which reinforces a convergence of all the facets of business for making profits by maximizing/optimizing the catalogue of efforts. It not only begins from the nascent/teething phase of the business but also exceeds beyond the customer/consumer delight.

This chapter infuses a 'learnt efficiency' to fillip competencies for enhancing the promotional–mix applied for products ranging from planning to framing roadmap for ultimate practice. Increase of market equity, enhancing impression/brand image of the company product through effective distribution system is the intention of MTM.

It also reflects on the touch points of media impact, particularly on the vital aspects of advertisements and other promotional mix elements germane to the context. Accountable spending on expenses of advertisement is another enchanting aspect. Lifetime customer values (LTV), Response Marketing (RM), Total Market Coverage (TMC) and value and lifestyles (VAL) have been related too.

Contd....

Indeed, certain significant areas have been elucidated in terms of grids and store boards, for enabling the reader to replicate and/ or experiment in the field. Small caselets and company's example make it further understandable. This chapter encompass a coverage with a newness in approach.

QUESTIONS FOR DISCUSSION

Q. 1. What do you mean by maxi-transnational marketing? Discuss.

Q. 2. How is selling process the key to maxi-transnational? Illustrate

Q. 3. Discuss the particulars of maxi-transnational marketing (MTM). Give relevant examples from the market you visit.

Q. 4. Which are the golden components that constitute maxi-transitional marketing (MTM) model? Discuss and elaborate.

Q. 5. What are the salient areas on which 'maximization efforts' are to be exerted for better results? Discuss with reference to the maximization related aspects. Explain with suitable examples.

Q. 6. How is lifetime customer value (LTV) attended by companies? Which are the methods employed for the purpose of LTV? Discuss giving reference.

Q. 7. How all the steps of maxi-marketing work together? Discuss.

Q. 8. What do you mean by targeting prospects? How do you analyze with respect to maximized targeting? Elucidate.

Q. 9. What are the five ways to find 'best customers or best prospects'? Express indicating on each of them.

Q. 10. What are the broad areas of personalized selling modalities? Illustrate.

Q. 11. What are the aspects employed to maximize media impact? Discuss in details.

Q. 12. How do media choices reach customers and what kind of impact it creates? Illustrate assuming a market patch of a region.

Q. 13. Write short notes:

(a) Modern domestic marketing vis-à-vis transnational marketing

(b) Maximized target

(c) Maximized media impact

(d) Maximized accountability and awareness in ads

(e) Maximized activation through induction

(f) Maximized synergy by advertisement

(g) Maximized linkage and perpetual markets

(h) Maximized sales and profit with satisfaction

(i) Maximized distribution with intensity

(j) Spelunking the prospect

(k) Fishing the prospect

(l) Mining the prospect

(m) Info-commercials

(n) Card decks

(o) Shared mail

(p) Telemarketing (Inbound and Out bound)

(q) Electronic shopping

(r) Sky tray

(s) Street selling

(t) Teleconferencing

(u) Sponsorships

(v) Door hangers

(w) Small billboards

(x) Movie theaters

(y) Lamp post.

Chapter 6

Maxi-transnational Promotion and Psychosomatic Customer Access

LEARNING OBJECTIVE

After going through the chapter, the reader shall be able to:

1. Define 'maximized accountability' on the impact of advertisements intended for target segments.
2. Explain the estimated value of expenditure incurred on advertisement from sales.
3. Recognize the essence of advertisement designated to create, promote and build a lasting brand image.
4. Understand the 'campaign theme and content' for influencing decisions for purchase.
5. Realize advertisement and marketing and the role of leftbrain and right brain advertising over a span of time.
6. Introspect the concept of USP in every product for creating mind share by true advertisement.

> *'Keep your thoughts positive, because your thoughts become your words. Keep your words positive, because your words become your behaviour. Keep your behaviour positive, because your behaviour becomes your habit. Keep your habits positive, because your habits become your values. Keep your values positive, because your values become your destiny'.*
>
> *— Mahatma Gandhi*
>
> *'Excellency is a fleeting term; a journey beyond infinity—an odyssey'.*
>
> *— Authors of TNM Book*

7. Identify the complex mechanical aspect of 'right brain' and creatively intriguing aspect of 'left brain'.
8. Interpret the 'strengths' and 'limitations' of advertisements.
9. Have an Insight into the domains of assessment grids, database marketing and their categories of approach to outreach the ultimate customer.
10. Assess the transnational maxi-marketing assessment questions that are conspicuously present in the ambit of promotional strategy.

MAXIMIZED ACCOUNTABILITY

Advertisements are made for a target segment with a goal to strike a buying decision. Propaganda that is popular with the people, kick-starts business in the market and overtakes competitors. Advertisements can be communicated through any means, from any direction, employing any method.

All the advertising campaigns, even those seeking mail orders, begin by fostering a favourable awareness of the product of services. They are advertised with a target in view. The biggest difference between direct and indirect marketing or advertising is that, the latter must create and build lasting awareness on the prospect. It builds impression for a prolonged period. This awareness lingers in the prospect's mind, until the opportunity or need arises at the retail level.

In the advertising made by the direct marketers, it can be known as to whether the attempt made to create favourable awareness for selling has become successful or not. This is revealed by the public response, towards the products during their visits to the retail counter. If we fail in reaching out the target customer, we can also find out where we have failed. It can also be done by breaking the messages in different parts and analysing g each of them separately. In the advertisements that are designed to create, configure and build a lasting image of a brand, a service company takes a much longer time to explore its loopholes and discrepancies.

Generally, we do not read about the failure and abandonment of a campaign theme in the weekly advertising press. These days the campaign themes

are conceptualized with such enthusiasm and confidence. How often we see the embarrassing excesses of cleverness in advertising and wonder! The question here is what is wrong with the research? The problem is actually 'attitude', and attitudinal changes are much more difficult to measure than are actions. The effects of awareness predisposition and image-building advertising depend not only on its content, but also on weight and frequency of its exposure. Thus, the prediction of attitudinal changes over a time is a very tricky business to gauge.

If our selling process is to be maximized at every step, we must maximize the power of our awareness-building advertising. It should emphasize on the awareness-fostering elements in our advertising. This calls for greater accountability and more precise measurement of advertising, while it is happening. It also calls for more and more exact comparisons of advertising alternatives—not just the old campaign versus the new campaign, but comparisons of a number of possible new campaign approaches and of different elements in the advertising tested against each other.

These questions of the actual sales effectiveness of a given advertising effort can be removed from both the realm of opinion and the imprecise evaluations of traditional advertising research. But it requires an open minded exploration of the options in transnational advertising, by a marketing fraternity still wedded to the past assumptions of the mass-marketing era.

MAXIMIZED AWARENESS

It is almost for hundred years, two warring camps have struggled for the soul of advertising and marketing.

> *'Be persuasive! Present a convincing advantage or benefit' is the battle cry of the first camp 'Be creative! Be entertaining'—insists the second camp. 'Ridiculous!' snorts the first. 'The public may be tickled to death with your advertising but will they buy your product?' 'Well, I would rather have them tickled to death, than bored to death! You cannot save the souls in an empty church!' says the second. 'Bah! You are arty, that is what you are!' 'Oh yeah? Well you are corny!'*

These two imaginative arguments given above represent the 'left brain' and the 'right brain' in the context of advertising. On these aspects, the principal arguments which have evolved over a period of time sincc inception are summarized below in the Box 6.1. It narrates the commentaries made by the seers in the field of advertising that are essentially pithy, concise and cascading with ideas. It scientifically delineates the motives cropping up in the psychological state of the mind, activated in term of actions. They are oriented to elucidate the theme. The leftbrain and rightbrain arguments are as follows:

Box 6.1 Left- and Right-Brain Advertising

Left Brain	Right Brain
Print the news of the store. No catchy headlines, no catches, no headings, no smartness, no brag, no fine writing, no fooling, no foolery, no attempt at advertising, no anxiety to sell, no mercenary admiration; hang up the goods in the papers, one at a time, a few today, tomorrow the same or others. — John O Powers, Wanamaker's Department Store (1895) True 'reason' why copy is logic, plus simplicity of thought, plus conviction, all woven into a certain simplicity of thought— predigested for the average mind, so that it is easier to understand than to misunderstand. — John W Kennedy, 'Advertising is Salesmanship in Print' (1904) 'Keeping the name before the public' is wrong and 'salesmanship in print' is right. — Lord & Thomas Pamphlet, The Book of Tests (1905) Style is a handicap. Anything that takes attention from the subject reduces the impression. — Claude Hopkins, My Life in Advertising (1927) Present day advertising research has a long way to go before it reaches the level of Claude Hopkins contributions to efficient advertising. — Alfred Politz, Consultant (Advertising) (1935)	Copy was not just the words but also 'that combination of text with design', which produces a complete advertisement. — E E Calkins, Calkins & Holden (1907) They were almost all pictures. It is the atmosphere in these that sells; the quality that gives prestige. — C Curtis, Pierce-Arrow Cars (1914) The actual effect of modern advertising is not so much to convince to suggest. — W D Scott, The Psychology of Advertising (1917) The psychoanalysts have learned this about human kind that nearly all of the important decisions of the individual are nearly made in the subconscious. — B L Dunn, Oneida Community Silver (1918) Reason—why advertising consists of a clever and semi scientific application of the thesis that all men are fools. I took upon the public as myself multiplied and they have not yet reached that stage of diffidence and humility, which permits me to write myself down as an ass. — T F MacManus, General Motors (1932) It is not what is said but how it is said that influences us the most. Any copy in advertising is an argument.

Left Brain	Right Brain
What this agency has done that is different from any other agency is to apply reason to advertising. Reason—non-unconscious starving for sex and security. — P Martineau, Chicago Tribune (1957)	It is literally throwing down a challenge to the reader, saying, Let's argue about this. The human reaction to any statement of claim is Wait a minute! Who says so?
Advertising began as an art and too many advertising men want it to remain that way — a never land where they can say this is right because we felt it is right. — R Reeves, Reality in Advertising (1961)	We are definitely again in the age of the eye. We have less time to read, browse, meditate and muse. There is a multiplicity of messages striking us from every side, so that it seems that only a lightning message of a picture can strike deep and hit home when we have a moment to spare. — M. Sherman, McCann – Erickson (1959)
They have never admired the belle's letters school of advertising. I have always thought them absurd, they did not give the reader a single fact. — David Ogilvy, Confessions of an Advertising Man (1963)	If an idea makes me laugh, that is a sure sign it is a good idea. All commercials should be entertaining, no exceptions made. Somebody's making the business too rational, which is wrong. Advertising is an emotional industry. Everybody ought to have fun. If you are not having fun then you are getting screwed. — Lou Centlivre, Lord & Thomas (1985)
I think people want information. They don't get it by advertising. Say you're buying a tape deck. Well you're up against it— especially if you've read the ads. A double entendre headline. Nice photo. But no real meat in the ad. Because the people who did the ad don't think, you really want to know. Advertising people argue that it is good to make it simple. But that's not the point. People want to know. Advertising ought to give them the information they need. — H Krone, Doyle Dane Bernbach (1984)	To make our creative effort from good to great, we add a healthy measure of our magic ingredient. We inject that absolutely necessary, positively critical element – style. — Bob Fearon, Fearon/GBA Group (1985)

The above ideas are self-explanatory. The following specs down below showcase the distinctions, which draw correlations between leftbrain and right brain. They highlight on the tangible reciprocity. These interrelated angles are placed to clarify the points further.

Left Brain		**Right Brain**
Unique product	⟷	Parity product
High involvement product	⟷	Low involvement product
Intangible product	⟷	Tangible product
High ticket sale	⟷	Low ticket sale

This above comparison is intended as a thought provoker and not as an infallible guide. Makers of high ticket computers, software and engineering goods require sophisticated technology but have often tried the right brain communication, contrary to the above diagram. Reeves argument states that, every product should use a unique selling proposition (USP), to fight for a share of the mind. As an example, one product named 'Coors Beer', in its commercial in the year 1984 showed a spokesperson standing in the 'Snow of Colorado Mountains' explaining that snow provides 'Coors' with unique pure water. This in fact is a visual and verbal USP.

The fact of the matter is that, there are 'four ways' of advertising, not the 'two ways' to do advertising. These four ways are left brain, right brain, whole brain and no brain. The above example of 'Coors ad' is an example of whole brain advertising. One other example of advertising is 'The first supper for a good solid start'. This is probably the artistic ad person's clever take-off from the concept of Da Vinci's 'The Last Supper' painting. This was designed for selling Mead Johnson's Pablum baby cereal. In this advertising picture composition, instead of 12 disciples, there are 12 babies in high chairs. It looks similar, appealing and funny. This advertiser did not consider having an impact on the new parents. What has been said about the product or company is not of great interest to new parents. This is an example of 'no brain advertising'. This is an example of suggesting ways and views to crystallize. For services, engineering goods, intangibles and for the emotion driven business, the trends dictate the idea that there is a special need for 'left brain communication'. In this case, words and skilled words are employed with the certain techniques to coach and groom the minds. This is also applicable for the 'video buffs', who claim that 'left brain' is the only answer. Leftbrain finds place in beer parlours, coffee bars, choices of cars and tasting cigarettes, etc.

However, right brain finds known products of low complexity for the users. It is sometimes mechanical in nature. Until products or services are sufficiently embossed in the public mind, it cannot create a favourable climate for the customer. All the prospective customers should be provided with

adequate information, stark facts, detailed explanations, reasonable rationale and emotional persuasion. Eventually, Calkins affirmed to the world in the first half of the 20th century that 'faith in appealing to the whole brain, when possible and wherever appropriate, is the most desirable'. Whole brain stimulation was ultimately the key to influence.

Interpretations on the ideas, thoughts and concepts have been innumerable in the domain of brain. They emanated with multi dimensional issues. It is product dependent and prospect hunted. In fact, top media consultant Maneloveg wrote, 'We are presently in a promotionally oriented marketing mode, where a more knowledgeable, more discerning public will wisely, calmly wait for a purchase, until the market puts it on sale or offers a deal. What we are seeing is the slow, inexorable erosion of brand loyalty for many product categories. The public is now selecting from the numerous product lines, it senses all as similar, with price break being the sole determining factor.' Today therefore, a substantial number of product managers are faced with problems in achieving sales targets that are below the planned objectives. Hence, they are gradually turning to a 'series of short-term promotional actions that move the product' with a lower profit margin. This is a kind of catch-22 situation that perpetuates the heralding dilemma that emerges from the crater of cut-throat competition.

Unfortunately, much of the advertising communication of the current times, particularly in the domestic marketing community, has become an unplanned culprit born out of the situation. The larger part of the problem is due to the abrupt, unescorted and zigzag communication plans. It is happening only because, the media houses are not reading the public mind correctly and transparently. It could be due to the reason that today's educated consumers want to learn more about a product that has been promoted and not less on the product in any case. Information curtailment is treated a crime against seller and customer.

❑ Strengths and Limitations of Advertisement

'Advertising creates an acceptable environment, and we push the products through the pipeline, but promotions ring the cash register'— goes the age-old adage. For this statement, there are a number of reasons that are stated below:

- A new product launch needs all the help it could optimize, including an aggressive promotion. Promotion can entice the curious customers into a trial and can pressure the retailers for shelf space in the shopping malls and kirana stores.
- Short-term gains are no less important, but not at the cost of long-term objectives. The product management system tends to support short-term gains and profits.
- A good increase in the company share points due to good promotion can make the product manager look like a hero in the short run. However, in the long run, when normal share of markets and profits per category decline because of over promotion, the product manager may not be there to receive the blame because he or she has moved onto a better job. Job switching is a phenomenon.
- Retailers expect it and demand it, even though it may accomplish very little in the longer run.
- It is hard to resist the 'defensive coupons' when one's competitor gives 'sales' in its stores. However, what is important is that 'who wins a sales promotion war'.
- The company may not have done long-term analysis needed to determine, what an over-promotion is doing to its brand shares and case profits.

❑ Sales Promotion can be Productive

There are a good number of possibilities for making the sales promotion more productive and accountable. Often however, sales promotion might not get the respect that is desired. Despite the huge sum of funds being spent on merchandizing and sales promotion domestically, they might continue to be treated as such. Most marketers see the promotional measures as not being quite integrated into the marketing programmes and also not consistent with the strategic thrust expected. However, in transnational marketing where the field is not yet promoted, we find the opportunity to beckon.

One method of assessing the efficiency of the promotion can be done through the testing of direct responses. Better testing of direct responses are done by measuring the 'comparative efficiency of the media source' or through the 'promotional effort over one another'. It is done out and out through a comparative study undertaken. This direct response testing is quick and inexpensive, reality based, potentially secret and can lead to database building.

❑ Effect of Coupon Promotion

The phase when coupon system of promotion was introduced consumed a lot of foreign exchange. By 1985, manufacturers were distributing over 180 billion coupons a year, with over 2,000 pieces per household. Coupon redemption rose to nearly US$7billion up, 75 percent over the previous four years. However, this was not a good practice as it eroded brand loyalty and focussed more on loyalty to coupons eventually cheating the consumers of quality products. The wastefulness of FSI couponing left no other way to shift the 'existing consumers' from that of the 'new prospects'. Electronic couponing was a further wrong step, in the wrong direction, as its appeal was for the 'current users only'. Subsequently, a new invention was super CFB couponing.

The divided the sales promotion into two kinds of activities. They were consumer franchise building (CFB) and non-CFB. In this case, CFB effectively registered the brand's unique advantages or attributes in the consumer's mind, through brand-image advertising, store demonstrations, recipes in service magazine ads and samplings, etc. It ruled out much of the couponing done through FSIs. However, non-CFB couponing candidly accelerated the buying decisions by reducing the price temporarily. It also happened by adding extraneous value or obtaining trade support with a trade deal or allowance. When the CFB/non-CFB ratio fell below 50–55 per cent, the profits almost always declined.

Min–max marketing promotion

Min–max marketing worked when the company believed that couponing the present customers and non-users is a valuable part of the promotion activity. In a variation of targeting the non-users, the company can mail to users as well as non-users, but send the former, a lower value coupon. It is also possible to combine it with high ticket couponing for high-priced items.

❑ Sampling Promotion

Sampling is one of the least expensive methods of promotion. It has been seen that, significant sales increases are possible through sampling. This yields an expression of increased desire for the product, engineered by the free sample. By virtue of charging a nominal sum for the postage and service handling, through doing multiple split-run tests to find the best way to maximize response, the company might be able to do free-sample advertising. It is close to being self-a nortizing.

This maxi–marketing approach is the super CFB to free sample advertisers. It involves preparation of six or eight different advertisements. Printing each on light card stock with a detachable business reply card on the flap, intermixing all six or eight uniformly and running them in a representative section of the target market publications is important. Then roll out the winning ad. A reprint of it would not only go with all free samples, but to all prospects.

Premium promotions

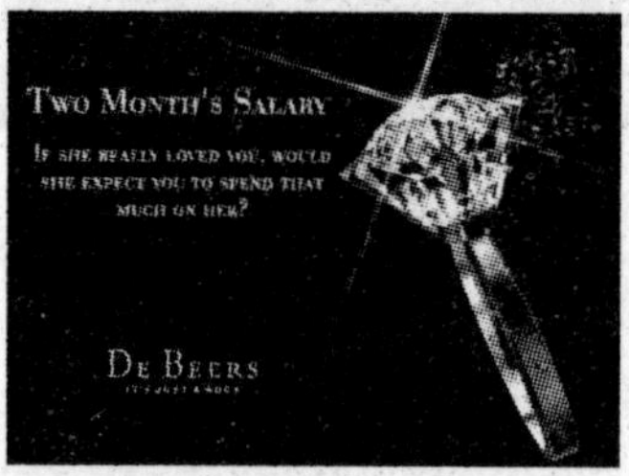

Premium promotions are prone to the ills of sales promotion. Good premium promotion does the following:

- Strengthen the image of the brand's unique benefit or positioning or personality;
- Encourage continued use of the brand;
- Stimulate the widest possible response from the public, especially from the real prospects;
- Related companies or brands can be jointly promoted;
- Involves the direct response multiple split-run tests for different premiums or single self-contained test in the same advertisement for different premiums;
- Test different price points for a self-liquidating premium via direct response. This might strike gold. The company might find that it could charge enough to cover the premium and the advertising that accompanies the offers. In addition, this might lead to free advertising for the premium;
- Premiums should be continuous, to be earned partially or entirely by continued use of the companies' product.

Sweepstakes promotion

Sweepstakes has been discussed before.

Send more information

Company sales promotion is a part of the broader function of activation. It is for the advertising audience to take up some immediate steps. The other principal means of activation is that of stimulating inquiries, inviting requests for more information, exciting them to ask more and more. This tool is cost effective and can accomplish more. Use of this device can:

1. Monitor the comparative effectiveness of latest advertising copies.
2. Rank and rate the value of each advertising medium used.
3. Give a chance to expose the people who are potentially the best customers.
4. It is capable of doing as much advertising for two-three times without multiplying the cost.
5. Start an in-house database of solid gold prospects, which the company can continue to cultivate.

In totality, it can be said that, if the company is aiming with tens of thousands of dollars for doing promotion and profit, to make a 'high ticket sale' or 'series of sales', in a transnational marketing. The company is not selling a parity product in an over-promoted field, then all these thoughtfully crafted, well integrated sales promotion and activation can turn the consumer awareness into blazing action. The very tools of direct marketing and direct response advertising can kick-start in the right direction and confirm that the company promotion is on the right track. The entire process of implementation has to be well planned, designed and synthesized to enter the market smoothly.

❑ Maximized Synergy: Double Duty Advertising and Marketing

Ways are innumerable but definite ways make hay. Similarly, there is a typical way to maximize the power of transnational market advertising. It can be done without adding a rupee to advertising budget. Contextual understanding is important. There is scope to add 'extra valuc', which can be extracted by arranging items to activate synergy in a single advertising effort. It shall optimize, in this process, the accomplishment of different jobs at a time. In order to do this, it has to look into the following aspects in detail. Here are some of the ways to do this:

- It can combine awareness and sales promotion together.
- It can promote two or more channels of distribution.
- It can do good and do well for better satisfaction. Advertising the brand name can associate the company with a cause and concern of the society.
- It can 'sell an event' while 'selling a product'.
- It can mutually share the advertising cost, with another advertiser. Co-branding is an economic way of making better impact in people.
- It can serve and support one medium,, while marketing in another. Gaming can be possible.
- It can promote any brand while promoting a separate profit centre. One can use brand advertising to support a new profit centre and then use this new profit centre to support that brand.
- One can build a database while building the brand simultaneously. It is important for one another.
- Company can use its brand name to sell at a premium and similarly use the premium to sell its brand name. They are both helpful for each other.
- One can advertise the brand while advertising the distribution channel.
- It can support the transnational culture, cause and the element of styles multiple.
- It can also bond, bridge and tie the product with an established transnational programme or company. It shall add fillip to the product for sales to happen.
- It can also use the marketing success in one market to uncover another.
- It can maintain a transnational marketing rules, code and mode.
- It can provide maximum information, tie-up and display material.

Maximization can happen through multiplying the factor effects in creating the advertising programme. Single method can create impact but more than one, rightly assimilated, can create magic. In the given context, 2+2 in advertising is proved to be more than 4.

❑ Maximized Linkage can Carry Business

Association, groupings and linkages in the market places, in all the spheres of life have become paramount. In the increasingly diversified and expanded market place, functions of mass advertising and for that matter marketing are destined to change. Act for change can be the name of the game. It shall have to become fluid and malleable like the size and shape of amoeba.

In fact, instead of trying to awe and influence 'everybody' in the media, the proper target function could be to attract, interest, identify, get together, gather and communicate, with the existing similar few buyers selling the same type of products, that are comparable. These selected few are the targeted few in the STP. They are the objective of advertising, who are the immediate prospects for advertisement. In fact, what happens next becomes important. It is as important as what has gone by before.

Curiosity of these focused minority section, which has been targeted, is converted into a 'firm-buying intention'. The additional advertising, pointed aids and promotion of equal quality of promotional measures create it. These are sent usually directly by 'mail to the interested prospect'. This form of marketing is called 'linkage'. It links the upfront advertising to the sale, reinforced with additional arguments and benefits, which the up-front advertising did not have the space, time and/or money to include. It is linked by virtue of an asserted entry into the prospective buyers.

This follow-up process that is 'given a more serious attention and funding' becomes an important and integral part of the marketing strategy. It is a nifty style of approach, which is essential in the case of smart transnational companies. These are often neglected by the companies but are ultimately inescapable for doing business across the boundaries of nations. Maxi-marketing restores this scorned Cinderella to the throne. The lack of attention to follow up the above approaches results in the following inadequacies. They are mainly:

1. Nobody in the company is 'in charge' of loving the customer prospect;
2. In the case of a unsold dress designed with a fad, nobody likes to know as to how or where, the dress/product is to be advertised;
3. Techno-products, not being able to learn easily are difficult to sell and make use of.

Building bridges and creating linkages for the promotion of products/services are an integral and vital part of transnational marketing currently. This is inevitable because, linkage is born out of demassification and

demystification. Linkages reduce the wasteful spending of massive marketing expenditure, which are usually and lavishly incurred on the prospects and non prospects alike. It saves and permits to channelize and direct some of allocated and budgeted marketing expenditure to connect, link, cultivate and convert the prime prospects easily. They do not have to beckon the company telling 'I am here'.

Research has shown that, contrary to popular belief, the power and profitability of designing the upfront advertising to support the linkage follow-up is much greater than the other way around. Empathizing with the customer through linkage has no substitute. It baptizes and converts the interested prospects into users and long-term customer kings. Eventually there are mainly 'five structural components' used in building good linkage with the marketplaces. They are:

Activation

Activation is integral to marketing and planning for advertising. This first step is to engage the prospect in a dialogue form exchanging views. It is a two-way communication. Advertising has to provide some reason for the interested prospect to respond to an offer. It provides the requisite information to find it, know a sample, a premium and the discount, etc.

Information

Information is warm, friendly and persuasive. Detailed information about the product is important. It is about all the things the company would like to tell the prospect.

Persuasion

Persuasion is important, information alone is not enough. Ideally, the advertisement should 'handle the reader by hand' and lead him emotionally from his present problem to the ultimate benefit.

Propulsion: Propulsion is to impel circumstantially. Direct marketers have learnt the hard realities of life. They learned that 'one of the greatest obstacles of success in sales is the human tendency of inertia and procrastination'. Propulsion converts the prospect to take a decision. It converts 'sometime' into 'right now'. Transnational direct marketers use, employ and put something in the hand of the prospect that propels him to act in a positive manner for striking a purchase. Examples could be an early-bird discount given for marketing a brand.

Consummation

In direct marketing, they try to make it as easy as possible to ensure an order being placed. Great care is exercised in designing a clear, simple, inviting and friendly order form. The retail equivalent of this is the sympathetic sales clerk who enables the things to happen coolly. However, the four main 'common failings' in the follow-up literature are:

- No letter/poor kind of letter;
- Typography or printing that is hard to read;
- Slow and apathetic response;
- Unclear or inadequate purchasing alternatives.

❑ Linkage Assessment Grid

Linkage assessment grid is important to evaluate the performances of linkages done. This is very useful in helping the company determine its stance and capabilities. It facilitates and ascertains as to when to do, to what extent it is to be done and whether to use the power of linkage. It absolutely relates to what the company is marketing. The grid's horizontal poles represent high ticket and low-ticket sales, the vertical poles, high involvement and low involvement. Details of the aspects have been delineated in the grid given below as at Fig. 6.1.

High Ticket	A. Most promising area for linkage advertising Example: Automobiles	B. Promising area for linkage advertising Example: Cheese and Wines	**Low Ticket**
	C. Possible area for linkage advertising Example: VCR and Fridge	D. Least likely area for linkage use Example: Paper towels	

Fig. 6.1 Linkage Assessment Grid High Involvement

Low Involvement

In the above grid all, the aspects are discussed and identified in their perspectives in the quadrants. Application of the 'principles of linkage' is seen in the boxes and is explained below:

- It is most desirable in the 'high ticket, high involvement' quadrant cited as (A).
- It is also desirable with careful financial analysis, in the 'low ticket high involvement' quadrant as at (B).
- It is possible but less likely in the 'high ticket, low involvement' quadrant as at (C).

- It is least likely in the 'low involvement' quadrant as at (D), with the possible exception of marketers who sell a number of related products.

In a cumulative calculation, it is seen that, the best of the awareness advertising currently intended for transnational marketing does not hammer on the prospects and non prospects alike. It cannot be a simple method of laying stress on all the aspects equally. It takes the first step in a continuum of communication, which ultimately turns the interested prospects into one-time buyers and then into customers who purchase for a longer period of time.

❑ Maximized Sales and Strategic Intents

The thought of too many marketing strategies for pushing the products into the market are usually halted with the completion of a sale. However, the strategies are slowly becoming sequential and are more engaged in continuity. Alternative strategies are becoming pivotal and paramount depending on the situation of the market.

Earlier, time and money were not invested for creating a special relationship with the company's best customers. No efforts were bestowed for making the customers loyal, for chasing through repeat purchase. Most of the companies, whether they are selling goods or services, failed to calculate and record the lifetime value (LTV) of a customer.

However, today in the age of competition, marketing moves have gone full circle in their quest of finer aspects of advancement in catching the customer prey. It has travelled incidentally from the person-to-person selling (see Fig. 6.2) usually done by the erstwhile village baker, to selling bakery products in the impersonal departmental stores. Impersonal selling has intruded into the shelves of shopping malls. Mass merchandizing by the giant supermarket are now going back, once again, to the highly personalized customer need. It has come up on a vast scale, meeting the demand of all kinds of customer capacity.

❑ Database Marketing

The rough calculation of long-term benefits, emerging out of the repeated sales, generated from repeated advertising no more exists. These benefits are

today being reviewed, as market share, mindshare and are quantified from the company assets. Inadvertently, now-a-days in the latest method a new kind of corporate asset is emerging. The emerging aspects are the customer database and the computerized compilation of the database, about each single buyer, which can be readily accessed to increase revenues and profits. This new asset base does not replace the share of market, nor minimize its importance. This customer database is slowly beginning to take its place alongside the market share, as a full-fledged partner in the maximization of corporate sales. Onslaught of the supercomputer has made this easier, less and less costly. This customer database has become a new private market opportunity, which can promote additional sales, cross promote, explore new channels of distribution, test new products, add new ventures, add new avenues to revenues and build lifetime customer loyalty. Fig. 6.2 below displays the ideal method of the evolution of database marketing.

Particulars	1870s	1970s	1980s	1990s
Appeal to prospects	Tangible product	Intangible service	Value-added benefits	Periodically replenished staples
Example	Catalogues and merchandize flyers	Money market funds	Frequent flyer programmers	Home delivery of dog food
Use of customer database	Repeat mailings–additional offers	Monthly statement cross-sell other funds	Record of activity–customerized plans and fares	Monthly statement – cross-sell of other income delivery offers

Fig. 6.2 Evolution of Database Marketing

The above formulation has a scientific intention to understand the kinesics of marketing adventures and advents, searching for business. By virtue of adding the power and prowess of a customer database, to the existing power of mindshare and or product brand in transnational marketing, the company communication can maximize the development of company's overall sales and profits. This can happen through the five important ways of approach. They are:

1. Maximized repeat sales;
2. Maximized customer loyalty;
3. Maximized cross-promotion;
4. Maximized line extension;
5. Maximized success of new ventures.

The above ways can be examined one by one, based on the antecedents that they entail for discussion. The aspects are empirical and meaningful and explained with examples.

Maximized repeat sales

As indicated before, the share of the mind as an aspect alone, leads the repeat sales to happen. Once the product is positioned in the mind, the product is bound to sale in a spree, purchased by the consumer. For example, if a customer likes the first packet of Kellogg's Raisin Bran Cereal , he is predisposed and determined to buy another when the packet is exhausted. If the Kellogg's product brand buyers are captured by their names and addresses in a customer database, they are again being sent with more of promotional literatures. These, as a result, will stimulate the customer to chose their products or services of the brand, over similar other products more frequently. They have three other basic ways to do, which are given below:

- Can establish ongoing reward programmes for enticing the customer base and penchant new customers;
- Can give preferred treatment to the best customers, statistics reveal that usually 80 percent of the business comes from 20 percent of the customers;
- Can offer custom-tailored special offers or benefits for the special segments.

Maximized customer loyalty

There is an old Latin maxim **'Qui non proficit, deficit'** which means 'he who does not advance, go backwards'. In the field of marketing, the opposite may come true. If the brand is not losing the customers that it already has, if the brand can maintain and deepen the loyalty of the customer, then it can become victorious and come up with flying buyers. All these can be accomplished through methods—sales promotion or direct marketing. It cannot happen through a single method. This is called maxi-marketing. One another way to sustain the customer loyalty, through a customer database is to set up a programme that will frequently re-promote the company's image and position. This way it can ideally get its customers and throttle other advertisers to pay for it.

Maximized cross-promotion

A company, which has a number of different products, services or divisions, under its roof, can use its combined customer database to introduce its other products to other customers. It can happen simultaneously by calling many opportunities, along with the one type of purchase that it has been into so far. If one product has a market appeal, other products of the same brand shall also appeal the customer base. A combined customer database is difficult to compile. Most of the business houses are trying for the same. Many large FIs are attempting to combine all their accounts into one accessible cross–promotional master list. This takes a whole lot of a time to develop, but once the database is achieved, it becomes a priceless asset for the organization. Only thing required is an up-to-date data, which is developed from time to time.

Maximized line extension

This can be of immense importance and is worthwhile for companies to make business. This mindshare can lead to a diversified growth of the company business. One path to diversified growth is line extension. As an example, if the people in the market like the Kellogg's commercial breakfast duly packed, they are favourably inclined to buy 'rice cereal'. Mindshare shall fasten them to similar brands in the product category. Hence, possessing a customer database and putting it to good use can also give a powerful boost/bonus to the existing demand. If the company comes to know, 'who all and where all are the best customers' it can jolly well spell out 'You loved our corn cereal and therefore you may like the rest'. The company can ask them to try rice cereal along with the corn cereal. It can trigger and belch business with a 30 percent coupon discount to get started. An interesting application of customer database to the line extension can be done by putting the existing famous brand name on a new product. It can be successfully launched without having to fight for shelf space in the usual retail outlets. All outlets and kirana stores look for the branded products.

Maximized success of new ventures

Launching of new ventures is important in the market competition. One of the most important uses of customer database is launching of new profit centres and new concepts, apart from updating the prevailing ones. Massive database provides all the innovative prospects for the entrepreneurs to galvanize the need for the satiating products and services. Even smaller database can help to launch new ventures for providing facilities for the definite customer segments. Hard-core special decisions evolving out of the database can yield benefits for the customers to profit. This immediacy can overcome the slow process of building business and can dissuade the battling outside sources of business, which are getting underway.

When companies are inclined for selling their products to the public through the wholesalers, dealers, agents and retailers, they search for need-based locations. In the absence of data, they become interested in direct marketing, which is a costly affair. It is employed for ensuring an asserted entry. Devoid of the data begets fear of the stumbling blocks, even the fear of being alienated from retailers. It appears scary for the business to go into about of competition.

However, with each passing year, as corporate ownership, distribution channels and retailing chains become more complexly structured, this fear becomes increasingly less. One solution to this problem concerned is to develop an entirely different product line, for direct marketing. Customer database can provide the foundation for building, creating and erecting new enterprises.

❑ Maximized Distribution

List of needed identifications, names of persons and agencies are the sources of power to sell products and services. A catalogue of names in the hands of merchants enables them to spot the best of locations in all nations. It can gear up and start retail outlets, supply the non stores and store merchants. It can prompt the business player to combine the store and the non-store distribution and can provide them with customers, the very first day. Database can enlighten a store merchant for maximizing distribution. They provide springboards for commissioning of profit centres in high rent locations, spaces and places to run the trade. Distribution channels cascade into levels of distribution, in accordance to the length and breadth of product requirement. Channel partners can even be co-created for reinventing the modus operandi of the business to gallop. Losses and dereliction in the line of distribution are impending lacunas in the allocation of products. It is by far one of the biggest of the problems faced by people. The ingredients that are immensely necessary for maximizing distribution are as follows:

- Need money for the circulation of products/services, and expansion of business to happen easily;
- Need dedicated stocks in the warehouse, flow of requisite periodic bulk, continuous flow, maintained inventory and timely filling of procurement orders/indents;
- Need the use of third-party credit for securitization of transactions;
- Need exchange of mailing lists for attaining reciprocal knowledge of the consignment;
- Need the usage of phone no, fax no., e-mail id and video conferencing, etc., for placing orders and receipt of the same;
- Need separate fulfilment of facilities for catalogue orders;

- Need different merchandize direction for the catalogue, emphasizing unique mail order items, rather than following the department-by-department, grade-by-grade approach in retail;
- Need the use of outside expertise for list maintenance and merge/purge.

In a given situation, when the company originates, distributes and circulates products/services, the list of customer names that already exist, along with the additional names added to the existing customer database, help the company broaden its distribution line and widen the geographical distribution. Moreover, the names belonging to the linking chains of mediators or intermediaries also become a source of marketing power to the company. As per requirement, the company can enhance and prune the prevalent channels of distribution, by shortening or opening up new channels. Channel changes are subject to the demand distribution. The power of distribution can penetrate into the untrodden zones of geographical pockets. It educates the customer, it dupes deceptively and it invades the market. It plays many roles clad with many hues. The power of selling is the best way to distribution. One of the ways of the power of distribution is depicted below.

Power of Selling in Distribution

90 percent	**10 percent**
I. Go to the dealer (Here is the name and address)	One may order directly
50 percent	**50 percent**
II. Order from your dealer	Mail coupons/ orders directly from us
10 percent	**90 percent**
III. Also available at retail	Mail coupon/order directly to us.

Thus, 'name' is the 'name of the game' in the 'game of distribution'. If any businessperson wishes to make effective and operate through efficient distribution, he/she should think of gathering, collecting and compiling names. He should classify the saved names of prospective customers and use them for calls. In the transnational market, this strategy can pull new customers directly to the distribution processes and/or push those clamouring for what the company have for sale. The company can even afford to sell the enchanted customers through the centralized depots, through sales agents, distant retail locations and so forth.

CONCLUSION

'Maxi transnational marketing' is a new direction in the field of transnational marketing, in which the prospects and the potential best customers are identified, located, cultivated, persuaded, motivated and converted in a way that maximizes sales and profits'. In simple terms, 'maxi-marketing is a continuum that forms and constitutes the likely prospects into long-term customers'. Nevertheless, conclusive interpretations shall logically justify the discussed aspects of 'transnational maxi-marketing. It has multi-pronged dimensions to market access, to maximize sales and enhance the level of the acceptance of product. There are certain chief characteristics and features that are common, which are embedded in the statements. Few comprehensive definitions of maxi-marketing are blended with all the characteristics that are described above. These are encapsulated in gist, which essentially explains the impact of maxi-marketing as a strategic step in the world of management. Each step in this process is logically linked to the next for creating a rhythm. The concise, brief and creamy steps are:

- Company targets prospects in each of the markets and across markets, who are clones of the best customers, in the companies collected customer database.
- Company strives to trace, discover and find the customers communicating effectively with them in the most likely and sought-after media promotion. Media help the companies to reach the pockets of customers. It could be for selling contact lens to the 40 plus for the cataract or clippers for the physically challenged people. It could be to avoid the exorbitant cost of imports by the falcons of business, supplying them with products at socially least price with fewer margins.
- Company appeal to the prospective customers for striking a deal with the whole brain or the left-brain, which is acknowledged for intelligence. This 'whole brain advertising' essentially invites a prompt response, taking them one-step closer to the sale. Sale is a phenomenon that can be provoked in a created environment, but to retain the customer quality is the key.
- Company designs the sales promotion strategy and follows up through advertising activities, for advancing into the strange corridors of business, battling wars for financial gains. Promotional communication and advertising follow-ups automatically will deepen into building and bridging relationship with the customers, not just making a sale happen.

- Company obtains the names, addresses and other requisite details of the customer prospects and feeds them into the company customer database. This database becomes the company's private marketing medium for planning the present and future moves.

- Company can maximize sales volumes through channels. Through the database, the company can begin to design and develop additional sales volume. It can be done through the study of the database by opening, if required even different channels of distribution, doing channel partnership and other modes that can be unfurled.

- The entire database directs the events that follow, shooting for maximizing distribution. This continuum adds to become much more than the sum of its parts and is not an arithmetic sum. It is because of this, the continuum makes possible a single unifying marketing strategy. Bits and parts in the systems treated in separation have become old. The piecemeal approach to marketing, selling, advertising, promotion, public relations, distribution, pricing, costing and all other aspects of communicating with the consumer is today replaced by a holistic new approach. It is done by involving addressability of the needs and wants of potential, demanding and actual customers. It is also done with accountability and assessment of cost-effectiveness in every step in the way. How to begin is important.

- This method of designing, calls for framing of a questionnaire factorizing the facets. The facets that shall be incorporated in the questionnaire are given below.

❑ Transnational Maxi-marketing Assessment Questions

The typical questions that are salient to the study of the above have been outlined below for the understanding of readers. They are a generic kind of questions, which need modification depending on the product, environment and issues. The questions are:

- How many different types of targeted prospects for the product or service can the manager identify and describe? What are the most efficient new media to reach and sell to them?

- How much advertising to non prospects does the company estimate in each type of media that the company uses? How can this percentage be reduced?

- Does the company marketing appeal or offer, which separates the prospects from the non prospects and the hot prospects from the warm prospects? If not, how could it be made?

- Has the company graded its media expenditure with a performance index, based on direct response?
- Is the company able to compare with the its exact public relations to the different approaches, in the company awareness advertising, using a reallife media environment?
- Can the company convince the person sitting next to you at a dinner party of the merit or superiority of the product or service the company is marketing? Does the present marketing do as good a job?
- Does the company's current marketing ask prospects to do something more specific than predispose the target audience to making a purchase some day? What can you add for activation?
- Has the company tested more than one creative approach for getting the public to respond to the company's current sales promotion offer?
- How do you know that the sales promotion your company is using is the most response-producing and brand-building approach possible?
- How much of the company advertising does double duty? Can you think of ways to make the company marketing do more than one job?
- What will you do, if you get many pages of advertising in the issues of a magazine without having to pay for more than one of them? Could you or your advertising agency find ways to fill those pages that could increase your sales? What would happen if you prepared those additional pages and mailed them to prime prospects who responded to your single page ad?
- If a TV station offered, you time for a 30 thirty minutes commercial message for the price of 30 seconds, then how would you use it?
- What will you do, if you prepared a thirty minutes commercial and tested it on cable or via a VCR cassette? If it is an offer what do, you do? How might you increase distribution of the thirty minutes commercial at little or no cost?
- When people see the company's commercial message or read the ad. do they get to know what to do about it? Do they know how to get in touch with the company concerned, if they have questions or want more information? When they get in touch, do you save the name? If you save the name, how well and how often do you contact the enquirer to build sales and loyalty?
- Is the company's country sale adaptable to third party or are the syndicated sales done by mail and phone? Is this potential being

exploited to build alternative distribution systems remaining out of sight of the company's present dealers?

- How often/far does the company help its retailers make more use of direct mail to promote the product or service? Can they manage to do by themselves?
- Does the company save the names and addresses of all the prospects and customers who communicate with the company by mail or phone? If so, are these names being entered in a computer database? If they are being put on computer, are they being correctly formatted for a wide variety of promotional and analytical uses?
- If the company has the customer and prospect names and addresses in the computer, how are they currently being used? What possible additional uses can the company think of? How could the company enrich the knowledge of each of these individuals by overlaying the existing list with the outside list/data? Does the company do anything to make them feel specially appreciated?
- If the company wishes to know 15 things about each customer in the database, what 15 things would you choose to know? Is the company database set up duly calibrated and adoptive to add new information and have it easily accessible for future use? How could the company make profitable use of the information?
- Does the company's direct-response marketing also create a demand at the retail level? Is the company able to benefit from this demand? If not, is there some other way through which you could create a demand at the retail level?
- Have you and your associates recently brainstormed for new ideas, for the additional products that you could sell to the existing customer database?
- Has the company overlooked any promising possibilities for profitable third party sales of its product or services? See how many can be listed.
- Can the company define and describe the image it presents to the public? Is there any way by which you could improve or sharpen your company image, while pursuing direct-marketing goals?
- Are there any new kinds of media promotion, which you should be testing, which you have been overlooking? It could be like video, card decks, FM radio, 30 minute commercial on cable, telemarketing and so forth.

- How do you customize your product or service to increase its appeal to different groups of prospects and customers? How would you have them achieved by conveying this news to them?
- Can the company benefit from the increased promotion of name-brand merchandize, backed by coop and money allowance?
- Is your company doing enough of the direct-response testing, which has historically given the company the kind of business, as a unique advantage over other forms of selling?
- What is keeping the company from using the transaction data in the files to identify prime retail locations for your products or services? How would you open up distribution—within existing channels or on your own?

These are a few of the brain-teasing questions that invoke a company to rethink on the business. Questions are different in different environments. They have their genuineness in identifying their slots of knowledge.

Summary

Maximized accountability has all along become the ultimate objective of any promotional strategy which is intricate and intrinsic.

Advertisements visualized for a customer segment have tangible results on sales. Stronger the brand image, customer loyalty becomes volatile and is dependent on the product quality. Theme and contents of all advertisement campaigns have to be sensible to the customer choice preference.

Indeed, the psycho-somatic aspect of brain of the buyer plays a key role. Left-hemisphere and right-hemisphere of brain respond ably different in the mental state. Evolution of left brain and right brain advertising has been reckoned by the icons in the arena. The USP of product and advertisement have indelible imprints in the mind-tree. Advertisement for influence has its limitations, in spite of the application of cutting-edge ads.

The grid's and provocative assessment questions provide ideas for scanning the viewpoints, making things believable.

The chapter has ample open-ended rebounding ideas to reflect back on.

QUESTIONS FOR DISCUSSION

Q. 1. Evaluate and discuss the maxi-transnational marketing model, as a paradigm for business.

Q. 2. Give an analysis of the modern domestic marketing, otherwise known as brand merchandizing or distribution. Illustrate, citing examples of situations in the organization.

Q. 3. What do you mean by maximized acccuntability and maximized awareness? How does advertisements intended for a target segment manoeuvre buying decisions in the customers? Illustrate.

Q. 4. How is estimated value of expenditure measured on sales? Discuses.

Q. 5. How does advertising campaign make maximized accountability? Analyse in the context of markets.

Q. 6. Critically examine the impact of advertising campaigns in the left brain and right brain. Explain the comments of seers in the subject.

Q. 7. Analyze the evolution process of statements offered by the seers in advertisement industry on the function of 'left brain and right brain'.

Q. 8. Under what conditions are correlations between left brain and right brain is utmost? Elaborate.

Q. 9. Do you think that products have USP? If yes, how? If no, why?

Q. 10. What are the strengths and constraints of advertisement? Describe the salient points.

Q. 11. Can sales promotion be productive? Elucidate on the promotion of couponing, min-max marketing, sampling, premiums and sweepstakes.

Q. 12. Identify the criteria that are responsible for maximized activation held due to advertising campaign. Illustrate.

Q. 13. What do you mean by maximized synergy? Discuss citing points.

Q. 14. Identify the ways for maximizing the synergy of transnational market advertising, without adding a rupee extra on a marketing budget. Elucidate the factors.

Q. 15. What are the 'five structured components' used in building good linkage with the market places? Elucidate.

Q. 16. Examine the linkage assessment grid for analysing the highs and lows of markets driven by advertisement.

Q. 17. What is the function of linkage assessment grid? Describe the aspects in the light of any business.

Q. 18. What is the function of database marketing? Describe the facets.

Q. 19. What do you mean by maximized distribution? Explain the necessary facets of maximized distribution.

Q. 20. Write five important questions for assessment of transnational maxi-marketing situations.

Q. 21. Write short notes.

(a) Left brain

(b) Right brain

(c) Maximized repeat sales

(d) Maximized customer loyalty

(e) Maximized cross-promotion

(f) Maximized line extension

(g) Maximized success of new ventures

(h) Personalized selling

(i) Maximized targeting

(j) Maximized media

(k) Repeat sales

(l) Customer loyalty

(m) Cross-promotion

(n) Share of mind.

Chapter 7

Planning for Transnational Marketing

LEARNING OBJECTIVES

After going through the chapter the reader should be able to:

1. Identify the main issues for planning the transnational marketing of public and private firms/companies.
2. Foresee future trends and schedule timelines as calculated objectives.
3. Recognize political risks and pressure for maintaining stability in business or foreign investments.
4. Analyse government actions that affect/influence transnational business planning.
5. Understand the criteria of country selection, considering market size, rate of annual inflation, fiscal scope, political will and market potential.
6. Interpret the factors of risk and possible antidotes for strategic strides for profit.

> *'Honest disagreement is often a good sign of progress'.*
>
> *— M K Gandhi*
>
> *'We are what we repeatedly do. Excellence therefore, is not an act but a habit'.*
>
> *— Aristotle*

Ascertain the phases of actions relevant to different countries that are negotiating a move. This may be done through engaging 'intermediate technology', assessing competitor's market, etc.

INTRODUCTION: THE APPROACH

One of the main issues faced by both public and private enterprises in planning their transnational marketing is concisely and forcibly summarized by Bertrand de Jouvenel in his book *L' Art de la conjecture* (1964). There he states: 'The great problem of our age is that we wish that things should change more quickly on the one hand and that things to come should be better known on the other'.

If this formidable challenge is to be met adequately, sufficient ability is required to foresee the trend of future events and their expected timing. In some cases even the skills to shape such events, or at least to influence them, have to be acquired. Moreover, there is the need to try to determine the part which is to be played, and the forces which have to be marshalled, to be able to play this part once it has been defined. On the transnational scene, where intricacy and complexity are often a multiple of what they are on the national scene, the preparation and execution of the required actions may prove to be of decisive importance. The aspect of timing is vital in this respect since 'being too early' might prove as costly as 'being too late'.

The essence of all transnational marketing planning can be summed up in one phrase: readiness at every stage of the activities. The greater the uncertainty to be faced, the more crucial this aspect of preparedness becomes. In these times when uncertainty in business seems greater than ever before, the plausible answer to this threat is to create sufficient flexibility. Such flexibility can be created in several areas of operations, the financial, the industrial or the marketing. The greater the expected uncertainty the greater the flexibility will prove to be.

As almost every branch of business has to acknowledge sooner or later that the flexibility needed to cope with every uncertainty is prohibitive in its cost, some compromise has to be reached. The compromise that is usually made is to learn to live with uncertainty, to try to recognize its effects as clearly as possible and to try to meet them with all economically viable means, both now and in the future.

POLITICAL RISK

The phrase 'political risk' covers the political pressures that influence three quite different activities—transfer, operations, ownership control—. All these can, in turn, be examined in the light of risks and social risks. This important, if rather simple, insight may well clear away some problems and misunderstandings.

It is curious that one writer who points this out then goes on to try to find a scheme for bringing the three different activities into a unified framework.

The political risks in a new venture can be quantified in terms which appraise probable political events and the consequential legal changes. Of course, the use of the words 'probable' and 'consequential' points to a problem of this whole subject; an attempt is being made to use numbers to clarify decision, but the numbers represent probabilities and are a guide to judgement not a substitute for it.

One popular recent method goes as follows: If the probable types of political interference are listed and the probabilities of their happening quantified, the present value of the adjusted cash flow produced by each possible situation can be worked out. From this, the possible gains and losses can clearly be seen and an informed decision can also be taken. One could add that this proposal provides the decision maker with a clear presentation in terms to which he is accustomed. The problem, as with so many of the methods, is that elaborate and apparently precise calculations are being made on a flimsy basis. The possibility of error in the weightage is high.

Nevertheless, an attempt has to be made as other schemes are more elaborate and not necessarily more reliable. Among these, there are proposals by Haner where he has suggested the use of Delphi method of consulting large panels of experts for assessing and reassessing a developing body of data. These produce a sophisticated body of economic forecasting which is but less sophisticated when it comes to political forecasting. The hazards of this are enormous but it is possible to bring together an evidence for a country, on a number of the subjects which influence political stability, and work out a scheme of probable future from the evidence assembled. These include short-term issues like the existence of neither a strong opposition nor an active guerrilla movement; medium-term issues like national, religious, racial or tribal antagonisms; and even longer-term issues like the existence of aggressive neighbours, the strategic position of the country, the known resources for development or the temperament of the people.

Table 7.1 is a proposal for assembling the characteristics. In the end the weightage placed on the chart for any given country must be subjective, and the further into the future, the more subjective will the weightage be. Nevertheless, much hard evidence can be collected to support them, and the criteria are framed with this in mind. Below the contrast between stability and instability are placed a number of options. It is naturally assumed that linking the characteristics to these options is even more unreliable but is, nevertheless, sometimes required. In the end, the limitation of risk is performed by bringing together a number of factors of which, forecasting is one. The choice of a less risky means of doing business, like licensing or management contract venture or the limitation of the term of the operation is another. The other means used is hedging which is commonly employed as a substitute for the other methods rather than as part of a package. No one goes quite so far as to say, 'Ignore the risks, and just make sure that every foreign investment is balanced by another'. But this is the import of much of the argument. One writer stresses that the greater risk is the lack of knowledge of the market and the environment. Enforced hedging is advocated, but in the light of market opportunities. The information requirements implicit in this discussion are considered later.

Table 7.1: A Selected List of Options for a Country and the Characteristics that may Influence Choice and Choice

Characteristics / Options	**Stable Political System**	**Opposition dedicated to Riot and Overthrow/ Guerrilla Movement**		**Religious, National, Racial or Trivial Antagonism**		**Strategic Position of Country**	**Aggressive Neighbours**	**Natural Resources**	**Temperament of People**
Stability									
Short									
Medium									
Long									
Instability									
Short									
Medium									
Long									
Dictatorship									
Military									
Right									
Centre									
Aligned to Russia									
Aligned to China									
Neutral									

Characteristics / Options	**Stable Political System**	**Opposition dedicated to Riot and Overthrow/ Guerrilla Movement**		**Religious, National, Racial or Trivial Antagonism**		**Strategic Position of Country**	**Aggressive Neighbours**	**Natural Resources**	**Temperament of People**
Democracy									
Single Party									
Two Party									
Multiparty									

Some Issues on Which Government Action Influences Transnational Business Planning

The role of the Government (Including that of state-owned enterprises)	**Selected Activities**
As a purchaser for	Construction Consultancy Defence Medical Supplies Office Equipment Transportation Equipment
As supplier of	The products of state-owned industries. The results of government research, statistical and other services.
As a competitor in	The products of state-owned industries. Consultancy
As a regulator of financial and business activities	Transfer of funds Regulations for founding and conducting businesses with their financial and management structures. Company registration, acquisition of property, contracts and so on.

The role of the Government (Including that of state-owned enterprises)	Selected Activities
As a regular of trade	Import and export controls, competition, legislation, price regulations, consumer protection, industry specific regulations, e.g., drugs and medicines.
As a raiser of revenue	Taxation on, for example; Profits Capital gains Machinery and equipment, payroll withholding tax tariffs and other duties.

GUIDELINES FOR A TRANSNATIONAL INVESTMENT STRATEGY

The last section assumed a company with most of its investment at home looking abroad for fresh sources of supply and new markets. This section starts from the assumption that a company is investing widely. The whole tenor of this study is that the different activities need to be looked at together by the planners; but they are considered separately here for convenience in order to build up a satisfactory set of criteria.

In considering transnational planning it is possible to ask a number of questions. For example: 'This company will have X resources available during the period under review, what proportion of these should be made available abroad?' and 'This company will have X resources available for the foreign side of the business during the period under review, should these be divided between regions and countries?' leaving aside for a moment whether these are the right questions, they are often asked and in many different ways.

The answers to the first question vary along a spectrum which, at one end, contains decisions committing all resources to the home market with an occasional export sale to use some surplus. Halfway along the spectrum is a company which determines that 50 percent of each year's investment is to be placed abroad. At the far end, is the company that decides it has reached the limit of expansion in its own country and that all the effort in sales and investment will in future be placed aboard. This limit may arise for a number of reasons: these include all those discussed earlier in this chapter from reassessing sources of supply, through matching the needs of customers, to the tapping of fresh sources of technical and management talent.

There are some disadvantages in being manoeuvred into either end of the spectrum of possible decisions; for instance, almost any transnational company has reasons for continuing to strengthen its home base. In the middle of the spectrum there are secure positions but there are also many ways of missing opportunities. Some arise from weaknesses in the planning process. The most common reasons for failure are:

Failure due to Lack of Effective Planning

- Cash flow problems in parent or subsidiary or both.
- Inadequate control system, producing a lack of reliable information at the head office.
- Anticipated increase in market did not materialize.
- Another subject which might have been included is a failure to recognize the impact of a venture on the total business, a typical error of planning.

Other problems could be listed, but these may aptly be called the killer snags. If the cash flow forecasts, the information coming back and the market research are too unreliable, something is almost sure to go wrong.

Table 7.2: Criteria for Country Selection

Size of market as measured by:

(a) Total population.

(b) The wealth of population in gross domestic product per head.

(c) The demographic structure and the relative affluence of different sectors of the market.

Inflation rate per annum calculated by the formula:

$$\frac{100\,(\text{Price index in latest available year} - \text{price index} \times \text{years ago})}{X\,(\text{price index} \times \text{years ago})}$$

Financial opportunities

(a) Availability of local equity

(b) Availability of loan capital

(c) Cost of loan capital

(d) Strength of local currency

(e) Corporate taxes

(f) Incentives for foreign investment

(g) Constraints of foreign investment

(h) Constraints on repatriating profits

Position of relevant industry

(a) How well-established is the local industry

(b) Competitive position in the industry

(c) Customer position

(d) Protection measures taken by the country

(e) Growth, actual and potential

(f) Existing markets for this particular company's products

Potential market

(a) Internal, including extension of the product life cycle

(b) Potential exports

(i) by trade agreements

(ii) by geographical position

(c) Strategic market and planning centre

(d) Distribution centre

(e) Centre for raw materials and other supplies

(f) Overall growth potential

Potential for development as supply centre:

(a) Availability of valuable raw materials

(b) Storage facilities, climate

(c) The extent to which the company needs extra sources of supply

Potential for development as a production and research centre:

(a) Legal constraints—building, pollution, etc.

(b) Labour costs

(c) Patent laws

(d) Transport facilities

(e) Other sitting problems

(f) Other suitable infrastructure

Political constraints and risk:

(a) The instability of the government

(b) The instability of the civil service

(c) Threat of nationalization or other forms of takeover

(d) The national ambition to industrialize the country

(e) Price control

(f) Safety and pollution regulations

(g) Restrictions on taking money out of the country

(h) Withholding taxes

(i) Other government policies and laws on such issues as labour, competition and ownership

(j) The options available to the government in future

Staffing aspects:

(a) Availability of scientists, technicians, skilled workers, unskilled workers

(b) Compatibility with existing employees

(c) Laws about the employment of foreigners

(d) Strength of the trade unions

(e) Attitude of the local people towards work, foreign firms and other relevant issues

(f) Labour costs (in industries where these are significant like electronics, footwear, toys and apparel) and labour productivity

Table 7.3: Some Risks and Their Possible Antidotes

Risk	Possible Antidotes
Political upheavals-nationalization or restrictive legislation	• Evaluate the risks and find appropriate constraints. • Investment insurance. • Enter more than one country. • Restrict investment by using licensing or management contracts. • Political forecasting. • Strategy analysis of competitors.
Action of Competitors	• Market research • Keep away from saturated markets or those with powerful direct competitors.
Over-extended resources (especially financial)	• Well-planned control system • Well-planned organization • Search for fresh resources (after defining criteria for their use)
Exchange losses	• Hedge
Financial risk	• Obtain local capital
Money transfer risk	• Try to utilize all transfer guarantee possibilities, e.g., know-how contracts.

Other criteria are not so critical; but naturally no problem has one single cause and all can contribute. Table 7.2 gives an outline of some of the main considerations in either selecting or rejecting a particular country. In addition, there are industry-specific constraints—prejudices, taboos, religious ideas which make some products unsaleable and cause others to be adopted.

❑ Some Risks and Their Possible Antidotes

The stage of development is very important in developing countries. Numerous efforts have been made to identify stages of development and from these to work out the market and other opportunities that can be predicated. An interesting proposal distinguishes ten different phases each with its distinct characteristics—the dormant, the traditional, the transitional, pre-takeoff, takeoff, innovative, rapid growth, technological maturity, high mass consumption and the affluent. While the distinctions may not always be precise, this does at least show some of considerations that are involved. If a company can decide at what stage a market for its products develops, then such a classification can be useful for planning. The scheme can be applied to parts of a country as well as the whole, which may be more relevant in some of the larger developing countries. In considering the relevance of such a scheme, it should be said it is easy to be overcome by the differences between countries, and

these are real enough and should not be underestimated. Nevertheless, some features are almost universal and only gradually change with the coming of industrialization. These include the influences of family ownership on business and the slow emergence of professional management and also the use of bargaining being replaced by cost pricing and then market pricing. The scale of industry and the nature of competition also change gradually.

The general issue of geographical diversification can easily become dominated by the shadow rather than the substance. Since, so many mistakes have been made for lack of simple techniques, it is easy to exaggerate the possibilities of the techniques. They are needed to ensure that errors are avoided.

Success is the result of a deeper understanding of fast changing situations. There is a creative as well as a calculative process in this aspect of planning. The goals and the constraints in societies are also changing, and these changes can have unpredictable effects.

The more advanced of the developing countries are likely to have constraints which may not be anticipated by the foreign company and which may influence the development of the local market in unexpected ways. The country is going through a process of adaptation, and there may be pressures to speed up the process and take shortcuts. This subject is much debated around phrases like 'intermediate technology'. Geographical diversification can no longer be assumed to be a useful way of bringing new life to obsolete products, although this will remain as a 'simple' strategy for some time to come. Product strategies are considered later, but it must be assumed that an approach which goes more deeply into technological forecasting is required.

Another more subtle approach is the one that depends on an assessment of competitors rather than on the opportunities of the company itself. The potential strategies of the opposition may be worked out by various methods, often some form of gaming technique, but quite appropriately by a straight survey of existing activities. The points at which the company can suitably meet the competition head on and those where evasion is most suitable can then be determined. This would give the outline of a suitable policy for transnational development.

Finally, some policies follow a preliminary decision as to whether the company is primarily a domestic concern using its operations abroad to fill any deficiencies in the home market, where its primary profits are made, or whether the reverse is true and the company is, as a matter of policy, scanning the world and making its profits at home or abroad. Many companies will claim to be in the latter category while actually falling in the former. The subtle policies emerge when the decisions are made consciously and the implications are considered.

If a company decides that its primary orientation will remain domestic, then it usually has two uses for foreign business. One is the provision of a market when the home market is slack. This may involve careful consideration of how to keep the necessary avenues open. The other use is to provide limited overseas investment to support the necessary export, but more especially to ensure adequate supplies. In this case, the foreign operations are cost centres when the domestic business is satisfactory, and they become profit centres when there is a decline at home. In either case the company maintains a steady income. This is an especially suitable policy at times when interest rates are high, and the expenses and risks of expansion are immeasurably increased.

Many writers have wrestled with the concept of a totally transnational policy, and some of the results have appeared more suitable for romantic than business writings. One problem is that such a policy cannot really be developed without an unmanageable flow of information. In one sense, however, this whole work is based on the view that a genuine transnational planning policy is possible. Here we have attempted to discuss the issues involved in determining a coherent corporate policy for deciding between countries while venturing into transnational business.

Resource–market strategies

The transnational company has a bewildering selection of possibilities in making systematic plans. These can be seen in terms of the search for foreign opportunities. In this sense, overall plans are intended, not the specific arrangements that derive from these plans in decisions about the setting of factories or sales facilities. Neither the decision making nor the planning often follows the approach set out here in practice, but this may establish a means of judging just what the possibilities are.

Many mixtures of the following approaches towards strategies are possible:

Resources

- To reassess the supply of raw materials in terms of cost, quality or reliability: This can only be done in terms of a particular material. The large corporate buyer can be an asset with some materials, like steel where advantage can be taken of temporary gluts in particular

countries. But a disadvantage in some commodities where the small local subsidiary can drive a more favourable bargain. A more sophisticated approach would mix the two, the larger buyer for some items and the small buyer for others.

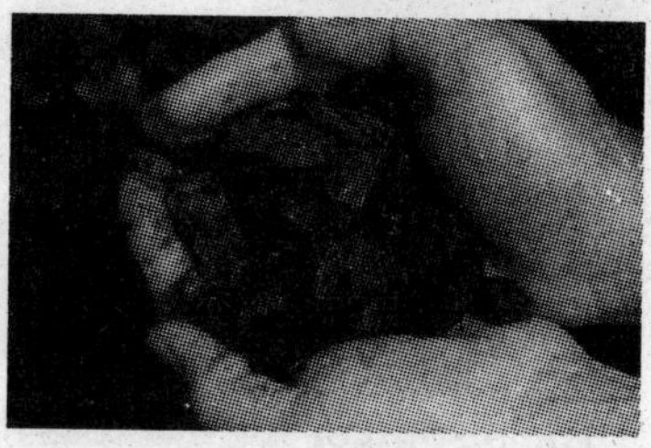

- To reassess the supply of components in similar terms.
- To reassess opportunities for reducing costs, and improving quality in the supply of the product or service. The bank or accountancy company which establishes branches in the same countries as its customers is an example of this, as is any policy designed to match the needs of the customer more closely by developing foreign facilities.
- To tap fresh sources of finance by having subsidiaries in countries with active money markets or where savings are strongly supported.
- To tap sources of personnel, especially technical and managerial, in countries where these are available.
- To tap technical knowledge and to plug into the general atmosphere of technical innovations in the most industrialized countries.
- To use other managerial capabilities. This includes the fuller use of expertise acquired in existing foreign operations.

Markets

- To sell abroad all products already sold in the home market.
- To sell abroad selected products. These may be products which are particularly subject to cyclical or seasonal fluctuations, or which are becoming obsolete at home (perhaps, because they are being replaced by goods that are more expensive but labour-saving) or products for which market research has shown special opportunities in particular countries.
- To sell abroad parts of products. The best-known example of this is where a product has a sophisticated component (the automatic control in a machine, the active substance in a pill) which can be profitably transported anywhere in the world; the simpler parts can then be manufactured and the finished product assembled nearer to the point of sale.
- To sell abroad all services provided in the home market.

- To sell services abroad primarily to existing domestic customers.
- To sell abroad technology and technical know how.

POLICIES FOR PRODUCT DEVELOPMENT AND DIVERSIFICATION

The resources from across the world of a multinational company should make new product development one of its great strengths. The fact that it often does not happen provides striking testimony to the need for more effective transnational planning. Most writers, with a few exceptions, take it for granted that the product development takes place at home and that the company takes little advantage of its global spread. New product development, in fact, is more circumscribed than some theoretical work on the subject suggests. Some of these, like the product cycle theory, are of great value to the transnational planner in suggesting where he may consider that there is market for existing, modified and new products. The theories that revolve around the location of maximum advantage may be important in negative sense, he may want to buck the trend and so win a competitive advantage. This may be won in other ways; for instance, R&D sometimes happen remote from the production centre on account of established centres of relevant knowledge. Examples of this are research into sugar beet seed in Sweden (where the seed is not grown) and into natural rubber in the United Kingdom. Work of this sort may lead to a technological push in one country which is then matched with a market pull in another or vice versa. A number of situations can be listed where some stress on transnational new product development is likely. Table 7.4 summarizes these situations, which include:

- A current or projected product has a limited life, but may be introduced elsewhere in a modified form.
- A product that is complementary to the company's range is available elsewhere, and can be bought and used at home.
- The company is dangerously dependent on one product but is also cash rich and can find more satisfactory diversification abroad.
- A company has research advantages, but for products that can only be produced in other countries or has products which need the support of foreign research.
- There are centres of special development in various parts of the world for the company's products or likely products.
- The company's products require adaptation to local needs in many markets.

- The company has suitable technologies for development in specific markets perhaps those that are highly developed or on the contrary those are poor.
- The needs of the market are not adequately translated into the product planning.

Table 7.4: The Development of New Products

The Trigger Situation	The Options and Analyses	By Whom the Research is Conducted
Over-dependence on limited product range	• Develop new products. • Consider joint venture with firm with complementary products.	• Planning R&D • Marketing
Need to operate different economies	• Adapt existing products. • Collaborate with local firms.	• Planning • Marketing
Apperance of special opportunities.	• Analyse strengths and weaknesses. • Select matching strengths and opportunities.	• Planning • Marketing
Low profitability	• Select profitable products. Redirect R&D. • Study competition.	• Planning • R&D Marketing
R&D overcapacity	• Study strengths and weaknesses of R&D. • Apply technological forecasting.	• R&D • Planning
Seasonal balance of products	• Use inventory to offset. • Seek new products with different seasonal pattern.	• Planning • Marketing • Production
Balance of life cycles and products	• Analyse existing products and their place in the life cycle. • Find compensating products likely to fill gap.	• Marketing R&D • Planning
Spin-offs from R&D	• Utilize for own new products. • Offer to others on contract basis.	• R&D • Marketing Planning.

The Trigger Situation	The Options and Analyses	By Whom the Research is Conducted
Marketing potential	• Analyse present utilization. • Identify new products to improve load.	• Marketing • Planning
Inventions	• Ascertain synergy with existing strengths develop and market new products.	• Planning R&D • Marketing
Excess liquidity	• Evaluate possible strategies for diversification.	• Planning

Table 7.5:
List of Multinational Product Strategies (MPS) Implemented (Observe Set)

(a) Products whose development occurred in the parent the firm.	Number of times observed: By product lines (30)	Number of times observed: For selected products (52)
1. MPS 1 = S1-S3-S4	10	21
2. MPS 7 = S1-S3	15	70
3. MPS 8 = S1-S4	9	10
4. MPS 9 = S3-S4		1
5. MPS 10 = S3-S1		1
6. MPS 11 = S4-S1		2
7. MPS 12 = S4-S3		3
8. MPS 14 = S3		3
9. MPS 15 = S4	2	
10. MPS 29 = S1-S3-S2-S4	2	9

(b) Products whose development occurred in the host country (ies) of the firm.

11. MPS 31 = S5-S7-S8		3
12. MPS 37 = S5-S7		5
13. MPS 39 = S5-S8	1	3
14. MPS 40 = S8-S5	3	3
15. MPS 42 = S8-S7		2
16. MPS 45 = S8	21	37
17. MPS 51 = S8-S6-S5	6	1
18. MPS 55 = S8-S6	12	11

NB: *The observations were performed in two ways, first in terms of the most-often used MPS for a particular product line, and secondly for a selected number of products from those product lines. The product line data were gathered to obtain a comprehensive coverage of the MPS implemented by those firms. In total, the MPS of 30 product lines and 52 selected products were analysed.*

Keys to Figure 7.1

K = The development of the product.

P = The characteristics of the production process and the location of the product centres.

M = Market characteristics and the countries where the product is sold.

p = Home country.

h = Host country.

Explanation to Fig. 7.1: A typology of basic states for a product is assumed to be (after acquisition) put up in a case to the main board, and gone ahead with after the necessary consents have been given). The consequence of this development has been an extreme difficulty in deciding where the future of the company lies. Some of the acquisitions have been in highly competitive areas, with low margins and a questionable future. Others have been in products with greater promise. Some have been in bulk producers for further manufacture. Others have been in speciality products for sale to customers.

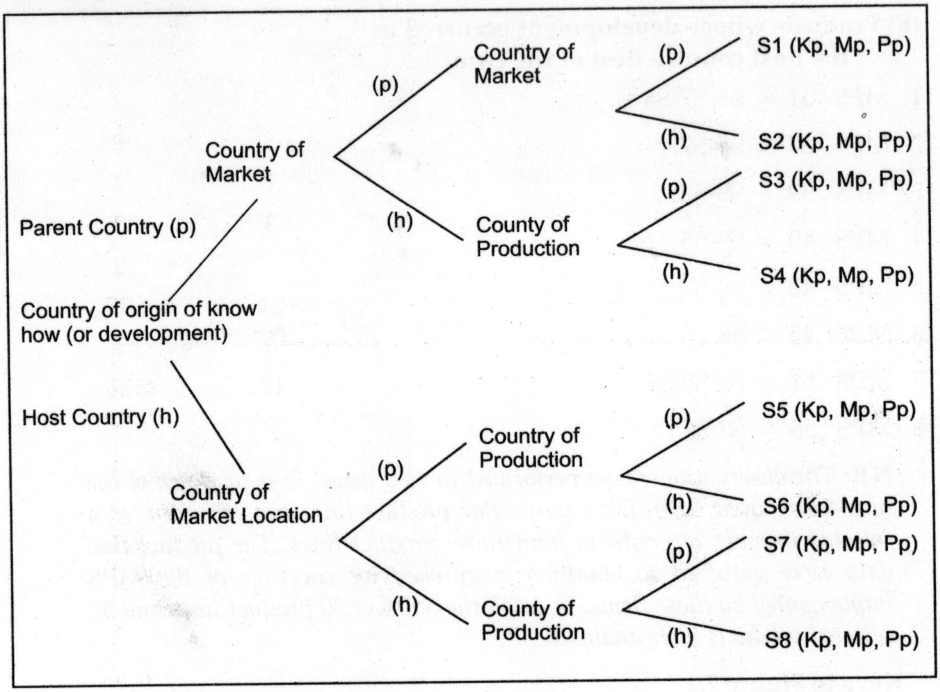

Fig. 7.1: Typology of Basic States for a Product

❑ Moving Abroad: Some Options

Companies can find themselves transnational because of the nature of their business. They operate mines or plantations in other countries, or they depend on these for their suppliers. Otherwise, they are in the business of transport or tourism. Some companies go abroad because they wish to enlarge their markets. Their product or service is thought to be saleable outside their home country.

For most of the large companies from across the world, the first moves abroad, are now a matter of past history. Accurate information about the problems encountered by them is unimaginable. However, each year several hundred new companies venture into the export field from India alone, and the world total must be enormous. This move to the foreign pasture has its share of problems and disappointments, especially with methods of foreign penetration that appears cheap. Some of these are:

- Sending samples to foreign buyers.
- Advertising or word-of-mouth recommendation in foreign markets.
- Contacts with foreign businessman made by chance at trade fairs or through trade delegations.

These haphazard routes produce problems which sometimes push a company, with eye on foreign markets, towards planning, and a number of possible strategies emerge. The costs include not only the expenses of actually sending the samples, but also the disillusionment which follows from lack of success. It has been estimated that the costs of planning can be repaid very early in the overseas operation, but that the costs of disillusionment are much higher. Available strategies include:

- Various arrangements for direct sale to the foreign customer.
- The employment of agents or distributors with specific contracts with the supplier.
- The use of selling subsidiaries.
- The sale of know-how or expertise of a technical or managerial nature through licensing, franchising or other contractual arrangements.
- The manufacture of goods or the provision of services through direct investment by whole or part ownership of a foreign subsidiary. This includes joint ventures with local businesses.

The list is not exhaustive and the subject is considered in more detail elsewhere. The significance of such a list is as a reminder of the range of choices available to the planner. He works with his hands tied behind his back if he is told, 'Our policy is only to operate through agents abroad', 'Our policy is to search for licenses outside Europe', or any of the innumerable such statements of policy which do limit the planning activity in many firms. The emergence of such statements often arises from disillusionment with just the sort of the unplanned development that has been mentioned before. Taking everything into consideration, it would be very difficult to suggest a guideline with universal application. Different strategies apply to different products in different markets.

The individual arrangements are discussed in books on transnational marketing, the planner is interested in the process of change, how a particular route for foreign business is chosen and under what circumstances. The difficulties caused by the overreaction to the problems of a particular route have already been mentioned. There are also difficulties caused by short-term actions which are ultimately incompatible with long-term policies. This is a common error; it is also the type of error which stems from an inadequate interplay between planning and practice. For instance, a selected collaborator may be adequate to play a part in the first move of a company into a new market, but may be unable to cope if that market expands. This may be because the collaborator is a small business without the potential for expansion, or because a different arrangement becomes suitable as growth occurs. Irrespective of the causes, the arrangements become suitable as growth occurs. Whatever may be the causes, the appointment of, for instance, an agent to handle a particular market for a limited period may produce intractable problems at the end of that period. The requirement is for a set of criteria for the route that is likely to be followed. These criteria stem from an understanding of the constraints and the potential in the situation. Some considerations are shown in Table 7.4. This provides a systematic background to the process that is summarized in Table 7.6, where by quantifying the options indicated, viewing of potential decisions are possible. Essentially, it is possible to view all the choices together. This may be impracticable for the small company, but even so, it serves a warning that to enter one market needs timely investment backing for a sustained operation. The decisions indicated in Table 9.1 in Chapter 9 are being made by some means or the other, although there may be no formal procedure. The table may be understood for interpreting what is happening or to reflect on what supposedly should happen. A format is provided which takes account of the opportunities and constraints and relates the decisions to the policy choices. The formula includes the industry group and the scale of business diversity as well as the technological content of both the product and the process. The structure of the market, the relationship of the industry group to the political and other aspects of the environment and the attitude of the leadership of the business are among the elements of constraints shown in Table 7.3. Each such factor can score advantages and disadvantages when put alongside the route. As a result, some routes will appear to have high or even critical advantages, others will be discarded.

Table 7.6: The Decision Support Chart

...weightings	Certainty	20											
	This decision	19											
	Market	18											
	Product	17											
	Company	16											
Investment		15											
	Wholly-owned subsidiary	14											
	Min. local shareholders	13											
	Major local shareholders	12											
	Joint venture	11											

Contd....

Sale of Knowledge		10											
	Management contract	9											
	Franchising	8											
	Licensing	7											
Sale of Products / Services min. investment		6											
	Selling subsidiary	5											
	Branch office	4											
	Distributors	3											
	Agents	2											
	Direct export	1											
	Subject no.		1	2	3	4	5	6	7	8	9	10	11
			Income	Growth	Sales		Tax implication	Political Problems	Quality & Control		Company key issue (s)	Product key issue (s)	Market key issue (s)

The purpose of this chart is to isolate the most important factors for final decision-to aid judgement, not to replace it. The final decision may be the answer to any of the following questions:

- Where do we go from here?
- How do we re-think existing transnational operations?
- How do we start new foreign operations?

- Are we using our existing opportunities/resources to the best advantage or are we meeting future threats adequately?

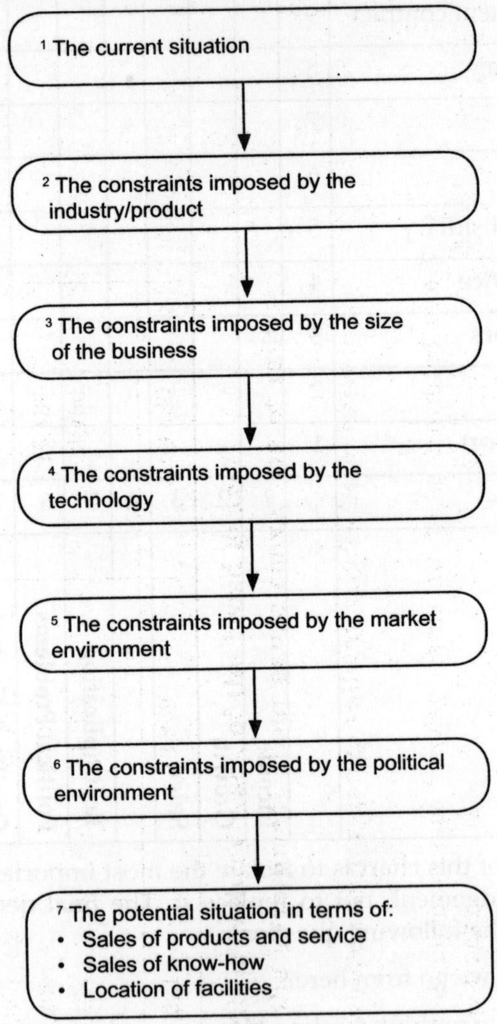

Figure 7.2: The Foreign Opportunity

How to use the chart?

On the left-hand side, fill in the decision subjects considered significant by the company. The subjects on this chart are only intended to serve as examples. These subjects should include:

Income	**Quality control**	**Competition**
Capital required	Financial control	Import constraints
Risk	Planning	Political stability
Technology	Market growth	Tax implications
Market share	Staffing-managerial	Investment constraints
Volume of sales	Staffing-operator	

Column 1-15 should then be filled in with a number from 1 to 5 representing the balance of profitability to the company of that decision. Thus, if under 'capital required' no more capital would be required to service direct exports then enter 5 in column 1; but if more capital would be required, reduce the number. In all cases, a high number indicates that this issue indicates advantage to the company under this heading; a low number indicates a warning.

Similarly, columns 16–19 should also be numbered. These will sometimes provide a corrective value to the numbers in the other columns. Thus, under 'capital required', columns 11–14 would have relatively low numbers, but in a company with surplus funds this would be offset by a high number in 16. The same effect could be produced in column 17 with a low capital product. Column 19 is arrived at by balancing 16, 17 and 18.

If any subject is of critical importance to the company, then the number in column 19 should be replaced by a 'C', and this subject is considered first in the final decision. Other subjects should be taken in order of the number in column 19.

Column 20 should be used as a counter-check and scored according to the reliability of the evidence in the other columns.

Column 18 can be used for any geographical areas under consideration—the world, a continent, a country, a province, a country and so on.

CONCLUSION

One great advantage of this method is that it can be used in any depth that a company requires. Thus, the whole process can take about an hour and hence be used to check against vague impressions, thereby getting a quick and inexpensive judgement. Otherwise, the process can take many months as a long-term planning tool where large sums are at stake. The range of numbers from 1 to 5 as suggested above can be increased, but this should not be done at first. Naturally a straight addition will not always be possible or useful, and some may prefer other symbols (+ or –, or A, B, C) to numbers. This chart should be understood as a proposed framework to be adapted for individual requirements. Some of the questions used to produce a rough score are:

1. What is the record of the success or failure of this firm in doing business abroad?
2. What is the record of other firms in the same industry group? What is the evidence of untapped potential in this industry group?
3. Are there sufficient resources in this firm – money, know-how, people – to develop abroad? If not, can they be found?
4. Is the technology suitable for use in the markets under consideration?
5. Is there sufficient evidence of demand in the markets?
6. Is there a likelihood of running into political problems in the countries chosen?
7. Even if all the answers favour the move abroad, are there still problems for this business?

The question numbers correspond with the numbers in Figure 7.2. These questions are only intended to be illustrative—both of the points made and of the difficulties involved. They, however, mask considerable complexity.

More important perhaps is to avoid framing the question in such a way as always to ensure the answer 'No'. So many of the techniques for evaluating market opportunity, often conservative at home, can produce paralysing results abroad. To avoid this, insertion of questions like that on the evidence for 'untapped potential' is also required. However, this raises problems, and most companies find the question in practice hard to answer— 'potential' is something that one has hunches about, collecting the evidence is more difficult and time consuming. To this end, the discussions on forecasting and information collection are discussed later.

One solution is for two sets of answers to be provided—one set gives a 'caution' reply, emphasizing the problems, and the other gives an 'opportunity' reply, stressing the gains that may be hoped for. The choice between the two replies must be a matter of judgement, but at least there is now a sound basis for the judgement. If the resources are available, then the opportunity reply may be preferred unless the caution reply shows the probability of bankruptcy. After re-emphasizing the width of the choices and their possible combinations, it is now possible to look briefly at each of the routes mentioned, beginning with the sale of goods abroad.

Summary

Planning a befitting strategy for transnational market requires analysis of issues governing companies. Issues like political risk, social risk, economic risk, etc., have to be evaluated for designing a plan-of-action for future development. All goals can be accomplished by empowering scientific techniques (Delphi technique) for being resolute on choices/options.

This chapter relates to the assessment of company status and exploring the reasons of company failure due to the lack of proper planning. It also speaks on the idea of selecting a market and country, analysing the factors of risk and its possible countermeasures for converting risk into definite profit. In order to ensure certainty in approach to business, 'technological forecasting' has been given weightage. These formulations realize the opportunities for defining new product development and diversification.

This chapter, under its purview, discusses techniques that enable a company to exploit the opportunities abroad by conforming to the decisions adopted through decision support chart applied in the marketplaces.

In the process of planning a strategy, categories are tested in the score sheet and judgements are validated for accuracy of decision. This strategy can thereby tap the untapped potentials of the foreign markets. This chapter shall guide the reader to infuse in him/her the ability to frame questions and apply in the field.

QUESTIONS FOR DISCUSSIONS

Q. 1. What are the vital issues that encompass the domain of planning for transnational marketing? Discuss citing suitable examples from companies.

Q. 2. How does forecasting of short-term, medium-term and long-term strategies help to manage risk in foreign expansion of business?

Q. 3. Describe government actions that influence the options of comp-anies for going transnational. Elucidate.

Q. 4. How does ineffective planning result in failure of a company?

Q. 5. What are the basic guidelines of government for encouraging companies for transnational operations? Illustrate.

Q. 6. What are the criteria of country selection? What are the main factors of risk and their possible antidotes for doing successful business?

Q. 7. How does intermediate technology help in overcoming cut-throat competition? Discuss.

Q. 8. How does evaluation of resources and market take place for searching foreign opportunities?

Q. 9. What is meant by new product development and diversification in framing policies to expand business outside the domestic country?

Q. 10. What do you understand by typology of basic states for a product? How does this happen for market acquisition in highly competitive and low-margin market? Discuss by citing examples.

Q. 11. How does selection by decision support chart implemented? Discuss.

Q. 12. Discuss how government actions influence transnational business planning.

Q. 13. What are the situations that entail transnational new product development? Give important points and discuss.

Q. 14. Elucidate on the decision support chart and its application in the field.

Q. 15. Write short notes.

(a) Delphi technique

(b) Political risk

(c) Gaming techniques

(d) Corporate policy

(e) Market size

(f) Inflation rate per annum

(g) Financial opportunities.

Chapter 8

Integrated Market Planning and Analysis

LEARNING OBJECTIVES

After going through the chapter the reader should be able to:

1. Identify provisions conducive for stepping up of exports in stages by domestic companies.
2. Organize investments and combat unplanned entry through 'cost advantage' in manufacturing at home and abroad.

EXPORTS MARKETING

The exact conditions under which one centre serves the world at the lowest cost and those under which the spread of facilities is more profitable are under constant reappraisal. It is an accepted wisdom among a majority of companies that foreign business, under all circumstances where this is possible is most profitable through export. But trade regulations in numerous countries, including a range of NTB make for increasing difficulties and emphasize the need for immediate policies, like assembly or part manufacturing abroad. There are many stages between a policy of domestic business supplemented by export and a full transnational policy.

> *It was a beautiful, bright day when we sat sail for the South Seas. I stood for a time on the deck while the sailors pulled up the anchor. They were singing while they were working and, in my heart, I was singing too.*
>
> *— R M Ballantyne (The Coral Island)*
>
> *Export marketing is methodological and mystic, yet strategic planning creates wonders in orchestrating the business.*
>
> *— Das and Satpathy*

It can be easily established that there is a considerable waste of resources by an unplanned entry into export; but the waste becomes much higher when some forms of collaborative agreements are agreed upon. Some of the most difficult problems recorded in research surveys have arisen from the unplanned development of agencies and distributors. Companies have extended themselves into investment prematurely, because of problems with agents and acquired expensive problems through a lack of understanding of the local commercial law. An example of this is a company that entered a market in a modest way through an agent, discovered that the market was inadequate. The cheapest way to continue in business, because of the compensation involved, was to buy the agent. This involved a totally unforeseen investment.

Countries try to reduce trade deficits, by ensuring that at least a partial manufacturing of a product is carried out in the domestic set up. If the capital is available, compliance with such regulations may be of benefit to the company. Indeed, some companies have arrived at such policies for commercial reasons and without any official pressure. There may be a cost advantage in manufacturing the more sophisticated parts of a product at home, while making or buying the others abroad. This applies to many branches of engineering, pharmaceuticals and other industries. Execution of labour-intensive assemblies is an advantage in countries with available cheap labour. Even where legal considerations do not apply, the actions of competitors may make some investments necessary.

❑ Planning Export Systematically

So far, the discussion on export was concentrated on the need to plan the export drive systematically and, where necessary, to support the export by investment. The latter is an issue, which has many implications for transnational planning. With about twenty-five percent of the value of world trade covering the movement of goods between different units of a company, it is clear that export and investments are increasingly mutually supportive. Equally, the increase of other ways of making money abroad, such as the sale of know-how again means that the relative importance of export in transnational planning is less than it was. The relative importance of a plan that examines a combination of routes becomes greater. Nevertheless, the absolute amount of business involved in exports is very large and continues to grow, especially in advanced products. This will continue to be the main route abroad for many smaller firms and those manufacturing specialized products. In this connection, there are a number of sub routes to consider—direct sales to foreign buyers

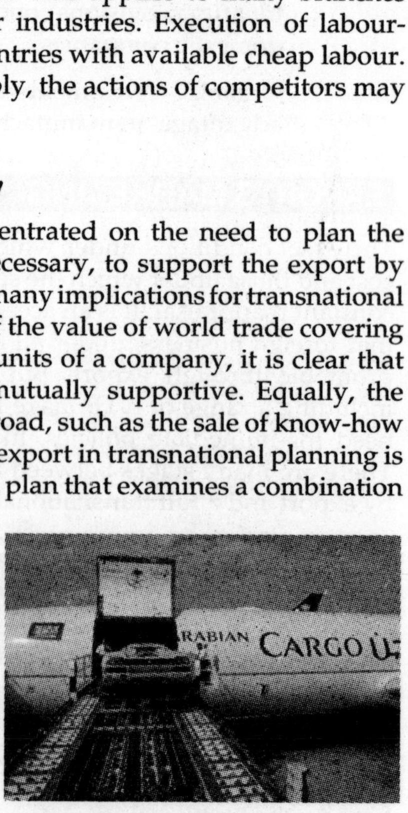

and the use of distributors, agents or other such collaborative agreements. The final stage, the beginning of investment is the setting up of a selling subsidiary. The choice of the sub route will depend partly on market considerations. Where a large market potential is established, considering an agent or distributor may be essential, but then, there are the difficulties of growth as mentioned earlier. There is a requirement of a set of guidelines for the selection, appointment and appraisal of agents. Haphazard methods seem to cause more failures than an incorrect appraisal of the market. These guidelines have to take account of the legal issues and a proper form of agreement is needed covering the pertinent issues. In France, out of the twenty types of different agents, normally only four are used. The legal implications of the different types are considerable and this must affect the selection. The same is true in other countries, where the agents of foreign companies have legal protection.

❑ Selling Subsidiary

The selling subsidiary usually follows where the other routes are inadequate. This replaces direct export, as a market grows in a particular part of the world, or an agent when there are problems of growth that cannot be resolved. Usually, there is no single argument for the establishment of a selling subsidiary; again, the planner needs a set of criterion. These should include the growth of the business, as mentioned above and its profitability. Also included are the expenses of gaining new business by the existing arrangements along with an estimate of the potential. Apart from the commitment of capital, the expenses of direct export, backed by the travelling salesperson are much lowering compared to those of a local operation and much less likely to win available orders, especially, when capital products are involved.

Another consideration for the selling subsidiary is that of after-sales servicing. These arguments are clinched when the selling subsidiary meshes with the other plans that the company may be developing, such as those for a regional policy outlined below. Exporting, thus, provides one set of routes to foreign business. Once seen as the normal way for most firms, this is now increasingly one among many; and all firms need to factor in other routes in their planning as well. In arranging for exports, a number of possibilities exist the costs of each should be carefully scrutinized. In any case, the most important criterion are not costs but profitability and continuing market penetration, this surely, is the object of the exercise, an exercise, which must be looked at in conjunction with the possible sale of knowledge.

THE SALE OF KNOWLEDGE

This includes a number of different kinds of arrangements classified, according to what is being paid for in terms of the contract—sale of technical knowledge, sale of commercial knowledge or sale of managerial knowledge. Naturally, there is much overlapping between the three. In addition, there are transnational service companies accounting for another small but growing proportion of the foreign earnings of the most industrialized countries; some of these service companies live mainly from the sales of knowledge abroad. There is little doubt that there is insufficient consideration by the planning department on the possible ways of earning money apart from sales of goods, e.g., know-how agreements, because they are not among the tactics used in the home country. Also reflected may be a conviction, not necessarily supported by the facts that agreements of this sort bring in a much smaller return on investment than sales. Paradoxically, restrictions on royalty payments and other developments make licensing arrangements less attractive, just at the time when more companies are coming to understand the possibilities. The reason for this is that counties especially, the less industrialized are coming to the conclusion that there is too much outflow of funds for the import of foreign technology. Hence, the efforts made to restrict licensing agreements in various ways, including direct controls and withholding taxes on the royalty payments. This does not necessarily mean that the opportunities for making money by the sale of technical knowledge are fewer. On the contrary, reduced royalty payments per sale may be compensated for by higher sales, especially in view of the fact that the regulations tend to be introduced as the country's standard of living rises. The constraints have altered, the advantages may well remain. Licensing to a third party is always a possible option; it becomes a probable option under a number of circumstances. These include:

1. A small company with patented products and inadequate resources to sell them directly.
2. A company with a product having a high technical content, enabling favourable royalty terms. Where there is good reason to concentrate on the direct marketing effort in certain regions, a carefully considered geographical strategy is involved.
3. A company with a product whose competitive edge is expected to be short-lived or where there is some other reason for wanting a rapid entry into multiple markets.

The last approach is the one that proves particularly difficult to organize in practice.

❑ Licensing and Franchisee

In general, licensing is often advocated for increasing market spread at lower risk; but the advantages can be cancelled out by the lower income unless it is considered in the light of more subtle strategies such as those listed. On the other hand, the view that licensing is normally a second best option and reserved for uninteresting markets is only sustained by extremely cautious arguments about risk. There are conditions where licensing is a preferred way for developing a market and for bringing money to the parent company The conditions will be obscured if a too-generalized policy is pursued. For instance, the fact has to be faced that licensing can produce a vigorous competitor. A well-known example of this is the manufacture of Fiat cars in Eastern Europe.

While technical knowledge is sold mostly by means licensing, commercial knowledge is usually sold by some system of franchising. Whereas licensing is a technical package with a technical content, there is a suggestion that the companies that succeed at either are those, which tend to blur the distinction. A company finds that technical knowledge needs supplementation by commercial knowledge. In both licensing and franchising agreements, there may well be patents and trademarks and one of the considerations will be to obtain the maximum protection for both in as many foreign markets as possible. There will be other legal issues, especially the framing and enforcing of contracts between the parent company and the foreign licensee or franchise-holders, but in both cases, the legal arrangements are ancillary to the commercial objective—profitable market penetration. Naturally, the legal inputs must be correct.

❑ Management Contract

Recent figures show that franchising in some form or other has become the most rapidly growing means of doing transnational business; this, of course, is a growth measured from a small base. Starting from an even small base, but likely to grow even more rapidly, is the management contract. This is the sale of management expertise in general, as opposed to the specific technical or marketing expertise in general, which dominates in the arrangements already discussed. Naturally, the distinction is not an easy one to make; it has already been stressed earlier that every know-how arrangement involves a contract, and that

the contract itself is not the most important part of the arrangement. The distinction between the different types of agreements is, based on what the foreign partner is willing to pay for the patent, the trademark or the skill in managing the business. The management contract can bring the company all the advantages of foreign investments without the need to find the capital for the investment although the firm's financial skills will also be used. This is because contractor has to assist the client in his search for funds. Furthermore, this method is acceptable in every country in the world and indeed, emerged as a separate means of doing business, because of the prohibition on foreign investment in countries that were anxious for foreign know-how. Almost any company, which is already successful transnationally, is likely to have a body of knowledge which would be saleable in some contract package. Hence, this method should feature in any planning. The legal control and other issues are the same as for licensing.

❑ Foreign management Expertise

When management contracts are discussed, the point often made is that they are of a temporary nature. A company or a country, accepts foreign management expertise until local skills are developed. A particular contract will certainly be short-lived, this is the nature of the exercise, but for planning purposes, the sale of the company's knowledge through contracts may well be a permanent activity—not more temporary than consultancy contracts, which too are similar exercise. Regarding the management contract as a consultancy activity for a company that normally conducts its affairs in other ways is quite apt. What is certain is that the management contract will only be a permanent way of doing business for a company that is well abreast with the relevant techniques and technologies. This is true of all the know-how agreements discussed in this section and is perhaps the critical point in considering the weightage given to these means of doing business abroad, according to the way the company plans, this is how expertise shall develop so, that expertise be, in part, paid for by transnational know-how agreements. Otherwise, as we have indicated, these agreements arise from the process of identifying where the company is in fact likely to draw its foreign income. A minimum investment is involved, but with it goes a maximum commercial package ensuring that the agreement achieves the full potential of the project. In each case, there is a legal apparatus for an arrangement, which depends on adequate controls and personal contacts. Indeed, the relationship between the parent company and the know-how partner needs to be as similar as possible to that between a company and a subsidiary. In many instances that have investigated, this has been suggested as the secret of business. We pass from this subject to one where the secret may be even more elusive—the development of the subsidiary abroad.

PLANNING FOR FOREIGN INVESTMENT

Most companies will be operating abroad through an agency, licensing and other agreements, before any subsidiaries or other ownership ventures emerge. If satisfactory commercial agreements are developed, there will, already be a rudimentary control and appraisal system, which will apply to the new operations; following from the last section. In fact, most companies fail to develop so smoothly and direct foreign investment causes a series of costly problems to the headquarters. Transnational corporate planning is much concerned with ensuring that this does not happen and that the management system expands to meet the changing conditions.

Another feature of the actual move from being a foreign trader to becoming a foreign investor is that it is usually a defensive move. A part of the business faces threat. In the case of manufacturers, this happens when changes in tariffs, import controls, transport costs, local competition or other similar factors, threaten a position in an important market. For service industries, the development is more likely to happen when important customers are increasing their transnational spread and are becoming impatient of bankers, insurers, consultants and other service companies, which only operate in one country. Naturally, there are some firms with carefully planned strategies, which take them abroad at an appropriate stage in their development, but for the majority this is not the case.

❑ Mechanics of Progress

The defensive development of transnational investment has the effect of placing the planning emphasis on the tactics and the mechanics of the move, rather than on the strategy. There is a world of difference between 'This is where we have to go' and 'This is where we need to be'. Comparisons are hard to make, but there is some evidence that manufacturing companies have developed abroad more rapidly and less expensively as part of a planned development. This is in contrast to a hasty measure for self-defence and is the intended action as opposed to the response to circumstances.

Undoubtedly, the planned extension requires skills, which many companies do not possess. In effect, the question being asked is not 'Where do we have to go?' but 'Where will we have to go? What are the chances of getting there first?' An outline of a systematic approach comes later. The difficulties are greater for service industries, but even for them, a more skilful sustained effort to build a transnational policy is not impossible. The need for such a policy becomes even more evident after examining the pressures that influence companies during their development abroad more closely.

PATTERN OF MOST JOINT VENTURES

- Equity capital.
- Bank guarantees for local loans (none of these had yet been called on, but borrowing elsewhere had been restricted by their existence).
- Component parts.
- Technical advice both in manufacture and in after-sales service.
- New product advice.
- Marketing advice, advertising and selling techniques, in most of the joint ventures, entail constant visits from head office experts.
- General advice from the representatives sitting on the local board.

The joint venture grows, succeeds and becomes profitable; but the original sponsor finds a number of frustrations, like putting in more than getting the returns out. An insistence from the start that the money must be repatriated in a number of different ways, would have avoided this problem. The same insistence can also be vital when establishing wholly owned subsidiaries.

Thus, the emphasis on planning for investment is on ensuring a return on that investment. In addition, all that has been said elsewhere in this chapter applies, especially that this investment—whether in joint ventures, selling subsidiaries, subsidiaries for manufacture or the provision of services—is to be regarded as one policy among the many and should be appraised regularly on this basis. The myth that foreign investment is in many conditions usually more profitable than other routes abroad, was put about first, in the 1960s. Subsequent investigation cast doubt on this dogma. Planning for investment is a process of answering questions about the conditions under which anyone of the company's markets needs investment support.

THE STRATEGIC SUBSIDIARY AND THE REGIONAL CENTRE

There has been a marked revival of interest in recent years in regional policies. This interest undoubtedly has been stimulated by the emergence of trading blocs, but the actual policies examined usually come within the geographical rather than economic boundaries. Larger companies set up regional centres, smaller companies simply give authority to a particular national subsidiary to oversee the business for a given part of the world. For either arrangement, the phrase 'strategic subsidiary' is appropriate. The parent firm has set up a local company, which will mastermind all the business activities in its area. The planning of supply and financing as well as of sales and manufacture, if undertaken at all, preferably managed locally with an integrated regional management. For the larger firm, especially the one with manufacturing in the area concerned, a regional centre may be an expensive luxury. National subsidiaries, well established in the region, may be frustrated and demoralized to no purpose when the regional centre is established. There may still be good reasons for such an institution to meet special business requirements, but the regional planning is almost certainly most suitably undertaken by a form of consultation with at least the larger of the national subsidiaries. The only exception is in a company in a business where substantial integration makes sense. Highly integrated regional organizations do exist, but are not common.

❑ Smaller Firms' Adventure

For the smaller firm, on the other hand, the subsidiary, which masterminds a regional policy in close collaboration with the head office, can become an effective agent for developing new business. In some types of manufacturing, as in capital goods and especially heavy machinery, this may be the first foreign investment of an enterprise. The travelling salesperson, a tradition in the British capital goods industry but also in lighter industries as well, ceases to make sense as soon as the firm grows. Yet, there may not be enough business in any one country to sustain a subsidiary. What is more, agreements with agents and licences can inhibit the establishment of national subsidiaries. Such agreements may also determine the likely site for the new subsidiary by ruling out some countries. Most companies go for the country where they already do the most business as a first choice and then, to an appropriate commercial centre, if the first choice proves impossible. Closeness to such a centre may well prove an important factor in masterminding the regional drive for the subsidiary has to be the 'eyes' and 'ears' of the company in picking up information that may lead to improved planning.

❑ Strategic Subsidiary

The vital feature of the strategic subsidiary is that, it provides the market and other knowledge along with planning proposals for the company for the region and at the same time, is an operating unit in its own country. Criteria for appraisal, framed in the light of success in the provisioning of corporate resources as well as in trading in the country where the subsidiary operates. Where the subsidiary is a full regional centre, naturally it will not trade in its own right at all. In either case, the subsidiary expectedly provides a flow of information in each function. Information on the purchasing of supplies is an example. The neglect of this function had led to extravagant claims about achievements, if more attention was paid to sources of materials and components for a company as a whole. These claims may be difficult to realize, the large buyer has his own problems in some markets, but at least the subsidiary should be able to watch the suppliers more carefully; other problems of purchasing, like quality standards and delivery dates, can also be handled more effectively.

Strategic Subsidiary: Finance

In the field of finance , the strategic subsidiary can employ at least one senior finance executive to watch the local money markets in the region, interest rates, and tax changes. All this information, can of course, be bought in by a small operation; but the incompany specialist can be a profitable resource, especially in a capital-intensive firm. The opportunities in marketing are clear enough, but in this case should not fall prey to exaggeration. Regional markets, in any meaningful sense exist mostly for only a limited range of products, mainly industrial goods. For most consumer goods, the region turns out to be too large as a unit. The small company may still need this unit, but it may become inappropriate as the company grows—providing an unwanted extra coordinator or an unnecessary link in a communication chain that is already too long.

Strategic Subsidiary: Technical and Marketing

For technical matters, the strategic centre often proves to have advantages that were unsuspected when established. These range from closer supervision of after-sales servicing in the region, through probing of fresh opportunities in manufacture or part(s) manufacture, to the establishment of limited research and development facilities. This last is an interesting possibility. As with marketing, the subsidiary's area may be of the wrong size for the purpose, but the possibility of a section of the central research and development department located outside the home country by itself is important. Naturally, such a section would have to be in close touch with the technical liaison work. Nevertheless, some of the problems that arise with research and development departments get over in a way, by contact with other operations, closeness to the market place and closeness to the source of funds. Recruitment might also be easier.

CONCLUSION

Thus, the strategic subsidiary is presented in such a way as to show how the transnational drive, can be masterminded through the carefully placed investments. A reliable agent or licence can certainly, perform this function, but this is an instance where investment appears worthwhile. Equally, it is true that, if there are strategically placed subsidiaries, not fulfilling the functions suggested in this section, resources are being wasted. From a particular facet of transnational management, in this case—the regional strategy, the next section considers more issues that are general across frontiers of the organization.

ORGANIZATIONAL PLANNING FOR THE TRANSNATIONAL COMPANY

It is necessary to understand, the possible links between the organizational system and the planning system. The former, has been classified according to the priority of the projections of management. The word 'projection' is used for one of the three major groupings of managers, according to which the appointments are named in the transnational firm—functional (finance, marketing and so on), product group and geographical (transnational, regional, national). The third grouping, geographical, adds the extra dimension, which accounts for so much of the complexity of transnational company organization. The word 'projection' applies to the first level, as it were, of the appointment. For instance, a corporate functional manager for functional projection, a product group finance manager for product group projection and the finance director of the transnational division for geographical projection. The projections derive from the establishment of priorities in the decision-making system—whether by functions, product, geography or services (inputs) and the organization types, are named accordingly.

❑ Type of Company and Reporting Style

If the company is not product group organized and does not have any specific transnational or regional management, then the organization type is called the overall or 'A' type. In this case, the subsidiary reports directly to the most senior level at the head office— the chief executive of the subsidiary—or to a member of the parent board. There is also a close relationship between the senior functional managers in the subsidiary and their counterparts at the centre. This type is called 'overall' because the executives who deal with the foreign side of the business are responsible for the domestic side as well. They have overall, company wide, assignments.

The 'B' type company is the product group organized at home. This means that most of the managers at the head office have responsibilities attached to a product group, whatever their particular function may be; but the domestic managers only have direct line responsibility at home. Executives, whose duties are for the world, a region or a country, manage the foreign operations.

If the product groups have worldwide responsibilities, then this is a type 'C' firm. This is usually referred to as a product group type, whereas the B type is called the geographical type.

There is a fourth 'D' type or matrix organization. The usual matrix is of product and geographical one. In this case, each product group has worldwide responsibilities for its own business and at the same time, there are geographical managers answerable for the foreign operations or their part in them. Less frequently, some central functional managers have direct links abroad.

❑ Other Organizational Systems

There are many other ways of classifying the organizational procedures adopted by transnational companies. The particular significance of the one adopted here is that it interprets the decision-making process. In a transnational company there are three main considerations in arriving at an important decision—the specialist functional, the product group and the geographical. For example, while a new investment proposal is under inspection by a product group finance department for an establishment in a remote part of the world, policies have to be set and plans have to be laid in line with each of the three considerations.

The organizational structure has two implications. One implication relates to the role of central planning. A number of units of the company will have departments that are involved in transnational planning, especially, the geographical units if they exist. The other implication for planning also relates to decision making—how is the requirement of the system actually met by the organization and, in particular, how does the required information become available? Even when the information required for decisions is not the same as needed for the plans the two must be assembled in the same way.

The product group worldwide organization has been shown to have certain disadvantages especially in the company's relationship with its subsidiaries; there is also the difficulty that the information system throws up much data about the performance of the products worldwide, but a smaller understanding of what is happening in particular countries. The geographical organization does just the opposite; it emphasizes the national markets as against the products. An information system that does both effectively is run by some large companies, but this is expensive to handle and imposes a burden on the smaller local subsidiaries. The collection of the information on which adequate decisions can be taken, has to be carried out without making life impossible for subsidiary managers. In any case, the data collection will determine to a very considerable extent how the tasks are performed. The subsidiaries will need to establish appointments capable of matching the information requirements of the head office. Sufficient appreciation to this fact is always not given.

Studies show that the sort of information that head office demands influences company/organization.

The organization can influence the planning in many ways, for instance, a disadvantage of the C-type company is that the management at home may devise global plans, but this may be ignored by the subsidiaries. The whole relationship between transnational and local plans becomes a difficult one. On the other hand, the transnational division can severely distort the range of ideas that get consideration in the planning. The managers in that division can also be unduly inhibited in their work due to their perception of what is acceptable to subsidiaries.

Wherever the planning is located, whatever the organization type is, undoubtedly there is a need for monitoring the progress in each market. Ultimately, the decisions made about developments abroad are in the light of experience and there is bound to be wastage where each division learns the problems afresh. The need is for an agreement which is sensitive to the local situations that arise, without allowing inhibition of the global considerations. The organization cannot, we repeat, take shape without influencing the planning and, therefore, its own responsibility for expansion or adaptation.

FUTURE DIRECTIONS

The reader should not expect science fiction, as one of the present authors wrote in a paper on corporate planning many years ago. No one has yet invented a time machine enabling a peek into the future. If we had, we might have done our readers a disservice. The company, which really knew what was going to happen in the future, might lose a lot of money by introducing new products too far ahead of demand. There is plenty of evidence that innovating too soon can be as damaging to a business firm as entering a market too late. We have already discussed how the arrangement of transnational business could be arranged so as to reduce the amount of future shock and provide sufficient options to meet the foreseeable emergencies. The need for flexible systems capable of matching up to the range of requirements is clear.

Few substantial companies are without their own planning departments, although there is considerable variation as to the role of transnational planning. This will certainly be the responsibility of all senior members of central planning, if it exists and perhaps, a specialist unit as well.

The argument for specialization has been in terms of the need to give extra attention to the foreign operations. To avoid their neglect, there is also the need to take account of all the special issues that arise in business deals in other cultures and other legal systems and, the various options available to the foreign operations, from export to foreign manufacture. Awareness of these and other differences from domestic operations is frequently lacking.

❑ Transnational Planning

Transnational planning, it has been argued, exists in every company with some business abroad, although the small firm cannot establish a specialist department. Nevertheless, a planned thrust abroad can exist, and may well be masterminded by a member of the board, or a vice-president, or someone who has acquired some relevant specialist expertise. The planning considerations are not greatly different from those of the large enterprise except that the information must be simpler, more direct and perhaps acceptable by an outside organization. The options for entering a market exist. The choice of methods of financing may be more restricted; but the chances of establishing a profitable niche may be better for the small company. In some ways, the firm, having limited resources, has the greater need of transnational planning, however conducted.

The penalties for failure are greater, and the differences from the domestic exercise may well be greater too, while less understood. The larger concern has to capture a substantial market share to justify its presence; it already knows the appropriate means of growth in the other countries where it operates. A sufficient sum can be budgeted for the market entry with the provision of writing it off without much damage if the venture fails. The small firm, on the other hand, may need its niche, its special sector of the market, as well as its market share. This is likely to be available in a different form than that at home, and the approach may even have to be indirect. To enter new market is too expensive unless the company has its presence in another market. For all these reasons, a small company may need specialized transnational planning more than any large company. The distinction made in this work between the conscious an unconscious activity is intended to emphasize that necessary planning can take place without the practitioner realizing what is happening.

Many operators, however, lack the improved techniques available and, in particular, the means to scan the world for more profitable options to find the particular share of the market that the company is equipped to capture and to identify the suitable routes for acquiring that share. These activities cannot normally be undertaken haphazardly, and the competition will ensure that rule of thumb methods are even more unlikely to produce results.

Transnational planning in corporates

The general sense of direction of transnational planning and its place in the corporate system are likely to remain the talking points for the future. It is likely that more specialist advisers are sought, both inside the companies and in the consultancy and accounting firms. The specialist will not replace the travelling salesperson or the technical adviser because he will never have sufficient all-round knowledge of the product, the market and the financing methods, this knowledge can only exist in a team. The transnational specialist has to know the 'when' and the 'how', to call upon a wide range of skills other than those with which he himself is familiar. Just as the personnel specialist has to offer a service to other managers who are dealing with staff, so a transnational specialist has to offer a service to other managers, with their sights fixed on foreign business.

This point ties in with the discussion as to whether the planner is staff or line. In the small company, he will have to be both and perhaps the large company would wish to retain as much of this dual activity as is compatible with accountability. It has already been shown, that the distinction is applicable differently at different stages in the planning cycle, an issue that will be re-examined below. Meanwhile, it can be asserted that the transnational planning consists of a number of insights and skills, which increasingly demand a specialized function. Where this is not possible, a systematic scheme for reviewing the foreign operations is indispensable. Unconscious inspiration has been an important source of transnational planning expertise in the past but cannot be relied on the future, a future which can be described as offering uncertainty as its main certainty; in any case, the intention of this whole work is to encourage a more systematic approach.

❑ Planning Cycle: Three Kinds of Activities

The three-fold distinction of activities within the planning cycle—decision preparation, translation and implementation, has been shown to be appropriate for interpreting most of the issues faced. Even if only one person is available to organize all the three activities, a systematic approach to each avoids many problems that will otherwise occur. In particular, in case of foreign subsidiary or foreign agent or the licensee, where planning problems are similar—the need to know for which part of the process is asked for contribution, when the various phases will be occurring and when the implementation will be agreed to. In this work, the emphasis is on the translation phase especially. This is not because of the importance of the objective setting or of the implementation, both of which have been considered in some detail, is belittled. The reason for emphasizing the translation is that neither the distinctive characteristics of this phase are always been recognized, nor are the special limitations for planning transnational operations. The translation stage involves a search for the most effective and profitable means of achieving the objectives; this is not necessarily the same as the most obvious ones, which are likely to be the means followed, if a phase separate from the decision preparation is not recognized. The translation phase also involves masterminding the transnational links and producing plans that carry conviction for implementation. In future, most likely the translation phase will be emphasized the most and that the increasing demands for global information, data banks and machine processing of the data will result. The small company, as well as the large, would recognize the importance of this stage, in terms of a thorough search, to find their place in the market, which can save disappointments and losses in the future.

There are three distinct phases of transnational planning, distinguishable by their time horizons. The first assembles evidence for determining the objectives; the second prepares the plans for realization of those objectives under the changing circumstances, while the third prepares the details for carrying out the plans. The separation of these stages helps to identify the need for new techniques and changing attitudes, among which reintegration is required. The future cannot be determined it must be provisioned for.

The planning for foreign diversification, not only seen to involve the search for new outlets, but the search for outlets on terms that would minimize the known dangers. These include lack of control in particular markets and production facilities with over-stretched communications. Among other examples are new products the handling difficulties of which by the present structure, is problematic and so turns out to be much more costly in corporate resources than anticipated.

The challenge of the changing business environment, with its increasing discontinuities, are met in general, by a planning that provides for the eventualities that the enterprise can expect to meet rather than seeking to determine the future. A number of existing techniques, becoming increasingly elaborate, would be used, of which scenario writing is likely to prove the most valuable.

❑ Role of Planning

The role of planning is likely to expand most notably, in making available a store of options for future activities on every aspect of the business of

the company, with a special responsibility of bringing together, plans in an integrated pattern and for the overseeing of the implementation. The most probable pattern of organization in the future is in small units with coordination, designed to ensure that corporate services are available from planners appointed as advisers to the different parts of the enterprise and that vital priorities monitored efficiently. This would further emphasize the interlinking role of the planning departments.

Information collection and processing are likely to become even more sophisticated and specialized, services of which would be available to planning and to other departments and divisions of the company on an integrated basis. Extensive stores with selective inputs would be built up to service the policy formation and the decision making.

❑ Future of Specialized Planning

The future of specialized planning is going to depend on recruiting of appropriate staff and this is going to be difficult. The main difficulty will be the need to insert some narrow specializations into a department that must remain small and at the same time open to regular interchange of staff with other departments.

Powerful realities are producing paradoxical situations and the potential contribution of transnational planning turns out to be easier to identify than to arrange. A skilled specialization, backed by suitable information technology needs to avoid isolation and irrelevance. Actual steps taken for these goals paradoxically produce contradictory proposals in the use of techniques, in the organization and now in staffing. This means that the unique contribution will be the priority, while constant watchfulness will be needed to prevent attempts to improve the contribution from becoming self-frustrating. In particular there is likely to be a concentration in a few sensitive areas where the enterprise needs the assistance most. One is the identification of future options for the decision preparation and for the laying out of contingency plans; another is the improved allocation of resources, including the required coordination; and yet another is the bringing of the short-term planning closer the scene of the action. The role of planning is likely to expand most notably in making available a store of options for future activity on every aspect of the company's business; with a special responsibility for the bringing together of plans in an integrated pattern and for the overseeing of the implementation. The most probable pattern of organization in the future is in small units with the coordination designed to ensure that corporate services are available from planners, appointed as advisers to the different parts of the enterprise and that vital priorities are sufficiently monitored. This will emphasize further the interlinking role of the planning departments.

Summary

This chapter introspects into the essence of export marketing, analysing the *modus operandi* of domestic company going transnational. It elucidates on the steps involved in the avoiding loses due to unplanned entry into the foreign market. Ideas are imparted for managing investments through cost leadership or cost advantage, reasons of trading and manufacturing in home country and abroad.

Besides generic aspects of export marketing, this chapter highlights the importance of channels of product distribution, particularly for specialized medical engineering products, per say, which has a thumping market potential. In the process of detailing, the chapter touches upon the parts of licensing, royalty, franchisee, contracts, trademarks, etc., for mobilizing investments, expertise, legal advantage and other benefits.

Eventually, concepts of planning foreign investment by trading, manufacturing and services business have been analysed in the content, laying greater importance on joint ventures, and collaboration is a tactics to expand business. It involves strategic policies adopted by big and small companies, cashing in on the symbiotic profit of 'strategic subsidiary' associated through regional agreement, trade agreement (blocs) and integrated management approach.

In relating avenues of expansion, the chapter deliberate on the function of 'planning systems vis-à-vis organizational systems' working in harmony. In the process, the pillars of management (marketing, finance, HR and operations) together with hierarchy in levels bearing job descriptions have blended with poise and sensibility. Moreover, factors of influencing decision making by specialist groups, product groups, geographical groups and other such groups have been diligently reiterated with reference to the macro strategic plan.

This chapter comprehensively engulfs a holistic view of corporate planning and transnational aggression, needed for opening inroads to business in the foreign soil.

QUESTION FOR DISCUSSION

Q. 1. What do you mean by export marketing? Discuss the provisions of expanding domestic business transnationally.

Q. 2. How does unplanned entry into exports result in waste of resources? Elaborate.

Q. 3. Other than 'cost advantage', what are the other strategies profitable for companies to go abroad for expanding business?

Q. 4. Do the specialized products like medical products have advantage in penetrating into foreign markets? Give reasons for your answer.

Q. 5. How does knowledge of market and after-sales service help the company for doing successful business?

Q. 6. How does legal aspects and expertise of foreign country help home country company to visualize transnational business better? Illustrate.

Q. 7. What do you mean by foreign investment planning? How is joint venture a part of strategy in foreign trade and services industries?

Q. 8. Is there any difference in the operational strategy associated with manufacturing industry and services industry? How is it different in transnational business? Discuss with suitable examples.

Q. 9. Discuss the strategic policy of big companies and small companies approaching through 'strategic subsidiary'. How are trade blocs, regional policy and trade agreements help in the integrated regional management?

Q. 10. How do 'organizational system and planning system' operate in tandem? What are the cross-functional relationships of employees working in the organization? Elaborate.

Q. 11. How does grouping of specialist function, product, geographical background, etc., evolve indecision making for working out strategic plan?

Q. 12. Write a holistic plan for approaching business transnationally. Discuss on the aspects that are salient to all business/marketing.

Q. 13. Write short notes:

(a) Licensing

(b) Franchisee

(c) Contracts

(d) Trademark

(e) Royalty

(f) Foreign investment

(g) Selling subsidiary

(h) Three phases of planning cycle

(i) Cost leadership

(j) Transnational planning.

Chapter 9

Winning Transnational Marketing — A Survey Approach

LEARNING OBJECTIVES

After going through the chapter, the reader should be able to:

1. Identify the facets of winning companies defined by management experts of transnational marketing.
2. Recognize the right attitude for winning in the field of transnational marketing.
3. Describe the attitude of self/executive for winning in the field of transnational marketing.
4. Ascertain important points from amongst the questions offered in four important factors, given under the title 'points-to-watch,
5. Define the scoring and evaluation of attitudes as per the rating provided.
6. Realize the attitude of a potential winner in the arena of transnational marketing.

'The new electronic interdependence recreates the world in the image of a global village'.

— Marshall McLuhan (The Gutenberg Galaxy 1962)

'Professional management is the great invention of this century, an invention that produced gains in organizational efficiency, so great that it eventually destroyed organizational effectiveness'.

— Henry Mintzberg (Mintzberg on Management 1989)

Various experts have variously defined the facets of winning companies. Eight factors emerge in common—leadership, autonomy, control, involvement, market orientation, getting back to basics (and staying there), innovation and integrity. Relevant considerations within these factors are described below:.

HOW TO KEEP ON WINNING IN MARKETING

Through Leadership

1. Visible top management
2. Sense of mission
3. Clear objectives down the line
4. The practice of leadership

Through Autonomy

1. Small headquarters bureaucracies
2. Small independent business units
3. Informal systems of working together
4. A positive attitude towards risk taking
5. Generalist managers

Through Control

1. Tight controls on finance
2. Constant feedback of results
3. Close attention to business planning
4. High standards

Through Involvement

1. Pride in ownership
2. High degree of communications
3. High pay and/or incentives
4. Promotion from within
5. Training
6. The social side of work
7. Genuine respect for the individual

Through Market Orientation

1. Brand strength
2. Customer relations
3. Quality control
4. Hunger for market information
5. Market oriented R&D
6. Action-oriented marketing

Through Getting Back to Basics and Staying There

1. Sticking to the last
2. Attention to detail
3. Eye on the ball

Through Innovation

1. Few barriers to change
2. Natural curiosity about how things are done elsewhere
3. Transnational prospective
4. Directed R&D
5. The role of the chief executive

Through Integrity

1. Integrity towards employees
2. Integrity towards suppliers
3. Integrity towards the customer
4. Integrity towards the public in general

Ability to handle a fundamental change in the market is the hallmark of an excellent company.

Of these, four factors based on transnational surveys are selected for special attention in transnational marketing and a questionnaire on their attributes is developed subsequently. These factors are—autonomy, control, market orientation and innovation.

Somewhere in the spectrum between total bureaucratic inflexibility and institutional anarchy lies the ideal blend of control and autonomy for each company in transnational marketing. That blend may not be constant. Like the ribbon in the middle of the tug-of-war rope, it moves back and forth according to the strength of competing influences. The level of 'autonomy and control', in transnational companies, may vary considerably even inside the same organization. The character and style of divisional heads in a decentralized holding company may create a wide variation in autonomy permitted to middle and junior managers. The kind of business may also have a significant effect. For example, businesses, where standardized customer services are essential may have less room for independence, while a high-tech development company may only work in an environment where new ideas can be tried out with the minimum of bureaucracy. Autonomy as a factor in transnational marketing works out in terms of the following features.

1. Small headquarters bureaucracies
2. Small independent business units
3. Informal systems of working together
4. Delegation down the line
5. A positive attitude towards risk taking
6. Generalist managers

Some businesses die because they have no 'controls'. They die either because they have the wrong controls or because they have too many. The small and even the big businesses sometimes pay so much of attention to customer service that cash flow is neglected. This is a common enough phenomenon. So too is the 'bureaucratic' company that pulls the reins so tightly that it throttles the growth. The more effective your controls are the more autonomy you can afford. What these companies forget is that controls are only of value if they assist in the primary purpose of serving the markets profitably. The problem is compounded by the fact that the transnational company and the environment in which it operates both change rapidly. But few companies systematically evaluate their control systems to ensure they still fit top management's objectives. As Tom Peters of *in search of excellence* wrote, 'A few (controls) that are believed are much more effective than numerous controls that are honoured principally in the breach'.

Worse still, the systems themselves can change in unplanned, often unexpected ways as people divert them to their own objectives. And the more complex they become, the greater the likelihood of failure or to put it in another way, the larger the system, the closer to infinity is the number of things that can conceivably go wrong. Before you can start to check your controls, you

have to know where you stand,—whether the controls you have contribute to the maximum efficiency or are against it and whether you have all the controls you need. The questionnaire on transnational marketing, provided below, looks at the following aspect of controls:

- Tight controls of finance
- Constant feedback of results
- Close attention to business planning
- High standards

One of the clearest differences between successful transnational and domestic companies lies in their attitudes towards their markets. If you wish to develop the winning streak in your transnational marketing, you must absorb the market and its requirements into the pores of your organization; the company and the market must become as one. It requires a high degree of sensitivity, reaction to market change and an instinct for how to direct it rather than simply swept along with it. The attributes of winning transnational companies can be described as:

- Brand strength
- Customer relations
- Quality control
- Hunger for market information
- Market oriented R&D
- Action-oriented marketing

'For most people, most corporations and to most management, innovation is an extremely uncomfortable and difficult process. The reason is that, fundamentally, 'innovation is by definition both disruptive and revolutionary' (John Demibitz). Of all the desirable characteristics of transnational management, innovation is probably the hardest to achieve since people and organizations are alike in being resistant to change. But too much of innovation and experiment are also not healthy for companies. The situation can be compared to a very common scene. Sometimes, when a car refuses to start, it often happens that the driver pushes it to make the engine. When the engine starts and the car gathers momentum, the driver needs to jump aboard and control it, otherwise, the car will race away and cause havoc. Same is the case with transnational companies. When these companies with the winning streak appear to have set the wheels turning, the management needs to jump into the driving seat before the companies move too fast. Before you can make innovation work for your company, you have to establish how hard it will be to get the vehicle (company or division) moving. Factors in the evaluation are:

1. Few barriers to change
2. Natural curiosity about how things are done elsewhere
3. Transnational prospective
4. Directed R&D
5. The role of the chief executive

The questionnaire provided below seeks to address the factors described above and their elements in a systematic way.

ATTITUDE TOWARDS WINNING IN TRANSNATIONAL MARKETING

❑ Autonomy

General

1. Which of the following statements best describes your company?

   (a) Top management believes that the only way to get the best out of people is to give them complete autonomy; if they want help they will call for it.

   (b) Top management believes in managing mainly by explicit rules and intricate procedures.

   (c) Top management believes in substantial autonomy within a clear and unobtrusive framework of simple controls.

   (d) Top management is afraid of losing control; it is constantly looking over people's shoulders.

2. What is your company's attitude to the idea of limited number of managerial and professional employees working some or most of the time from home or elsewhere, linked to their office by computer?

   (a) Positive, it has already carried out on a number of successful experiments.

   (b) Cautions, it foresees many practical problems.

   (c) Totally opposed, how would it know what they are doing?

❑ Small Headquarters Bureaucracies

1. How big is your group headquarters?

   (a) Just a handful of people

   (b) 100 or so

   (c) 100 to 500

   (d) More than 500

2. Where are most of the major operating decisions taken?

   (a) In the field

   (b) At headquarters (HQ)

   (c) Jointly by HQ and recommendation from the field

3. Which is more important to the management—foyer or back offices/ shop floor?

   (a) Spend more on the back offices because people deserve comfort.

   (b) Think it's more important to have an impressive foyer than comfortable offices.

4. Compare the annual running costs and the asset value of the headquarters building with those of the production units. Which of the following statements is nearest to the truth?

   (a) Running costs and/or asset value of fairly small production units are significantly higher than those at the HQ.

   (b) Running costs and/or asset value of fairly small production units are about the same as those of the HQ.

   (c) Running costs and/or asset value of HQ are moderately higher than those of an average production unit.

   (d) Running costs and/or asset value of HQ are very much higher than those of an average production unit.

5. How many levels are there between the (group) top management and the first level of supervision?

   (a) Three or less

   (b) Four to seven

   (c) More than seven

6. (a) Where do young managers see the greatest promotion prospects?

   (i) In the field

   (ii) At the HQ

   (b) Where are the most talented junior and middle managers in the company concentrated?

   (i) In the field

   (ii) At HQ

❑ Small, Independent Business Units

1. What is the average size of the major operating units in your company?

   (a) Less than 500 people

   (b) 500 to 1000 people

   (c) More than 1000 people

2. How frequently does the unit head have to refer upwards for an approval?

   (a) Never

   (b) A few times a year

   (c) Monthly

   (d) Weekly

   (e) Daily

3. How much on-the-spot decision-making authority do your company's people in the field have compared with the competition?

   (a) Far more

   (b) Somewhat more

   (c) About the same

   (d) A bit less

   (e) A lot less

4. For which of the following functions does total or near-total responsibility (within an agreed budget) rest with the operating unit?

(a) Marketing

(b) Production

(c) Sales and distribution

(d) Capital investment

(e) Industrial relations/personnel

5. How close is your company to being an entrepreneurial organization?

    (a) Totally

    (b) Quite

    (c) Not very

    (d) Quite the opposite, it is a pure bureaucracy

6. Has your company set up any semi autonomous subsidiaries, where entrepreneurs (from inside or outside) retain a significant share in the business?

    (a) Yes

    (b) No, but intends to

    (c) No, but thinking about it

    (d) No, not likely to

    (e) No, totally opposed

7. How do unit managers perceive corporate headquarters?

    (a) As a lifeline when things go wrong

    (b) As a cost centre

    (c) As a bank

    (d) As a priesthood

    (e) As an ivory tower

8. Does the general climate in your company encourage entrepreneurial behaviour?

    (a) Yes

    (b) Partly

    (c) No

❑ Informal Systems of Working Together

1. How are the conflicts of interest between different operating units usually resolved?

   (a) Swiftly by discussion

   (b) Slowly by discussion

   (c) Slowly by explicit written procedure

   (d) Allowed to fester till top management intervenes

2. How long does it normally take between requests from the operating units and decisions by top management?

   (a) A matter of days at the utmost

   (b) Up to a week

   (c) Up to a month

   (d) Over a month

3. Taking the basics of your industry (e.g., in manufacturing, bringing a new production on stream). Does the company do this in?

   (a) A significantly shorter time than its competitors

   (b) About the same time as its competitors

   (c) Significantly longer time than its competitors

4. (a) Does the culture of the organization as a whole make it easy for ad hoc teams to be formed for tackling problems and opportunities?

   (i) Yes

   (ii) Often

   (iii) Seldom

   (iv) Never

   (b) Do these teams automatically assume a degree of authority?

   (i) Yes

   (ii) Often

   (iii) Seldom

   (iv) Never

5. How much notice is taken of the recommendation of such teams?
   - (a) They are there to make decisions.
   - (b) Top management usually acts on their recommendation.
   - (c) To management occasionally acts on their recommendations.
   - (d) It is just a talking shop the ideas are rarely implemented.
6. How often does top management give direct orders?
   - (a) Hardly ever
   - (b) Sometimes
   - (c) Frequently
7. If asked whether they were allowed to use their initiative sufficiently what would be the reply of most junior/middle managers?
   - (a) Yes
   - (b) Sometimes
   - (c) Not often
   - (d) Never
   - (e) No one would ask such a question.
8. What do managers in your company feel about being seen to delegate more and more of their job?
   - (a) Improves their chances of promotion and new responsibilities
   - (b) Increase their chances of being made redundant
9. How many middle managers does you company have, compared to junior managers?
   - (a) One middle manager for twenty or more junior managers
   - (b) One middle manager for ten to twenty junior managers
   - (c) One middle manager for less than ten junior managers

A Positive Attitude Towards Risk Taking

1. What is the differential in rewards for taking 'high risk' managerial jobs compared to the normal 'safe' job in a successful operation?
   (a) Very high if you perform
   (b) High
   (c) Moderate or no differential
   (d) Lower than in successful operations
2. What happens to managers whose projects fail?
   (a) They are encouraged to try again with a better product
   (b) They are encouraged to try again but given a black mark
   (c) They are shunted aside or demoted
   (d) They are fired
3. How does your company reduce the risk in new ventures?
   (a) By pursuing, only those ventures that appear to be profitable even with a very large margin of error.
   (b) By pouring money and effort into detailed planning, preparation and market research.
   (c) By not pursuing new ventures at all.
4. How easy is it for a manager with a good idea and a detailed case, to obtain unbudgeted finance to pursue it?
   (a) Straight forward
   (b) Complex
   (c) Virtually impossible
5. Do people in your company feel free to admit mistakes?
   (a) Yes, it is expected.
   (b) No, you are asking for trouble.
6. There often seems to be a connection between the size of risk taken and the size of a person or company's ambition. In the past five years has you company taken:

(a) Numerous large investment risks

(b) A few large investment risks

(c) No large investment risks

❑ Generalist Managers

1. At what age does your company expose specialist managers to general management experience?

    (a) At age 25 – 30

    (b) At age 31 – 40

    (c) At age 41 plus

2. If you, as a manager of your operating unit were able to buy it out of the company tomorrow, what would you do?

    (a) Make very few changes – we are already running it/we can run it in the way we think best.

    (b) Make moderate changes – we would throw out some of the reporting systems.

    (c) Make major changes – I know how to run this operation most profitably, but top management would not let me.

CONTROL

❑ General

1. How often does top management change the control system?

    (a) Frequently

    (b) Occasionally

    (c) Almost never

2. List the formal controls in your company that apply to you. What proportion of them are designed to help you do your job rather than tell someone else what you are doing?

    (a) All or most

    (b) About half

    (c) Very few

    (d) None

3. Are the same basic controls applied across the company?
   (a) Yes
   (b) No
4. Do you fully understand the reasoning behind and need for ...?
   (a) All the controls
   (b) Most of the controls
   (c) Some of the controls
   (d) None of the controls
5. What is your attitude towards control systems?
   (a) Simple to operate
   (b) Fairly simple
   (c) Difficult
   (d) In need of an expert to interpret them
6. What proportion of the control systems would you jettison tomorrow if you had the opportunity.
   (a) More than half
   (b) A quarter
   (c) Less than quarter
   (d) None
7. Has anyone in the company ever tried to put the control systems into context for you as part of the overall corporate objectives?
   (a) Yes
   (b) No
   (c) Other
8. Does top management have as its key controls:
   (a) Fewer than five critical measurements
   (b) Six to ten critical measurements
   (c) More than ten critical measurements

❑ Tight Controls on Finance

1. Are tight financial controls the result of poor profit and cash flow generally in the company or of a planned diversion of resources where they will do most good?

   (a) Latter

   (b) Former

2. Which of the following statements is most accurate?

   (a) Our company approves of capital expenditure readily if there is a sufficiently large demonstrable saving to be made.

   (b) Our company only approves capital expenditure reluctantly.

   (c) Our company approves of capital expenditure – if the money is available.

   (d) Our company hardly ever queries capital expenditure.

3. What, in your view is the primary purpose of financial controls in your company?

   (a) To hold expenditures down at any cost

   (b) To act as an early warning system of financial problems

   (c) To give top management the flexibility it needs to plan market response

   (d) To keep everyone in line

4. How much of the financial information you provide on a regular basis is used in your job?

   (a) All

   (b) Most

   (c) Some

   (d) None

5. How much of the financial information that you provide on a regular basis is being used by senior management?

   (a) All

   (b) Most

   (c) Some

   (d) None

6. How closely are cash controls tied to personal reward?
   (a) Very closely
   (b) Loosely
   (c) Very loosely
   (d) Not at all
7. How quickly are the last month figures consolidated and presented to the top management?
   (a) Within 36 hours
   (b) Within 72 hours
   (c) Within a week
   (d) A month or more
8. How far down the chain are those results communicated?
   (a) To all employees
   (b) Down to supervisor level
   (c) To middle management
   (d) To the senior management only
9. What proportion of junior managers knows the profit and loss status of their departments from week to week?
   (a) Most
   (b) Few
   (c) None
10. At what frequency management appraisals in other key critical areas carried out?
    (a) On a daily basis
    (b) Six monthly
    (c) Annually
    (d) Rarely, if ever
11. Do you always know how well you are performing in the areas that matter to your company?
    (a) Yes
    (b) No

12. Do you know what the controls that really matter to top management are?

    (a) Yes

    (b) Guess quite reasonably

    (c) No

❑ Close Attention to Business Planning

1. Is business planning implemented in your company?

   (a) An ongoing affair, part of daily routine

   (b) An annual event

   (c) Less frequent than annual

2. Who gets involved in the financial side of business planning?

   (a) Everyone

   (b) All management and supervisory levels

   (c) Middle level/functional manager levels

   (d) Senior management/board members only

3. How much personal ownership do you feel towards your portion of the business plan?

   (a) A good deal

   (b) Some

   (c) None

4. In a typical year, does your company/department:

   (a) Come out pretty close to plans

   (b) Miss the plan by miles every time

5. When the actual sales fall below those predicted in the business plan, what does your company typically do?

   (a) Keep changing the plan to fit the real world

   (b) Change the real world to fit the plan, by throwing in additional effort

   (c) Bury its head and hope for the best

6. At the end of the financial year, does your department typically:

   (a) Push all possible expenses into the closing year on the basis that it was so bad a bit more will not matter

   (b) Push all possible expenses into the coming year on the basis that you have to do something to make the figures look better

   (c) Present an accurate financial picture of events

❑ High Standards

1. Does your company clearly state, for all employees, the general standards of the performance it requires from them?

   (a) Yes

   (b) No

   (c) Other

2. Are you personally clear about the performance standards expected of you?

   (a) Yes

   (b) Somewhat

   (c) No

3. Does the top management provide an example of high standards for others to follow?

   (a) Yes

   (b) Somewhat

   (c) No

4. Is there company folklore—a set of anecdotes—that reinforces the standard expected of employees?

   (a) Yes

   (b) Some

   (c) None

5. How do managers in your company react to substandard behaviour or performance?

   (a) Jumping on the employee concerned immediately, wherever they see something wrong

(b) String up a catalogue of complaints until they have enough to confront the employee in a rap session

(c) Tolerate the bad performance until it either corrects itself or becomes sufficiently serious that action has to be taken.

MARKET ORIENTATION

❑ General

1. Does the board of your company genuinely understand the difference between sales and marketing?

    (a) Yes

    (b) Party

    (c) No

2. What are the positions of sales department and marketing department in your company?

    (a) Sales subordinate to marketing

    (b) Sales is equal in status to marketing

    (c) Marketing is subordinate to sales

3. What is the attitude towards marketing department in your company?

    (a) Consulted or involved in every other major department's activity

    (b) Consulted or involved in some major department's activities

    (c) Obliged to mind their own business

4. Does the top management establish clear objective for the marketing plan, based on and in harmony with the overall corporate objectives?

    (a) Yes

    (b) Partly

    (c) No

5. At what stage of the budgeting process is the marketing plan, domestic and transnational drafted:

    (a) At the end

    (b) At the beginning

    (c) As the other plans become clear

6. Transnational marketing is seen as an activity, which should involve:

    (a) All senior managers

    (b) Some senior managers

    (c) Only the transnational marketing managers

7. A new product flops because people do not like some of its characteristics. How would this be normally seen as?

    (a) A problem for marketing, sales and production together

    (b) A marketing problem

    (c) A sales problem

    (d) A production problem

    (e) Anybody's problem as long as it's not mine

❑ Brand Strength

1. Does market research show that people regard your company as different from its competitors?

    (a) Yes

    (b) No

2. What is the general attitude towards main brands?

    (a) Better regarded than the competition

    (b) Equally regarded with the competition

    (c) Less well regarded than the competition

3. Have any major products from your company become 'commoditized' in recent years (steel is now bought without regard to who supplies them in spite of the brand name people treat the product or service as a commodity)?

    (a) Yes

    (b) Partly

    (c) No

4. Is the company spending on brand planning?

    (a) Yes a consistent, planned operation spanning at least five years

(b) Yes a spasmodic injection of advertising according to an annual plan

(c) Little and not very often

5. Is the company spending on 'new products' planning?

   (a) Yes a consistent, planned operation spanning five or more years

   (b) Yes a spasmodic injection of some finance and advertising according to an annual plan

   (c) Little and not very often

6. How important is the achievement of market leadership to your company?

   (a) Very, it is central to our philosophy—we will buy market share if we have to

   (b) Moderately, we would rather be the most consistently profitable company than the one with the most volume

   (c) Moderately, we rarely have the resources to seize or hold market leadership – we don't like to become targets

   (d) Unimportant

❑ Customer Relations

1. Have senior managers in your company ever posed as a customer with a compliant to test the complaints handling system (or hired an outside agency to do the same task)?

   (a) Frequently

   (b) Occasionally

   (c) Rarely

   (d) Never

2. Does the top management see copies of or analyse customers' complaints?

   (a) Frequently

   (b) Occasionally

   (c) Rarely

   (d) Never

3. What is the status of the manager directly responsible for customer relations (if any), i.e., who signs the replies to service complaints?

   (a) Board level

   (b) Senior management

   (c) Middle management

   (d) Junior management

   (e) No such function in our firm

4. How swiftly, does your department/company acknowledge the written or telephonic complaints?

   (a) Within 24 hours

   (b) Within 48 hours

   (c) Within a week

   (d) Within a month

   (e) We do not bother to respond at all

5. How closely are parameters of the complaints analysed?

   (a) Very

   (b) Moderately

   (c) Not at all

6. How often does the top management personally contact the aggrieved customers?

   (a) For any serious complaint

   (b) For some serious complaints

   (c) Never

❑ Quality Control

1. How closely can you identify the source of each problem that leads to a complaint about some of your products?

   (a) Up to the individual employee

   (b) Up to the individual department

   (c) Up to the plant

   (d) Not at all

2. What percentage of staff in your estimation, comprise the quality ethic in your company?

    (a) All

    (b) More than half

    (c) Less than half

    (d) Negligible

3. What level (if any), of involvement does your company have in the quality control methods of its suppliers?

    (a) Close

    (b) A little

    (c) Not at all

4. Which of the following best describes your company's approach to quality control?

    (a) Get it right the first time: quality begins and ends with the operator and his equipment

    (b) Test and check by sample

    (c) If it is not right, the customer will soon tell us

5. Does your company openly value product quality as an employee motivator?

    (a) Yes

    (b) Partially

    (c) No

❑ Hunger for Market Information

1. Is any market research, including transnational marketing research, done in your company?

    (a) Allocated a formal budget

    (b) Updated regularly

    (c) Rarely used

2. Do you know your competitor's domestic and transnational strengths and weaknesses?

    (a) Better than they know themselves

(b) Pretty well

(c) Moderately well

(d) Hardly at all

3. How closely are sales, production and advertising activities tied to the research data?

   (a) Closely

   (b) Partially

   (c) Hardly at all

4. What does your company do while developing new products and processes?

   (a) Form Interdisciplinary teams with finance, marketing and production strongly represented

   (b) Make R&D produce what marketing or sales says it needs

   (c) Let R&D produce what it thinks marketing or sales should be selling

5. Does your company send its R&D people into the field, in India and abroad, to gain the customer's view points?

   (a) Yes

   (b) Sometimes

   (c) No

❑ Action-oriented Marketing

1. What level of contingency planning does the marketing department do?

   (a) High, we want to cover any likely eventuality

   (b) Moderate, we have contingency plans, but it takes a while to bring them on stream

   (c) Low, we make a plan and stick to it

   (d) Low, we make a plan and change it to fit the circumstances as they happen

INNOVATION

❑ General

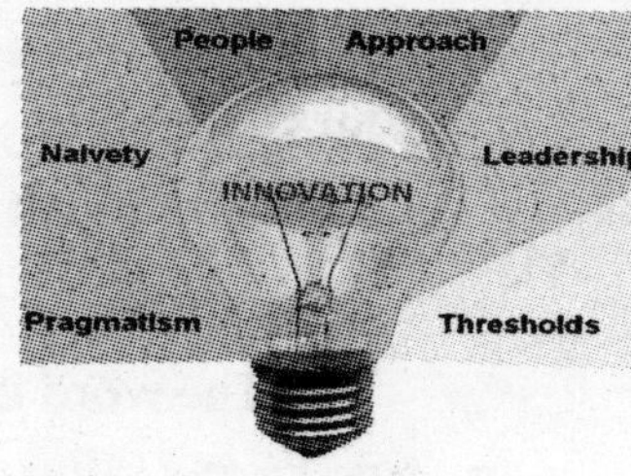

1. Does success belong to the company that innovates?

    (a) First in its business sector

    (b) Second in its business sector

    (c) Last in its business sector

    (d) Sometimes first, sometimes second in its business sector

2. What proportion of your company department's sales turnover goes into R&D?

(a) Manufacturing industry

(i) Over 5 percent

(ii) 3 to 5 percent

(iii) 1 to 3 percent

(iv) Less than 1 per cent

(b) Service industry

(i) Over 3 percent

(ii) 1 to 3 percent

(iii) Under 1 percent

(iv) None at all

3. Do you have a policy for innovation?

    (a) Yes

    (b) Partially

    (c) No

4. Does your company have long-term innovation objectives, i.e., does it have a clear idea of the products it expects to sell after those you are researching now become obsolete?

    (a) Yes

    (b) Somewhat

    (c) No

5. How does your company see innovations as?
   - (a) Just a matter for R&D
   - (b) Affecting every part of the organization
6. How strongly does innovation figure in the corporate strategy for your company?
   - (a) Very much
   - (b) A little
   - (c) The word is not mentioned
7. What is the reputation of company's top managers?
   - (a) Have a reputation for being innovators
   - (b) Have a reputation for being conservatives
8. List the five keys developments in your industry over the past ten years. Your company_______________.
   - (a) Embrace them all immediately
   - (b) Dismiss some initially as minor significance
   - (c) Dismiss most initially as of minor significance
9. How many departments are there in your company that appear never to innovate?
   - (a) Most
   - (b) Some
   - (c) None

❑ Few Barriers to Change

1. Does your company:
   - (a) Reward managers for valuable new ideas
   - (b) Assume that innovation is part of the job description and does not merit additional reward
2. When your company has had an expensive failure in a particular market or technology sector. Does it:
   - (a) Evaluate why things went wrong and invite people to suggest ways of doing it better next time

(b) Cut its losses and refuse to countenance any forays into that sector again

3. What proportions of managers in your company have been given training in creativity techniques?

   (a) 100 percent

   (b) More than 30 percent

   (c) Less than 30 percent

4. When faced with a revolutionary but apparently sensible new idea does your company typically:

   (a) Look to see if it can be tested without great expense

   (b) Keep referring it back for 'further evaluation'

   (c) Decide it is too radical

5. What happens to persistent mavericks in your company?

   (a) They are promoted quickly

   (b) They are promoted till someone chops their head off for being disruptive

   (c) We encourage them to move to a more suitable employer

6. Do the shop floor employees have guarantees that labour saving ideas they generate will not mean that they lose their jobs?

7. (a) Is there a clear, formal structure for reviewing and testing new ideas?

   (i) Yes

   (ii) Partly

   (iii) No

   (b) Does everyone know what the structure is?

   (i) Yes

   (ii) Often

   (iii) No

8. (a) When a dynamic young manager with lots of ideas quits, does your company attempt to establish why he felt he had to go elsewhere to further his career?

(i) Yes

(ii) Often

(iii) No

(b) Does the evidence you have suggests that these people mainly leave:

(i) Because their ideas have been evaluated, but do not fit the corporate portfolio

(ii) Because no one will act on one of their ideas, although it has been evaluated positively

(iii) Because no one will listen to their ideas at all

9. (a) How fast do new ideas move through the corporate hierarchy from junior management to board level?

(i) Within days

(ii) Within weeks

(iii) Within months

(iv) Most never get there

(b) And how fast does the initial response come down?

(i) Within days

(ii) Within weeks

(iii) Within months

(iv) What response

10. You are told that tomorrow there will be major changes in your part of the company and that the content (though neither the status nor salary level) of your job be affected. Is your reaction most likely to be?

(a) Excitement at the prospect of tackling something new

(b) Excitement tinged with worry

(c) Sheer panic

❑ Natural Curiosity about Things Done Elsewhere

1. How close a watch does your company keep on the development activities of the competition?

(a) Very close, we know their R & D programmes in great detail

(b) Quite close, we monitor them regularly

(c) Not closely at all, we just read the trade papers

(d) Not at all, we don't believe they are doing anything of interest

2. How long does it take your company to follow up on an interesting new idea elsewhere, to see if the idea could be applied to its own operations?

   (a) Within a few weeks

   (b) Within a few months

   (c) About a year or so

   (d) Only when everyone else is doing it

❑ Transnational Practice

1. Does your company regard transnational conferences and symposia mainly as:

   (a) A vital opportunity to keep up-to-date with what other people are doing

   (b) A reward for good performance

   (c) A waste of time

2. Has your company established transnational links for the specific purpose of keeping up-to-date with threats and opportunities from overseas?

   (a) Yes

   (b) In part

   (c) No

3. How many board directors have transnational experience (i.e., working at a senior level overseas)?

   (a) All

   (b) More than half

   (c) Less than half

   (d) None

4. How much time on an average do board members spend overseas?
   (a) 20 percent or more
   (b) 10 percent or more
   (c) 2 to 10 percent
   (d) Less than 2 percent
5. If you are a technology-based firm, do you have an internal engineer or scientist capable of scanning the Japanese technical literature in Japanese?

DIRECTED R&D

1. Does top management set clear commercial objectives for R&D?
   (a) Yes
   (b) Sometimes
   (c) No
2. What proportion of junior R&D staff could tell you the market and production cost objectives for the products they are working on?
   (a) 100 percent
   (b) 75 percent
   (c) 50 percent plus
   (d) 25 percent plus
   (e) Less than 25 percent
3. Are the present teams concerned with new product development and business development?
   (a) Located on a single business functions
   (b) Isolated with frequent communications with other functions
   (c) Isolated with infrequent communications with other functions

THE ROLE OF THE CHIEF EXECUTIVE

1. (a) How often does the top management visit the laboratories/ research facilities?

    (i) Weekly

    (ii) Monthly

    (iii) Quarterly

    (iv) Rarely

    (v) Never

   (b) What does the top management do on these occasions?

    (i) Talk to small groups or 'individuals' at any level

    (ii) Talk to department heads

    iii) Talk to the R&D manager only

POINTS TO WATCH

1. Autonomy without controls is abdication. Companies with the winning streak combine autonomy with simple controls.
2. Companies with the winning streak go overboard neither on back room offices nor on shop floor. The golden rule in both cases is to be smart but functional.
3. Unit managers should perceive corporate headquarters as a bank. This is regarded as a healthy attitude.
4. Reduction of risks in new ventures by pouring money and effort into detailed planning, preparation and market research characterizes the winning streak in companies. Anything that seems so risk free that it cannot fail usually has a very serious catch, even if you did not see it now. Hence, the importance of market research, to expose underlying assumptions.
5. While it is true that constant change in the market requires corresponding changes in the company and its organization, most of the useful controls will be fundamental to the business. If a company

changes its controls frequently, it is an indication that the control systems are too complex. Simple controls rarely need much change, whatever happens outside the company.

6. When actual sales fall below those predicted in the business plan, ideally the financial objectives of the plan should remain, only the means of achieving them should change, i.e., sound alternative is the only one that makes sense in terms of winning. It would be very surprising if managers keep changing the plan to fit the real world , which is, in effect, equivalent to no planning.

7. Generally, employees think that managers should hold their peace on little things. After all, surely people become very irritated and resentful at constant nit picking. Important point is that, properly handled, constant vigilance by managers are actually appreciated far more by his subordinates.

8. The debate regarding whether sales and marketing are equal is status or whether one is at a higher level in position than other is a minefield. In theory, sales should be subordinate to marketing. In practice, the relationship may depend on the calibre of person and the role of marketing. If the primary function of marketing is simply to pump out statistics and sales-support literature, it can be disastrous to place it in charge of sales. If the top management wishes marketing to assume its proper strategic function however, it must give marketing some measure of responsibility for directing where and how the sales efforts are applied. It must also ensure that the person in the marketing hot seat has the ability to perform that demanding role. One of the key attributes is team-building ability.

9. While much of the research into competitive advantage suggests that market leaders are usually more successful (i.e., more profitable) than market followers, it is easy to fall into the trap of chasing market leadership for its own sake. It may, in many cases, be more profitable in the long-term to redefine the market that one is in.

10. Companies (transnational) with the winning streak tend to innovate first where it really matters, second where it is less important.

11. If a company regards transnational conferences and symposia mainly as a reward for good performance then probably it has many bored and frustrated executives. If you want them to relax, send them on a

paid holiday. Give them a single major problem to think about and ask them for a one page report on it, a week after they return. Send them to transnational conferences as well, of course, to work and listen.

12. If borad members of a company spend 20 percent or more time in a year overseas, then who is there to mind the shop? It is very rare that any but the transnational manager or export director needs to be overseas that much. A good average is 5 to 15 percent. There are people who can use air travel as thinking time, but they are rare.
13. The earliest way to find out about long-term threats and opportunities to your business from is to simply ask the Japanese themselves. The local representative office of the Ministry of Transnational Trade and Industry will supply you a copy (in English) of Japan's plans for your industry.
14. One of the lessons of *in search of excellence* is that effective project teams having once been given clear guidelines and containing the interdisciplinary skills, work best if they are cut off and left to it. These teams are referred to as 'skunk works'.

Table 9.1: Scoring and Evaluation of Attitudes in Transnational Marketing

Score	Rating
0–30	The winning company in transnational marketing.
30–60	A potential winner in transnational marketing.
60–150	The average transnational marketing company.
150–240	Need to watch its transnational marketing.
240–325	Poor transnational marketing.

To determine how well your company is doing in transnational marketing; choose the most appropriate of the multiple choice answers to each of the questions. Each of multiple choices has a score ranging from zero to four. Tally the entire score and consult the chart below. A 'Potential Winner' in transnational marketing has a score ranging from 0–60.

Summary

This chapter is based on the aspects of understanding about the 'winning companies'. In order to assess and evaluate, various factors relevant to the study have been offered by the experts in the domain. These eight factors are leadership, autonomy, control, involvement, market orientation, getting back to basics and staying there, innovation and integrity. Out of the above eight factors, four factors have been selected for special attention based on which a typical questionnaire has been prepared. These four factors are autonomy, control, market orientation and innovation.

Prior to attending the given questions, relationship in between the four factors has been discussed with distinction. This included a wholesome idea on the entire aspects associated in the field of transnational marketing strategy.

Moreover, on each of the four factors, certain questions have been slotted which are chiselled for the subject. In each of the factors certain classified types of questions have been given in different required categories. Categories include general types and specific types, leading to estimated stores for obtaining a rating in the final stage. The scoreboard of each candidate can be seen in the rating chart. This chapter is scale-based illustration of the questions, which can be tried for testing the attitudes of company.

QUESTIONS FOR DISCUSSION

Q. 1. What are the main eight factors defining the facets of winning companies?

Q. 2. What are the four important factors selected for special attention in transnational marketing out of the eight factors given? Discuss.

Q. 3. How do the factors of 'autonomy' get assessed for winning companies?

Q. 4. How does 'control' as a factor get assessed for winning companies? Elaborate with respect to the given questions in the category.

Q. 5. How does 'market orientation' as a factor get assessed for winning companies? Look into the category break-ups and illustrate.

Q. 6. How does innovation as a factor get assessed for winning companies?

Q. 7. Discuss on the aspects of 'points to watch' and relate to transnational marketing.

Q. 8. Discuss on the scoring and evaluation of attitudes as per the table.

Q. 9. Try these questions on three executives and ascertain the status of their company. Give your analysis on the ratings.

Q. 10. Write short notes:

(a) Leadership

(b) Autonomy

(c) Control

(d) Involvement

(e) Market orientation

(f) Getting back to basics and staying there

(g) Innovation

(h) Integrity.

Chapter 10

Some Do's and Don'ts in Transnational Marketing

LEARNING OBJECTIVES

After going through the chapter, the reader should be able to:

1. Identify some of the do's and don'ts in the field of transnational marketing.
2. Recognize the do's, nurture the best customer, making quality control the core of business in the entire organization.
3. Explain the don'ts, making results and not efficiency the main stay of the business.
4. Understand the ultimate of transnational marketing beyond qualitative assessments, evaluations and score sheets.
5. Describe the qualitative aspects of transnational marketing.

'The first and best victory is to conquer self'.

— *Plato*

'Develop the business around the people; build it, don't buy it; and, then, be the best'.

— *Richard Branson*

SOME DO'S

1. Learn to deliver on promise, even if it takes a great deal of effort.
2. Be open, suggestive and persuasive in communication.
3. In talking to the customers, sticking to the relevant detail, but provide as much information in as little a space, as you possibly can.
4. Listen to your customer before you begin talking.
5. Take a personal interest in your customer, his country, his culture, his background, his company, etc.
6. See how you can provide the personal touch in dealing with customers, actual or potential.
7. Maintain a flexible and responsive system for dealing with customers and servicing them. Be accommodating, for example, have separate cells for customer complaints, which are answerable for performance.
8. Always try to learn more about the market and the customer before you take a stand or commit yourself or your company.
9. Respond immediately to customer complaints and requests, even while they are under investigation. Senior management may answer serious complaints.
10. Be committed to serving your existing customer better. In the initial stage, not losing a customer may be more important than gaining one.
11. Be humble and respect the client. This quality has fetched many a deal for the discerning company and executive.
12. Encourage risk-taking attitude. Those with initiative must be given the freedom of operating on the transnational turf.
13. Always stress on the value of your service before you present your product. As the transnational giants, like AT&T claim, 'we are in the service business', is a very effective and selling slogan.
14. Just claims of service are not enough. Back up your claims, with a service strategy, marketing ethics, game plan and more efficient and effective service operations.
15. Adopt a penetration pricing policy, even if it means selling below the total cost (sometimes), in order to get a foothold in some markets and to win repeat orders from the targeted long-term customers.
16. Try to broad-base the product to the extent feasible.

17. Study the industry and national economic plans of target countries before you seek to enter them. Just the size of the market and the growth rates are not enough.
18. Study the current and likely regulations and concessions affecting industries using your or related products in the target markets/ countries.
19. Examine the stability of, and the long-term implications—economic, political and others, such as ethnic populations of doing business in particular markets.
20. Make sure that your product is good enough or is better than the desired specifications by a third-party quality inspection before you attempt to sell.
21. Identify who your precise competitors are and seek information about their product offerings and competitive advantages.
22. Study the sales volumes, product ranges and markets of competitions to see where you have a differential advantage, at what levels and volumes of sales and production.
23. If you sell substantially through agents try to find out to what parties, in what industries and in which locations are the final sales made.
24. Evolve plans for choosing the right products for the right growth markets at the right time and start networking in advance.
25. Evolve person-based management practices as opposed to formal bureaucracies or the single-contact line executive or purely entrepreneurial practices.
26. Keep a long-term strategic perspective. Sacrifice short-term profits for a niche in the market and a sustainable economic advantage over competition.
27. Study the values and cultural symbols that prevail in target markets and use them.
28. Be constantly opportunity sensitive. The search for opportunity by the entire organization must be ongoing and continuous.
29. Seek and encourage creative and original personnel as opposed to seeking maturity, experience and control.
30. Have a product design strategy as opposed to a product positioning strategy. Thereby, retain the flexibility of selling a standard product, customized product or the standard product with customized options, i.e., retain the flexibility and competitive advantage of low-volume

product markets as opposed to mature high-volume standardized product-marketers.

31. Constantly renew sales motivation among your personnel through incentives, recognition and training programmes.
32. Concentrate your marketing efforts on key areas where you can have a competitive advantage, particularly in terms of geographic location, viz., shipping and freight costs.
33. Learn to coddle, cajole, persuade, appease, gratify and arouse the curiosity the customers in your dialogue with them.
34. Have a specialized cell in export-import financing, not just for budgeting or payments, but trained to look for opportunities in transnational financing. Banks are usually given this job. But they cannot be satisfactorily relied upon.
35. Based on customer response, have a flexible product line permitting the design and sale of new products.
36. Calculate the hurdle rates, associated risks, cost and expected returns at what sales levels and prices for each new product. Test and compare the pre- and post-launch figures.
37. Whatever market you enter, be committed to it until you decide to exit.
38. Constantly emphasize the significant businesses to be in as opposed to running a delineated business.
39. Shortlist three competitors and plan to do better than them.
40. Planning should be according to external factors such as, technology, market, price, society, law, government, and transnational trade competition trends.
41. Fill out your product range by line extensions, based on market information and technological adaptation.
42. Concentrate resources on the most vulnerable or well-disposed non-domestic market segment.
43. Choose products/markets that require the response rate beyond an identified competitor's ability.
44. Recognize the commercial potential of new technology or its new uses early, through a well-defined search process.
45. Choose product markets, which require capital or other resources that an immediate competitor is unwilling to commit.

46. Exploit managerial differences in style, method and systems, such as overhead rate, distribution channels, market image or flexibility. Downplay your transnational disadvantages, particularly 'image' by stressing the quality and advantages of doing business with you.
47. Be aware of the 'politicizing of economic decision making' implications, seek opportunities, and curb ambitions accordingly. But be quick to capitalize on nuances of change and legal pockets of even restricted opportunity. Your company should have transnational political awareness.
48. Have a transnational marketing mode and a code based on the areas suggested above.
49. Strive to be agents of transnational social responsibility.
50. Be able to raise long-term capital at low cost to finance projected transnational plans, domestically through EXIM banks, etc., and also transnationally.
51. Examine 'ease of entry' and 'exit barriers' before taking up or rejecting any major transnational market.
52. Have a positive hunger for market information.
53. Engage in formal long-term marketing planning.
54. Transnational marketing should be integrated at the top in your organization that is, a transnational manager should only report to the top management, while horizontal communication is maintained.
55. Advertising/promotion programmes should be measurable and be measured in their response, while being part of an overall plan.
56. Cut prices to the bare minimum and thrust into virgin territories, which others considered too barren to approach.
57. If the price difference with your competition is not much, do not cut price, but better quality. Offer more for the same price.
58. If you cannot pare the price, try the pack—the minimum volume you are prepared to sell the customer.
59. Getting things right significantly depends on knowing where you are going. A low price strategy could be to penetrate new markets, build up market share and knock out competition or merely to get rid of stocks. Unless the objective is clearly defined, it is very easy to get derailed somewhere along the line.
60. Know the mathematics. Lowering the prices is all very fine but it needs increased volume of sales to keep profits at the same level. It

is a simple mathematical exercise but most people seem unaware of it. The accompanying table sets out what it takes, if, for instance, the current gross profit is 5 percent of sales, it will take 400 percent more sales to earn the same gross profit after a 4 percent price cut.

Percentage of increase in sales increase needed to earn the same gross profit as before a price cut.

Table 10.1: Mathematics of Pricing Sales and Profits

Expected Price Cut	Current Gross Profit (percent) 5	10	15	20	25	30	35
1.	25.0	11.1	7.1	5.3	4.2	3.4	2.9
2.	66.6	25.0	15.4	11.1	8.7	7.1	6.1
3.	15.0	42.08	25.0	17.6	13.6	11.1	9.4
4.	400.0	66.6	36.4	25.0	19.0	15.4	12.9
5.	400.0	100.0	50.0	33.0	25.0	20.0	16.7
6.	400.0	150.0	66.7	42.9	31.6	25.0	20.7
7.	400.0	233.3	87.5	53.8	38.9	30.4	25.0
8.	400.0	400.00	114.3	66.7	47.1	36.4	29.6
9.	400.0	1000.00	150.00	81.8	56.3	42.9	34.6
10.	400.0	1000.00	200.0	100.0	66.7	50.0	40.0

61. Protect the weak markets or products. The onus to cater to all market segments is the responsibility that the market leader has.

62. Price a product low and then cut prices further because of economies of scale, marketing efficiency and technological advances.

63. The true price warrior needs also be the lowest cost producer.

64. The lower you price the product, the greater is the potential market expansion. At the top of the pyramid, there are people with small volumes and premium prices. At the bottom, are the mass marketers with massive sales and low margins. Ironically, those at the bottom are actually sitting at the top of the pile. Learn how to be one of them. Keep the prices so low that others will think twice before going into your segment.

65. Have a permanent vigil strategy. Many me too products miss on this. A cheaper product will not necessarily sell if the price difference is marginal. Retain the premium image, while actually pricing the product at the bottom end.

66. Have a knife-edge marketing strategy; for the high-volume markets, keep the lowest price, but raise the price where competition is relatively less hot.
67. Maintain a one-to-one relationship with the customer.
68. Contact your end users for their views on quality, usability and other features on your product offering and their feedback including satisfaction with your product, in general.
69. Develop a prospect database that allows you to approach your target prospects as individuals. Store in memory, not only their names and addresses but also every bit of information about your targets that you would like and that can realistically be gathered. The only condition that targets should fulfil is that they must be ready and able to buy your product.
70. Test media effectiveness in your promotion. All expenses should accountable and made to prove their value, wherever feasible, by tabulated responses.
71. Rank media and media buys by promotion and advertising cost per prospect response or purchase, not per copy.
72. Engage in either whole-brain or left-brain advertising that reinforces information with reason and emotional persuasion (see Chapter 6 for details).
73. Indulge in activation advertising—an advertising that influences a customer consider buying.
74. Use synergy in marketing. Make your advertising do double duty, serving two purposes such as, educating the customer about your company and informing him about the nearest dealer. Combine awareness advertising and sales promotion in an explosion of energy and profitability.
75. Combine your marketing message with that of a compatible fellow marketer, to share the cost, lending both credibility and providing both with a transnational image.
76. Maximize linkage by providing an idea to the prospect of what to do next, where to buy or how to obtain more ready information. Focus your expense on the most desirable, most interested prospects (not all), in ways described in earlier chapters.
77. Try to achieve a share of market and a share of mind. Use your customer database to win over both prospects and exciting customers, using the concept of lifetime customer value.

Use your customer database to:

(a) Stimulate repeat sales and consolidate market share,

(b) Increase the chances of success of line extensions,

(c) Cross-promote different products in your line,

(d) Build lasting loyalty of your best customers,

(e) Help open up new channels of distribution, in ways described earlier.

❑ Know and Cultivate your Best Customers

78. Use direct mail, coop mail, ambient video, electronic shopping, infomercials (15–30 minutes video films informing the prospect about your product offering, company concerns, etc.,) and other techniques of min-max described earlier in the book.
79. Educate the prospect in not only the product offering but also about how you do business.
80. Synergize two or more distribution channels or methods. Establish a new form of distribution and help the new distribution channel nurture the way you have done business before or change your business practices.
81. Calculate the arithmetic of marketing directly to known users of competing brands or companies, before you actually do so.
82. Make full use of the available public database and telemarketing, for marketing and in gaining information about the markets abroad.
83. Go in for immediate action in response to promotion, queries or marketing plans, both yours as well as those of known competitors.

❑ Empathize with your Customer

84. Provide maximum pertinent information about the product, company, country, way of doing business and perception of the client, etc., and the tie up and display material.
85. Promote at least two channels of distribution.
86. Advertise the brand while you advertise the distribution channel.

87. Support elements of a transnational culture of cause and element of style and use that in your marketing message.
88. Tie up your product(s) with an established transnational programme, industry or company in your marketing message. In other words, highlight and capitalize on your transnational successes.
89. Use marketing success in one market to uncover another.
90. Brainstorm about additional products you could sell to your present customer database.
91. Use profitable or effective measures for third party or syndicated sales of your products or services.
92. Examine how direct response advertising can create demand at the retail level in different markets.
93. Examine how you might customize your product or service to increase its appeal to different groups of prospects of customers. How would you find them and convey the news to them?
94. Does your marketing method have a process or appeal or an offer, which separates the prospects from the non-prospects and the hot prospects from the warm prospects. If not, elaborate how it could be done.
95. Could you convince the person sitting next to you at a dinner party of the merit or superiority of the product offering and service provided by your company? Examine how your present marketing could do a better job than this.
96. Encourage top management's views of autonomous transnational marketing groups.
97. Maintain small headquarters bureaucracies.
98. Provide comfortable work environments for backroom offices and the shop floor in addition to headquarters.
99. Have small independent product based business units.
100. Give on-the-spot decision-making power to marketing personnel in the transnational field.
101. Make a differential reward system in favour of personnel taking high managerial risk successfully, while encouraging the rest to try again with a better product.
102. Encourage ambitious people to do their job freely while giving them a specified degree of budgetary support.

103. Enlist tight financial controls but ensure that proper financial information is disseminated widely first, especially to those who take care of the action.

104. Make sure that financial controls that top management sees as vital are communicated to all levels of management.

105. Make transnational business planning continuous.

106. Ensure participation, commitment, motivation and remuneration for transnational business planning.

107. Examine the plan assumptions in light of gaps in attainment.

108. Keep performance standards high and person based, communicating them to the persons concerned.

109. Keep performance standards in tune with the transnational strategy and plans of the company. Always examine failures instead of just punishing the guilty.

110. Make sure that your prospects are aware of your brand strengths and your attainments in market leadership.

111. Test your customer relation responsiveness even by using top managers as dummy customers.

112. Test and improve your response times in all critical areas of strategy and operation. Be aware of your organizational strengths and timing of response to the full. Make commitments accordingly.

113. Send sample copies of customer complaints and your response details to the top management and act on their feedback.

114. Use Juran total quality concepts, quality circles, total marketing, theory and management techniques or others seriously, in building the 'quality' ethic in your company. Do not wait to hear from the customer on quality.

115. Make quality control the business of your entire organization by making it an employee motivator.

116. Fuel the hunger for market information by making transnational market research a continuous part of operation.

117. Use interdisciplinary teams drawn from all spheres from marketing to production, through research, for customer oriented problems and solutions.

118. Have a policy of innovation not just in training, recruitment or customer-driven R&D, but also in knowing where the company wants to innovate, in tune with what design, strategies, plans and goals and how they can be measured in innovating actions and processes. Evaluate and improve company response to market and technological developments.

SOME DON'TS

119. Do not commit yourself to what you cannot deliver.
120. Do not spend too much time on telling the customer why it cannot be done his way. Spend the same time in thinking of how else it could be done to suit the customer.
121. Do not always try to show your best side to the customer. It is often better to be frank.
122. Do not be boastful about your achievements.
123. Even if the client is wrong, do not be aggressive, argumentative or inattentive.
124. Never try to short-change the customer. Trust lost is seldom regained and often magnified.
125. Do not keep harping all the time on the virtues and quality of your product. Let the customer speak himself.
126. Do not try to pass the buck in handling transnational marketing problems. Immediacy of response and solutions are critical, even at the risk of being proved wrong.
127. Do not be infatuated with a 'grand design'. Learn to move ahead and stay systematic step-by-step.
128. Do not hesitate to tell the client how doing business with you is better or different from others.
129. Do not be satisfied by merely allocating resources to promotion, advertising and spending it intuitively. Develop a promotion plan, a media plan based on the promotion mix and marketing strategy and an overall action package, of which, advertising is a part. Other factors include customer, product, marketing and environmental considerations.
130. Do not always go for volumes in the market. Sell at cost plus or below cost sometimes, even in small or marginal markets to win long-time customers.

131. Do not aim for the same rate of growth across different markets. Make plans realistically, based on your relative share of the market and to the extant you want to be in business.

132. Do not make the mistaken assumption that the biggest market is also the most profitable. Better deals may be there in the smaller and lesser-known markets.

133. Do not consider every transnational company in your business as a competitor. Only those with similar backgrounds, advantages, disadvantages, products, price offerings and having similar sales volumes and comparable market shares are to be studied in depth and improved upon.

134. Do not pass on more paper work to the customer than the minimum necessary.

135. While proceeding under the assumption that the potential customer wants to learn more about your product and company do not burden him with unnecessary and irrelevant information and force him to respond to any other matter than bringing him closer to the point of sale.

136. Do not begin with assumptions that sales are the primary criteria of success in transnational marketing. It is marketing effectiveness, how so ever defined.

137. Do not accept that in the end, harvesting or generating sources of income as traditionally prescribed will be successful in transnational marketing.

138. Identifying all or even the major competitors is not as important as that of deciding, which competitors to follow and whom to lead.

139. Forget what they teach in business schools. Improvise and learn to organize your business and its methods according to the way the markets demand.

140. Do not spread the marketing effort over the entire range. Concentrate on key markets as defined above in the terms, type of market, nature of customer, geographic location, time of entry and commitment.

141. At the same time, do not concentrate all (or most) of your effort on a single market, regardless of the size of the market. In other words, diversify the market risk.

142. Do not try to peddle untried or yet to be accepted products in large markets. For large markets, it is better to aim for the market price competitive 'me-too' products, provided a minimum quality is maintained.

143. Do not hesitate to prune out marginal and unpromising markets. This requires a willingness to drop some traditional markets in favour of new growth markets.

144. Aim not at profits but market share.

145. Do not plan the environment but plan with the environment.

146. Do not plan on immediately entering a new business or providing a new product where information about it is purely judgemental.

147. Plan not products but products that are market based on explicit information about combinations of technology, customer function (that the product performs) and customer segment(s).

148. Do not treat transnational merchant wholesalers, brokers and agents as you domestic distributors, but as special customers in their own right.

149. Sell not a product but an aura, an appeal, a package (of function, service, comfort and benefit) and idea. Package your product with an idea or appeal that will have transnational recognition in the market.

150. Follow not domestic strategies of 'growth with industry', 'harvest', 'withdrawal' or 'divestiture' but typical transnational strategies or 'start-up' (new products generated through customer re-sponsiveness), 'find niche', 'hold niche' and 'fast grow'.

151. Do not ignore antimonopoly laws, import restrictions, other controls such as anti-dumping acts or levies but seek to work around them by shipments through third countries, etc.

152. Do not ignore the potential of semi-legal 'grey markets' in unbranded goods where possible, but without committing legal breaches.

153. Do not be completely dependent on domestic packaging standards. Learn about packaging developments worldwide. Encourage, even finance or arrange finance for your packers and shippers to have transnational collaboration or even import directly the resources and technology necessary to improve your packaging and shipping quality.

154. Do not burn your fingers in high involvement categories. A high involvement product generally commands a high-degree of brand loyalty. In low involvement products (LIPs), brands do not really count for much. LIPs are a more succulent prospect than high-involvement products (HIPs).

155. Forget about LIPs and HIPs, if you are extending the market by creating a new segment.

156. If you do not have the staying power that competitive markets demand, do not venture. A low-price product operates on water-thin margins. But it needs a tremendous product offering and heavy promotion to get it moving to reach the required high volumes.

157. Remember, that price alone will not sell, it is the total perceived value of the product, the company and what it stands for, along with the country. You have also to get the marketing mix, production, price, promotion and distribution right.

158. Do not rely on advertising alone while advertising. Have your complete marketing package ready.

159. Do not attack a market where the competition is well entrenched and aggressive, unless you are prepared for unexpected expenses.

160. Do not think that low price is a panacea for all your ills. A problem with a low-price strategy is that the business is vulnerable if the competition adopts a similar strategy. This often happens in transnational marketing. Therefore, keep other cards in your hand.

161. Do not go in for the approach of branch merchandising but for personalized selling.

162. Do not demand written, explicit and elaborate procedures for resolving conflicts among operating units.

163. Do not prevent ad hoc teams from being formed in the organization to tackle problems and opportunities in marketing, production, etc., on the contrary give them authority.

164. Do not prevent officers from feeling that delegation down the line will improve promotion chances.

165. Don't prevent managers from feeling they have a free hand, in general, in running their units that is, encourage changes through generalist managers.

166. Do not overlook the primary fact that for any system of controls, the purpose of controls is to enable you to do your job better.

167. Do not have a system of rigid controls. Have loose-tight controls based on their degree of importance to company objectives.

168. Do not fudge figures in plans. If you cannot come up with adequate statistics, plan alternatively, but do not use data superficially.

169. Do not confuse sales with marketing. All marketing should be seen in light of the marketing plan or its omissions.

170. Do not overlook tardiness in response to customers or prospects. Build a culture, an informal style of working, quick thinking, readily organized information base, to support an instantaneous variety of marketing. A late response may be worse than no response.

171. Do not become paralysed by information. Develop an action-oriented marketing through contingency planning and situational analysis.

172. Do not build barriers to change. Seek to overcome them particularly in cases of expensive failures for the company. Be open to experimenting with new ideas, particularly in marketing.

173. Do not make employees, particularly workers feel threatened by labour-saving ideas generated internally or externally.

174. Do not let barriers to new ideas emerge in communicating them throughout the organization, particularly to the operators in the transnational marketing field.

175. Do not fail to test the duration it takes for the organization to respond to new ideas.

176. Do not but make employees feel that nothing except a degree of security of employment can be taken for granted in your company.

❑ Make not Efficiency but Results your Business

177. Do not overlook that your executive directors should spend up to 25 percent of their time on developing a transnational perspective, orientation and image for your company.

178. Do not ignore the role of R&D in transnational success but only market-led commercial R&D.

Summary

This chapter reveals the core of transnational marketing, highlighting the essence of do's and don'ts of business, revolving around the holistic aspects.

It emphasizes on cultivating the best customers, making quality control the quintessence of business. It harps on the results and not on measuring efficacy. Beyond quantitative score sheet methods, the chapter emphasizes on the need of qualitative know-how and knowledge.

This chapter offers 118 do's and 60 don'ts which are time tested and holds true for any business.

QUESTIONS FOR DISCUSSION

Q. 1. What are the usual 'do's and don'ts' in transnational marketing management? Discuss assuming real life experience.

Q. 2. Write short notes:

(a) Maximum linkage

(b) Know your best customers

(c) Inter disciplinary teams.

ADDITIONAL QUESTIONS

1. How do you differentiate between marketing management and strategic management? Discuss.
2. What do you mean by a transnational product strategy and domestic product strategy? Illustrate with examples.
3. What do you mean by the transnational company and domestic company promotion strategy? Illustrate.
4. What do you mean by the promotion-mix strategy? Discuss.
5. What do you mean by market commitment strategy? Explain with examples.
6. How do you measure transnational market potential? What are the steps used? Discuss.
7. What are transnational new product strategies? Illustrate with the processes involved.
8. Explain the three dimensions of market boundaries.
9. What are the aspects of transnational distribution channels? Discuss.
10. Elaborate on the 'strategic thrust' in the domain of transnational marketing. Discuss on the perspectives.
11. Illustrate on the governmental constraints on the transnational growth. Discuss with examples.
12. What are the transnational corporate public and its concerns? Explain and discuss.
13. What are the strategic factors in transnational business? Discuss.
14. What are the contributing factors to competitive rivalry? Explain.
15. How do you rate the marketing effectiveness in transnational companies? Discuss.

16. Evaluate and discuss the maxi-transnational marketing model, as a paradigm for business.

17. Give an analysis of the modern domestic marketing, otherwise known as brand merchandizing or distribution. Illustrate, citing examples of situations in the organization.

18. Give definitions of:
    - (a) Personalized selling
    - (b) Maximized targeting
    - (c) Maximized media

19. How does advertising campaign make maximized accountability? Analyse in the context of markets.

20. Critically examine the impact of advertising campaigns in the left brain and right brain. Explain the comments of seers in the subject.

21. Under what conditions are correlations between left brain and right brain is utmost? Elaborate.

22. Identify the criteria that are responsible for maximized activation held due to advertising campaign. Illustrate.

23. Identify the ways for maximizing the synergy of transnational market advertising, without adding a rupee extra on a marketing budget. Elucidate the factors.

24. Examine the linkage assessment grid for analysing the highs and lows of markets driven by advertisement. Explain.

25. Outline the importance of database marketing. Discuss.

26. Write short notes:
    - (a) Repeat sales
    - (b) Customer loyalty
    - (c) Cross promotion
    - (d) Share of mind

27. Discuss the aspects of planning for transnational marketing. Elucidate the pros and cons.

28. How does 'political risk' and 'social risk' influence the transfers, operations and ownership control?

29. What actually influences the choice and change in a transnational company? Discuss with respect to a selected list of options for a country.

30. What are the issues on which government action influences transnational business planning? Analyse and discuss.

31. Assume a company and apply the guidelines for the transnational investment strategy. Elaborate with fictional data wherever required.

32. What are the salient criteria for selecting a country market? Examine the criteria in detail.

33. 'Risks are inevitable and possible antidotes are bound to be available'. Outline the main considerations in either selecting or rejecting a particular country. Discuss.

34. 'Making of a systematic plan by a transnational company needing an assessment on the foreign possibilities on resources '. Discuss.

35. Why do multinational companies go for new product development? What policy is adopted for product development and diversification based on the country resources? Elaborate.

36. Market competition needs product planning and calls for the development of new products. Discuss.

37. Why do companies opt for moving abroad? Relate the issues encompassing home country product and services and foreign country buyers.

38. Which foreign country opportunities are attractive and profitable? Make a survey on the 'Decision Support Chart' for two companies availing database from the Internet.

39. How do exports take place? What are the favourable preconditions of exports? Explain citing examples.

40. What do you mean by sale of knowledge? Discuss and explain the aspects related.

41. How do companies operate abroad? How do companies plan for foreign investments?

42. Are there different patterns for the joint ventures? Give reasons for your answer.

43. 'Large companies set up regional centres, smaller companies simply give authority to a particular national subsidiary to oversee the business for a given part of the world'. Discuss.

44. How are organization systems and the planning systems related in the activities of transnational companies? Discuss.

45. What are the future companies? Discuss in the light for transnational companies and domestic companies.

46. What are the facets of winning companies in the international market? Discuss in details.

47. Compare and contrast the application of autonomy and control in the winning companies forging for transnational market share. Explain.

48. How are customer relations and quality control associated as building blocks for the making of a transnational company? Discuss.

49. What role does market information has in the transnational market?

50. What are the facets of winning companies in the international market? Discuss in detail.

51. Compare and contrast the application of autonomy and control in the winning companies with eye on transnational market share. Explain.

52. How are customer relations and quality control associated as building blocks for the making of a transnational company? Discuss.

53. What role does market information have in the transnational market?

Index

Symbols

A

B

C

D

E

F